The
DRIVING
INSTRUCTOR'S
HANDBOOK

KU-737-513

Driving Schools Supplies Ltd

Supplying Driving Instructors Nationwide

ROOF SIGNS ➡ Hard brilliant white gloss finish that stays white. Tri-pac Version - Roof sign plus two matching door panels on soft, all over magnetic flat white material.

DUAL CONTROLS ➡ Supply only or have them professionally fitted at our Birmingham fitting bays.

LETTERING SERVICE ➡ Computer designed layout for a really good message impact.

BOOKS & MANUALS ➡ Full range of training and reference manuals for ADI trainees. Also audio/visual aids. ADI training aids, road layouts, lesson plans etc. Discounts available.

THEORY MOCK DRIVING TEST PAPERS ➡ Latest questions from the DSA theory bank. 35 questions per sheet in full colour.

DRIVING THEORY TEST CD ROM ➡ The UK's best selling Driving Theory Test CD ROM. Contains the entire official DSA Theory Test question bank for cars and motorcycles. Highly recommended.

FULL MAIL ORDER SERVICE DIRECT TO YOU
Order our latest catalogue,
for all your Driving School requirements

ALL MAJOR CREDIT CARDS ACCEPTED

DON'T BUY YOUR NEXT SIGN UNTIL YOU HAVE CHECKED OUT OUR PRICES!

DRIVING SCHOOLS SUPPLIES LIMITED
2-4 Tame Road, Witton, Birmingham B6 7DS
Tel: 0121- 328 6226   Fax: 0121-327 1864
Email: sales@d-ss.co.uk
Web: www.d-ss.co.uk

The
DRIVING
INSTRUCTOR'S
HANDBOOK

A reference and training manual

ELEVENTH
EDITION

JOHN MILLER and MARGARET STACEY

**KOGAN
PAGE**

First published in 1982 by Kogan Page Ltd
Second edition 1983
Third edition 1986
Fourth edition 1988
Fifth edition 1989
Sixth edition 1991
Seventh edition 1993
Eighth edition 1994
Reprinted 1995
Ninth edition 1996
Reprinted 1996
Tenth edition 1997
Reprinted with revisions in 1998
Reprinted 1998 (three times), 1999
Eleventh edition 1999
Reprinted 2000 (twice), 2001 (twice)

Apart from any fair dealing for the purposes of research or private study, or criticism or review, as permitted under the Copyright, Designs and Patents Act, 1988, this publication may only be reproduced, stored or transmitted, in any form or by any means, with the prior permission in writing of the publishers, or in the case of reprographic reproduction in accordance with the terms of licences issued by the Copyright Licensing Agency. Enquiries concerning reproduction outside those terms should be sent to the publishers at the undermentioned address:

Kogan Page Limited
120 Pentonville Road
London N1 9JN

© Autodriva Training Systems 1982, 1983, 1986, 1988
John Miller and Margaret Stacey 1989, 1991, 1993, 1994, 1996, 1997, 1999

British Library Cataloguing in Publication Data

A CIP record for this book is available from the British Library.

ISBN 0 7494 3085 0

Typeset by Saxon Graphics Ltd, Derby
Printed and bound in Great Britain by Clays Ltd, St. Ives plc

Contents

RCM
Marketing Ltd

20 NEWTOWN BUSINESS PARK, ALBION CLOSE, POOLE, DORSET BH12 3LL
TEL:01202 737999 FAX:01202 735909

We supply almost everything needed by the driving instruction industry:

A FULL RANGE OF TRAINING AIDS, BOOKS, SIGNAGE,
STATIONERY, THEORY TEST PAPERS, DUAL CONTROLS,
MIRRORS, STICKERS, MAGNETIC SIGNS, ETC, ETC.

WE ALSO HAVE A FULLY EQUIPPED ON - SITE PRINTING
PLANT FOR ALL YOUR BUSINESS CARDS, FLYERS, ETC.

MANUFACTURERS OF SCANASIGN THE INDUSTRY'S
LEADING ROOFSIGN.

We are also the official supplier to the **MSA**
Motor Schools Association of Great Britain

Call or write today

for our new

FREE brochure!

WE HAVE FULL MAIL ORDER FACILITIES WITH MOST ITEMS AVAILABLE FROM STOCK
ALL MAJOR CREDIT CARDS ACCEPTED

About the Authors

John Miller and Margaret Stacey are Driving Standards Agency Approved Driving Instructors and qualified tutors. They each have well over 20 years' experience within the driving instruction industry and have been involved as consultants with many national organisations and committees. They both conduct practical training courses for the ADI examination as well as for updating and retraining experienced instructors for their Check Test. John Miller operates a driving school for car and lorry drivers.

Together with Tony Scriven, John and Margaret are co-authors of *Practical Teaching Skills for Driving Instructors*. This book is also published by Kogan Page.

Practical Teaching Skills for Driving Instructors is recommended for candidates preparing for the ADI examination and also for experienced instructors preparing for their Check Test. It is useful resource material for all instructors in their everyday work of teaching drivers at all levels of ability.

Margaret Stacey is also the author of the best-selling Kogan Page titles *Learn to Drive in 10 Easy Stages* and *The Advanced Driver's Handbook*. These books are widely used by instructors at all levels throughout the UK and in the Republic of Ireland. Margaret produces and regularly updates a *Home Study Programme* for those preparing for the ADI Part 1 Test of Theory. This is proving so effective that it has now been incorporated into the training syllabus of numerous training establishments throughout the UK. Also supplied by Margaret is a *Visual Teaching System* to help instructors simplify their explanations to drivers of all levels. This may be used by candidates during the ADI Part 3 Test of Instructional Ability. She also contributed to the interactive CD ROM entitled *The Driving Test – Your licence to drive* produced by RIVA International in conjunction with the Institute of Advanced Motorists.

More recently Margaret has been involved, as a member of the ADITE Management Committee, with the setting up of the new single register for ADI trainers. This register, ORDIT, which is supported by all of the ADI Consultative Organisations, is administered by the DSA and regulated by the Industry and has been set up to promote better control over the ADI training sector.

Every effort has been made to ensure that this book is up-to-date at the time of publication. However, because of the changing nature of legislation and all the new procedures being introduced within the driver testing industry, some differences may have occurred since going to print. We therefore strongly recommend that you read the latest trade magazines to ensure that you are completely up to date.

John Miller
MILLERS
57 North Street
Chichester
West Sussex PO19 1NB
Tel/Fax: 01243 784715
e-mail: john.miller@cwcom.net

Margaret Stacey
AUTODRIVA
35 Bourne Square
Breaston
Derbyshire DE72 3DZ
Tel/Fax: 01332 874111
e-mail: mstacey@
autodriva.freeserve.co.uk
Web site: www.autodriva.co.uk

DeskTop Driving Ltd

DeskTop Driving Ltd

DeskTop Driving Ltd

DeskTop Driving Ltd

If you are training or already qualified we can help you with all your training supplies

DeskTop Driving Ltd

Order Lines: 01903 882299

Sales e-mail: sales @desktopdriving.com
Catalogue Request: catalogue @desktopdriving.com
Customer Service:custserv@desktopdriving.com

Fax: 01903 885599

MARGARET STACEY

A well respected name in the driving industry and the author or co-author of the following titles:

- **The Driving Instructors Handbook**
- **Practical Teaching Skills**
- **Learn to Drive in 10 Easy Stages**
- **The Advanced Drivers Handbook**

has published 3 new books to help PDI's with the Part One examination.

In total these 3 books contain 750 ADI test questions

Available individually at £14.99 or all 3 for only £34.99

Book 1 contains 225 Theory Questions   Order Ref: 489
Book 2 contains 225 Theory Questions   Order Ref: 490
Book 3 contains 3 Mock Test Papers   Order Ref: 491
All 3 Books   Order Ref: 492

AVAILABLE NOW FROM SOLE UK DISTRIBUTOR

01903 882299

Foreword

The Driving Instructor's Handbook was first recommended by the Department of Transport (now the Driving Standards Agency) in 1989. It was chosen because of its coverage of material relating to the ADI examinations and in particular to the Part 1 Test of Theory. The book has been regularly updated and therefore continues to be recommended both for those aspiring to become ADIs and for those already on the Register.

The knowledge required to pass the Part 1 Test of Theory is wide ranging. Not only does this book cover much of the syllabus, but it also gives practical advice for the Part 2 Test of Driving Ability and the Part 3 Test of Ability to Instruct.

The Check Test is becoming much more searching in its assessment of ADIs' skills at identifying, analysing and remedying driver faults. Many driving instructors who have been on the Register for a number of years are beginning to struggle to retain their ADI grading, with a higher proportion than ever now being graded as sub-standard.

With the volume of traffic on our roads on a continually increasing upward trend, it is vital to ensure that the standard of driving continues to improve. This is one of the reasons why the driving test has recently undergone its first major overhaul since it was introduced in 1935. More emphasis will now be placed on the candidate's on-road skills and failure will result not only from one serious or dangerous fault, but also from less serious driver faults.

Trainee driving instructors must therefore be aware that they need to seek an adequate amount of good quality training, not only to ensure that they are properly prepared for all three parts of the qualifying examination but also to prepare them for teaching new drivers 'safe driving for life'.

Experienced instructors who have not sought to keep up-to-date with their teaching methods must realise that those qualifying now will be much better placed to compete in the market-place. It is therefore recommended that instructors at all levels read this book and put into practice the methods of teaching which will result in newly qualified drivers being able to cope more effectively with the problems facing them on our roads. They should also consider that it may be more sensible to have some refresher training prior to taking their Check Test, than finding themselves in a situation where they are downgraded and at risk of losing their job.

With the many changes currently taking place over the whole range of activities within the driver training industry, those involved at all levels of training are strongly recommended to use the Handbook as resource material.

That the Handbook is now in its 11th edition (the sixth update since we first began recommending it) is a tribute to its authors and publishers in keeping it up to date. Whilst we may not agree with every view expressed by the authors (since the opinions expressed are their own), we strongly feel that you can learn much from them which will be to your advantage.

Mike Ambrose, Registrar
Approved Driving Instructors

Introduction

The Driving Instructor's Handbook was first published in 1982 and since 1989 has been recommended by the DSA as a text book for the ADI examinations. This, the revised 11th edition, contains all the latest information on driving licences, driving tests, teaching skills and the ADI examinations.

Drivers of most motor vehicles and motorcyclists are now required to pass a theory test. In addition to this, those passing the test for a motor car are restricted to driving vehicles of up 3,500 kg and with a maximum of eight seats. Anyone wishing to drive a larger vehicle with more than eight seats or with a gross weight of more than 3,500 kg will need to take an extra test; as will anyone wishing to tow a large trailer behind a car or small commercial vehicle.

Under *The New Driver Act*, any newly qualified driver who accumulates more than six penalty points on their licence within two years of passing their test, will lose their licence, have to re-apply for a provisional and re-take both the theory and practical tests.

All of the above means that, as well as preparing drivers for the 'L' test, ADIs need to be able to deal with drivers at all levels of ability and experience. To do this, they need to be effective teachers who will be able to develop safer attitudes.

Teaching people to understand is far more complex
than simply telling them where to go and what to do!

Training to become a driving instructor is therefore neither easy nor cheap. However, the time and effort taken to prepare for all three parts of the ADI examination, and the fees involved, should be considered an investment for your future.

A wide variety of training courses is available to the prospective instructor. Before you make your choice, or pay out any large sums of money in advance, study carefully Chapter 2 of this book. This explains the structure of the examination and how long it may take you to qualify. Chapter 3 goes on to explain, in more detail, the training you will require and the different types of course available.

It is important that you select a tutor who is completely up to date with the examination syllabus and who trains ADIs on a regular basis. Although your local driving instructor may be extremely good at teaching new drivers, there is a vast difference between 'teaching to drive' and 'teaching to teach'.

Listen to the advice given by your tutor. As there is a limit of three attempts on the Part 2 Test of Driving Ability and the Part 3 Test of Ability to Instruct, you should make sure you are well prepared before you attempt these elements of the examination. There are no short cuts! Remember, if you fail, there will be more pressure on you at the next attempt.

When you have qualified, you should bear in mind that you are now a professional. You are your best advertisement! Make sure you set a good example by driving correctly at all times. Dress smartly, keep your car in a clean and good mechanical condition. Treat all of your clients with respect and put your best effort in with all of them. If you follow these simple rules you will get lots of recommendations and your business will flourish.

As a practising ADI you will need to continuously consider the changing trends within the driving instruction industry. The 'L' driver market has been declining over recent years with the fall in both the birth rate and the middle-aged learner market. This trend is likely to continue until there is an increase in the number of 17-year-old pupils in a few years' time.

The number of instructors in the ADI Register remains relatively constant. Therefore, with a changing market and the sustained level of competition, there is no time to sit back and wait for the telephone to ring. You must be prepared to seek out new markets for yourself. Chapter 1 gives a few ideas and suggestions for maintaining an adequate level of business and keeping ahead of the competition.

As a practising ADI, are you happy with the grading you achieved in your last 'Check Test'? Even though you may have a reasonable pass rate, your teaching style may be a little out of date. If you have been an ADI for a number of years, you may find it helpful to update your knowledge and teaching style so that it is comparable with that of your newly-qualified competitors. Listen to the advice given by your Supervising Examiner/Approved Driving Instructor (SEADI). Make sure that you are completely up to date with modern driving and teaching techniques and that you are working with the latest editions of *The Highway Code, The Driving Manual* and *The Driving Test*. These should also form the basis of your lessons given over to preparing your pupils for the theory test.

With the many changes which have been introduced over the past year or so, we have included as much information as is relevant on subjects such as the theory test, the licensing and testing of LGV and PCV drivers, and the licensing requirements for new drivers. However, because of the changing nature of legislation, some differences may have been introduced since this edition went to print. We do recommend, therefore, that you read the latest trade magazines to ensure that your information is up to date.

John Miller and Margaret Stacey
Summer 2001

The Role of the Driving Instructor

This chapter gives an outline of the driving instruction industry and includes information on:

- the instructor's job;
- the qualities it takes to become a good ADI;
- the ADI qualification;
- how to select your trainer;
- further qualifications;
- driving instruction opportunities;
- the major ADI associations and organisations.

THE ROLE OF THE DRIVING INSTRUCTOR

In today's fast-moving and complex road and traffic systems, the driving instructor's role is becoming much more diverse than when the driving test was first introduced in 1935.

Although the newly qualified ADI's main occupation is in the teaching of new drivers, there are now far more opportunities to extend that role to include:

- theory and pre-driver training;
- teaching people with disabilities;
- defensive and advanced driver training;
- company and fleet training;
- minibus driving;
- training in the towing of caravans;
- corrective training for traffic offenders;
- assessments for older drivers;
- schemes run by police forces and local county councils.

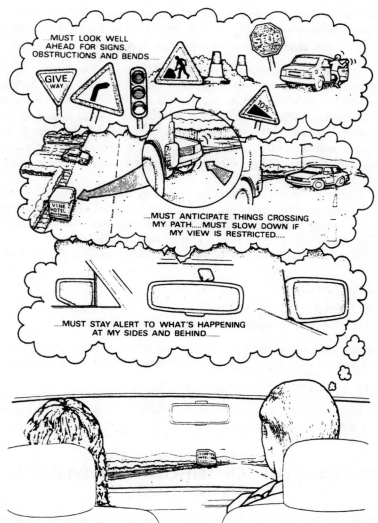

With the speed and density of today's traffic, together with increasingly complex driving situations, the job of teaching new drivers is not an easy one. It is not enough to be a good driver who enjoys motoring. The professional instructor needs to have a serious interest in improving the standards of new and experienced drivers in order to reduce the numbers of accidents and casualties suffered on our roads.

To become a good driving instructor you need to:

- have a thorough understanding of the rules and principles involved in safe driving;
- be able to put these principles into practice by driving thoughtfully and efficiently;

- be able to patiently teach drivers how to apply those principles, while everyone else around you is trying to get from A to B as quickly as possible;
- instil in clients, at all levels of ability, safe attitudes.

One of your main aims must be to produce drivers who will make our roads safer, while at the same time ensuring that they also enjoy their driving. The number of motorists killed in road accidents is far too high, particularly among the newly qualified, younger drivers. You will need to encourage pupils to develop better attitudes towards themselves, their vehicle and, last but by no means least, towards all other road users. Drivers who are taught to accept and compensate for the mistakes of others are far less likely to become involved in the 'road rage' epidemic.

To be able to carry out all the skills necessary to today's driving instructor, you must be prepared to study hard for the Part 1 Test of Theory and have sufficient, good quality training to stand a reasonable chance of passing the Part 2 Test of Driving Ability and the Part 3 Test of Ability to Instruct.

The exam pass rate figures for the twelve-month period ending January 2001 were:

Theory Test	54%
Part 1:2 Eyesight: Driving Ability	45%
Part 3: Instructional Ability	30%

This meant that, from a total of 10,810 applications at the written stage, 2,264 actually qualified to become Approved Driving Instructors at the end of the period.

From these figures, you should be able to work out that the exam is not an easy one, especially Part 3. You should therefore be prepared to invest in good quality training and a lot of hard work!

THE QUALITIES OF THE GOOD DRIVER AND INSTRUCTOR

As far as your own personal driving skills are concerned, you should be aware of the qualities required by the good driver. These include:

- Responsibility – you should always show proper concern for the safety of yourself, your passengers and other road users. As a driving instructor, you should always have the safety and well-being of your pupils at heart, particularly those in the early stages of their driving career. Don't take them into situations with which they are not ready to cope – you are responsible for their safety.
- Concentration – you must concentrate at all times. Even the slightest distraction can have disastrous effects in today's heavily congested and fast-moving traffic. Your concentration when sitting next to inexperienced drivers is even more essential. You must read the road further ahead and

take into account any developing situations so that you can keep your pupils safe, relaxed and eager to learn more.

- Anticipation – the ability to predict what might happen is part and parcel of the good driver's skill in keeping out of trouble. This is even more important when you are sitting in the passenger seat with someone at the controls of your car. You need to understand the individual needs of each pupil and anticipate how they may or may not respond to changing situations. You have to plan well ahead and anticipate potential problems so that you can help your pupils to deal with them early and safely.

- Patience – always show restraint and patience with other drivers, particularly when they make mistakes. This will not only set a good example to others but, if you have your name on your car, it makes good sense to demonstrate good driving practice. To lose patience when a pupil makes a mistake will only compound the problem. Normally, pupils know when something has gone wrong. Be patient, even if you have explained things a number of times previously. Your patience should build up your pupils' faith in you. It should also help to build up their confidence, because they feel safe in the knowledge that anyone can make a mistake, and patience and practice can put it right.

- Confidence – the efficient driver displays confidence at all times. This results from being totally 'at one' with the vehicle – travelling at a safe speed with the appropriate gear engaged and in the correct position on the road. Planning well ahead and anticipating changes in the traffic situation also helps to avoid the need to make any last-minute, rushed decisions. Every action should be planned and carried out confidently. When training others – no matter what their level of driving – the syllabus and route selected should be matched to their ability. Avoiding situations they cannot cope with will help to build up their confidence in you and in themselves.

As well as the above qualities, you also need the following attributes to be able to teach safe driving:

- Knowledge – although driving is mainly a practical skill, to be able to survive, you need:
  - a sound knowledge of the rules and procedures outlined in *The Highway Code* and *The Driving Manual*. Not only is this essential for the ADI examination, but you will also have to prepare your clients for the Theory 'L' Test;
  - to keep up to date continually with any changes taking place – your clients may ask for advice on anything from changes in road procedure to the category of driving licence they may need, or how to change a wheel;
  - to be fully aware of the principles involved in teaching and of keeping the teaching environment safe;
  - to develop vehicle sympathy – for this you need to know the principles of how the car works and how it responds in different conditions;

- a basic knowledge of vehicle mechanics and routine maintenance requirements. The car is the tool of your trade – if you are unable to recognise problems before they become serious, your car may break down and you will be unable to work.
- Communication – as a driver you need to communicate with other road users through a system of signalling. This includes using the indicators, brake lights, reversing lights, arm signals, eye contact, positioning correctly in the road, and using the warning instruments – the horn, flashing headlights and hazard lights.

To communicate with your clients, you need to develop different ways of explaining facts in a way that can be understood clearly by each individual. Their understanding of new principles and techniques will lead to greater confidence. This means that you must not only teach your pupils how to do things, but also why they are done in that manner. There are a number of ways in which you can communicate, including:

- establishing the level of understanding of your pupils and how best to communicate with them;
- explaining new principles in a clear and simple way;
- using visual aids so that your pupils can 'see' what you mean;
- giving practical demonstrations of complicated procedures;
- developing confidence and success by talking pupils through new procedures;
- giving your directions and instructions in good time for pupils to respond safely;
- giving encouragement through positive feedback and praise;
- finding out whether pupils understand your instructions by asking them questions;
- encouraging pupils to ask questions if you feel they do not understand.

Although driving has been made relatively easy through better car design, efficiency and safety, road and traffic conditions are becoming more and more complex. In order to keep your clients safe, you need to be aware of the major causes of road accidents. These include:

- ignorance of, or total disregard for, the rules of the road;
- lack of concentration and attention to developing situations;
- carelessness;
- driving while under the influence of drink or drugs;
- driving when feeling unwell;
- driving with deficient eyesight;
- a willingness to take risks;
- using a vehicle in an unroadworthy condition.

Because of the ever-changing road and traffic conditions, and the regular modification to rules and regulations, driving procedures need to be continually adapted. The driving test for new drivers has undergone its most major overhaul since it was introduced in 1935 and is far more relevant to today's driving needs. New drivers have to be taught to a far higher standard, with hazard awareness playing a major role in their development.

It is up to the instructor to ensure that drivers at all levels are taught to:

- handle their vehicles sympathetically and economically;
- drive with courtesy and consideration;
- look and plan well ahead, anticipating what may happen;
- compensate for the mistakes of others;
- understand what they are doing and why they are doing it.

To be able to do all of these things, you, as an ADI, must be prepared to keep yourself up to date with all of the changes relevant to driving and the teaching of it. The DSA sends a copy of its magazine *Despatch* to all ADIs. This contains some of the latest information. However, most instructors tend to work in isolation and it is very easy to become complacent and just 'plod along' without giving any thought to either updating themselves or improving their skills.

In order to keep up with the times, it is sensible to join some sort of ADI organisation. There are a number of national associations which provide information to their members on a regular basis.

The main ones are the:

- ADINJC – Approved Driving Instructors' National Joint Council;
- ADI Business Club;
- DIA – Driving Instructors' Association;
- MSA – Motor Schools' Association.

THE ADI QUALIFICATION

If you wish to teach driving for money or money's worth, whether this be to complete beginners or experienced drivers, the only official qualification is the Driving Standards Agency Approved Driving Instructor (car) (or in Northern Ireland, DoEADI). You must have had a specified minimum number of years' experience as a driver and you must meet all the other requirements laid down in the Road Traffic Act. A full explanation of the qualifications for registration is given in Chapter 2.

For an application form and full details of what is involved in the qualification, you should apply to the Driving Standards Agency (DSA) for their information pack *Your Road to Becoming an Approved Driving Instructor (ADI.14)*. You should send your request, together with your payment (currently £3.50) to: The ADI Register, Stanley House, Talbot Street, Nottingham NG1 5GU. Applicants in Northern Ireland should apply for an ADI.1 (free of charge) to the Driver & Vehicle Testing Agency, Balmoral Road, Belfast BT12 6QL, Tel: 0289 068 1831.

To qualify as an ADI, you have to pass an examination which is conducted in three parts: Part 1 – Test of Theory; Part 2 – Test of Eyesight and Driving Ability; Part 3 – Test of Ability to Instruct. You must take and pass all three parts of this examination within a two-year period. The format of the examination and how to apply is explained in Chapter 2.

HOW TO SELECT YOUR TRAINER

Proper preparation for each part of the examination is extremely important. To pass Part 1, you need to ensure that the materials and books which you study are all up to date and that any questions which you don't understand are explained by your tutor. A regularly updated *Home Study Programme* is available from Margaret Stacey. This enables you to fit in your studies around your other commitments.

As there is a limit of three attempts at Parts 2 and 3, it is essential that you seek good training from a properly qualified tutor. There are some very good tutors around. A list of those who have been inspected by the Driving Standards Agency is included in their information pack *ADI.14*.

The Approved Driving Instructors' National Joint Council (ADINJC) also has a list of tutors who have qualified through their Tutor Training Courses. For a list of these contact: John Milne MBE, 121 Marshalswick Lane, St Albans, Herts AL1 4UX (tel: 01727 858068).

There is an extremely high failure rate at the Part 3 Test of Ability to Instruct – the most complex part of the exam. It is therefore essential that, before committing yourself to a course, you ask your tutor to specify:

- how much individual in-car training you will receive;
- when this training will be given in relation to the examination appointment.

Beware of paying out large sums of money for intensive courses – there may not be any refund should you fail to complete the course, or if you fail to reach Part 3. Chapter 3 explains how to prepare for this examination.

FURTHER QUALIFICATIONS

The level of competence you attain to pass the ADI examination is the minimum standard required by law to enable you to teach driving professionally. However, road and traffic conditions, the driver training industry, and also the law, are in a continual state of change. You should strive to keep yourself up to date and also improve on your own knowledge and personal driving skills. This will help to equip you for driver training at all levels and not to limit you to basic 'L' driver training.

You can consider the various optional qualifications and driving tests. The Institute of Advanced Motorists (IAM) and the Royal Society for the Prevention of Accidents (RoSPA) are probably the most well known of the advanced driving organisations. Their tests are outlined in Chapter 4 of this book. The Cardington Special Driving Test and the Diamond Advanced Motorist's Test are industry based and an outline is given here for your information.

The Cardington Special Driving Test

This test is available to all Approved Driving Instructors. The standard required is much higher than that needed to pass the ADI Part 2 Test of Driving Ability.

Tests are conducted by permanent Staff Instructors at the DSA's Driving Establishment at Cardington, near Bedford. You will have to demonstrate that you can handle your car efficiently and accurately on all types of road and while carrying out a variety of manoeuvre exercises.

At the end of the test your examiner will complete a report which will be discussed with the Chief Instructor before a grading is given. Results are normally sent out within 48 hours. If you attain a grade 'A', you will be eligible to receive the Special Test Certificate.

The fee for this test at April 2001 is £65. For further information write to: The Special Test Booking Section, The Driving Establishment, RAF Cardington, Bedford MK42 0TJ (tel: 01234 742134).

The Diamond Advanced Motorist's Test

This test is administered by the DIA, whose examiners use the standard DSA marking system. During the test, which incorporates a wide variety of road and traffic situations, you are allowed no more than six driver faults.

Tests are conducted by Diamond Advanced Examiners. These are normally ADIs who have achieved the Diploma in Driving Instruction, have passed the Cardington Special Driving Test and have also passed the DIA Diamond Instructors' Course.

Once you are an ADI, this extra qualification should help you in marketing advanced and defensive driving courses.

The Diploma in Driving Instruction

This professional qualification is awarded jointly by the Associated Examining Board (AEB) and The Driving Instructors' Association (DIA). It is not restricted to ADIs. Anyone involved in driving instruction, road safety or other occupations related to driving may apply. The overall aims of the diploma are to improve standards of driver instruction and to provide wider public recognition of the services offered by those who hold it.

The examination consists of five modules, each tested in a two-hour examination. These are:

1. Legal obligations and regulations.
2. Management of a small driving school.
3. Vehicle maintenance and mechanical principles.
4. Driving theory – skills and procedures.
5. Instructing – practices and procedures.

A certificate is awarded for each module and, when all five have been passed, the Diploma in Driving Instruction is awarded.

Examinations are conducted in April/May of each year and entries are accepted at any AEB centre which takes external candidates (normally Colleges of Further Education). For full information on this qualification write to either the AEB or the DIA.

The City & Guilds Further Education Teacher's Certificate

Now that the theory test for learner drivers is firmly established and a wider driver training market is opening up, you may find this qualification particularly helpful. It will help to build up the confidence which is needed to adapt your teaching from the normal one-to-one in-car situation, to standing in front of a class to teach your subject.

This certificate is relevant to anyone teaching in adult education, no matter what their specialist subject may be. It will give you a greater understanding of the different teaching techniques and you will discover how and why people learn at different rates.

One of the main advantages of achieving this certificate is that it is a recognised teaching qualification accepted by most educational establishments. You will therefore have an advantage over your competitors when you apply to run driving courses through schools and colleges.

Courses are held at Colleges of Further Education throughout the country and are normally run on a part-time basis. For full details, contact your local college or education authority.

Certificate in Education (CertEd)

This certificate is aimed at those who wish to develop as more professional teachers. It is normally a continuation of initial teacher training (such as the FE Teacher's Certificate) and is designed to build on current teaching experience.

The scheme is modular, being broken down into four parts. Continuous assessments are made throughout and there is no examination involved. Depending on current qualifications, this part-time course can be taken over a one- or two-year period.

The CertEd fits into the Credit Accumulation and Transfer Scheme (CATS) which, by accumulation of credit points, opens up a wide range of further training and development opportunities.

For information on course availability contact your local Education Authority.

The National Vocational Qualification in Driving Instruction

The driving instructor's biggest potential market is the young learner looking for 'L' driver training. Most young people now leaving schools and colleges are aware of the NVQ system. They recognise the qualification as a guarantee of a minimum standard of achievement.

To gain an NVQ, all you have to do is collect evidence of the everyday work which you carry out. Your evidence has to show that your work is conducted in line with the DSA syllabus. Your portfolio of evidence then has to be verified by assessors who have been qualified by the awarding body.

Although the ADI qualification is the only official requirement that allows you to give driving instruction for payment, the title is not always recognised. There is nothing to determine the quality of instruction between one ADI and the next, and sometimes selecting a name from *Yellow Pages* can be a hit-and-miss affair. If you have an NVQ, this will immediately be recognised.

If you would like the added recognition this qualification will give you, and would like further information, contact: John Milne MBE, 121 Marshalswick Lane, St Albans, Herts AL1 4UX (tel: 01727 858068).

THE DRIVING INSTRUCTION MARKET

The 'L' Driver Market

About 1.6 million 'L' tests are conducted every year by the DSA. Over 90 per cent of candidates have some tuition with an ADI. This is therefore normally the largest source of business for instructors.

The biggest market for 'L' driver training is in the 17–20 age range. There are various ways of finding out about population trends and the viability of opening up a driving school in your area; these include:

- consulting the local electoral register;
- contacting the local sixth form schools and colleges.

The driving instructor's job sometimes has to be a delicate balance between conscience and reality. Teaching driving as a 'skill for life' requires much more practical training these days than it did when the Driving Test was introduced in 1935. However, too many learners seem to think that a driving licence is a right, not a privilege, and only want to pass the test as quickly and as cheaply as possible. Even though road systems and the volume of traffic are changing all the time, some parents still compare learning today with 20 years ago. All too common is the statement 'Well, I only had 10 lessons!'

You obviously want to keep your clients. You therefore sometimes have to reach a compromise between your ideal standard and what they will accept. Your main consideration when reaching this compromise is whether the pupil will be safe.

Teaching driving should be a combination of theory and practice. This means that while the pupil is studying, he or she can be taught how to put the principles and procedures into practice, resulting in a better understanding of why the rules and regulations are in place.

There are ways in which you can make your training more effective. *Learn to Drive in 10 Easy Stages*, written by Margaret Stacey and published by Kogan Page, covers the syllabus for practical training in a step-by-step format. This is used by numerous instructors throughout the UK to give pupils some in-between lesson guidance. Where pupils are getting private practice, they can be encouraged to study this book with their supervisors so that the confusion and differences of opinion which so often occur can be avoided.

To teach 'safe driving for life', as well as all the books you have to study for the ADI Part 1 Test of Theory, you will need to have a thorough understanding of the DSA's recommended syllabus for learners. You will find this information in the HMSO book *The Driving Test*.

Theory Test Training

It will be your responsibility to ensure that new drivers are made aware of the importance of understanding the principles and rules for driving safely. Candidates have to study a number of books for this test and you can increase your own earnings by buying some of these in bulk at discounted rates for selling on at the full price.

Try to emphasise to pupils that the more time they spend studying for the Theory Test, the better they will understand the rules, and that this could result in their needing fewer practical lessons.

Preparing pupils for the Theory Test does not necessarily mean investing in your own classroom facilities. There are different ways of organising training for this test and at the same time you can increase your earning potential. These include:

- taking some time off each practical lesson to cover elements of the theory syllabus;
- teaching small groups of clients in your office;
- hiring a room once a week to run a modular course so that clients can attend at their own convenience and still cover the entire syllabus;
- giving talks at youth clubs;
- setting up a classroom and offering theory training for pupils of other ADIs who do not wish to become involved with theory training.

Because of the personal contact you have with pupils as a result of running theory courses, many of the above schemes may result in an expansion of the practical training element of your business.

Information Technology

Theory tests are all computer-based and most pupils have access to computers – whether this is at home, at school or in college. It is therefore important for you to be able to offer your pupils the appropriate CD ROMs for effective learning. Interactive programmes can be particularly helpful for pupils who have learning difficulties such as dyslexia.

The right computer programmes will also enable you to prepare personalised business stationery, hand-outs and other training aids. You should also be able to reduce the cost of professional fees by 'balancing your books' on computer.

Pre-driver Training

Driving is now accepted as a life skill. Bearing this in mind, getting yourself known to those in the pre-driver age group can be extremely useful.

Setting up pre-driver training courses will not only give the pupils a sound knowledge before they take to the roads, but it will ensure that your name will be recognised by them when they reach driving age.

To discuss the benefits of these courses for young people, you should contact:

- the local education authority;
- schools with sixth forms;
- sixth form colleges;
- youth organisations/groups;
- the local road safety officer.

The 'Pass Plus' Scheme

Set up by the DSA in an effort to encourage further driver education through post-test training, this scheme is available to all ADIs. The object is to give new drivers experience in a wider variety of situations and conditions than is required for the L test. You can encourage your pupils to take the extra training by emphasising that many insurance companies offer substantial discounts to successful participants, usually equivalent to a one year's no-claims bonus.

Pass Plus is designed to 'make newly qualified drivers better drivers'.

The course consists of six special training sessions covering driving:

- in towns;
- out of towns;
- in all weather conditions;
- at night;
- on dual carriageways;
- on motorways.

Training can be taken up to a year after passing the practical L test. The insurance discount can be deferred for a further two years if the participant is driving on someone else's insurance.

Although the number of newly qualified drivers taking Pass Plus is slowly increasing, this is still a vastly untapped market with very few instructors taking advantage of its potential. When asked by the DSA for the secret behind successful promotion of Pass Plus, some of the tips given were to:

- mention the scheme when pupils first contact you for information;
- try and involve parents, getting them to recognise the added reassurance Pass Plus gives;
- give a reminder about the scheme before and after pupils take the practical test;
- inform pupils and parents of the statistics of newly qualified drivers being involved in accidents.

Since the major part of an ADI's work is teaching new drivers, the Pass Plus scheme gives a little more variety.

To become involved with the scheme, an instructor's starter pack, including all the necessary course material, is available from the DSA at Nottingham for £20. Refill packs cost £16.

The College of Driver Education (CODE)

This is a charitable organisation set up with four main aims:

1. To help raise the general standard of driving.
2. To ensure that driving instructors are thoroughly trained.
3. To assist in funding and developing research into driving matters.
4. To provide a counselling service to victims of road accidents.

Members of the public who wish to update and improve their driving skills are invited to take an assessment with a CODE-approved assessor. There is no pass or fail element involved in this assessment, which eliminates, to a large extent, the pressures involved in taking one of the advanced driving tests.

When you have had some experience in driving instruction, CODE may be a means of introducing more variety to your work. It must be remembered, however, that assessing experienced drivers is totally different from teaching new drivers, and assessments must be made at the appropriate level. It is therefore essential that you have had some experience at dealing with drivers at varying levels of ability. Those applying for the post of assessor will themselves be appraised by an Area Assessor as to their suitability for the position.

Anyone who applies to become a CODE assessor must be a qualified ADI. To apply, write to: Bernard Rogers, Chief Assessor CODE, 12 Queensway, Poynton, Stockport SK12 1JG.

Defensive Driver Training

There are now more than 30 million full licence holders in the UK. A significant number of them would benefit from some form of 'defensive' driver education.

Company drivers: Many companies and organisations employing groups of drivers will be looking for professional expertise in order to conduct driver assessments and remedial training for their employees. The latter might include drivers with a record of accidents, or potential new employees.

In order to demonstrate a professional approach to clients, you will need to have a properly structured system for the assessment of driving and presenting reports. Your possible customers might include:

- local companies;
- voluntary groups;
- education departments;
- health authorities.

All of the above are employers of groups of full time and part time drivers as well as voluntary drivers.

Traffic offenders: Some traffic offences now attract a compulsory or discretionary order for disqualification and/or a requirement to take a further driving test. Your local solicitors would be interested in a professional assessment and reporting service which could benefit their clients in preparation for court hearings.

Drivers requiring updating: there are large numbers of drivers who may have held a licence for many years, but have not driven for a while, or who have simply lost their confidence. You could advertise re-training or refresher courses to bring drivers up to date with the latest rules and regulations and to re-build their confidence. You could also give short talks about defensive driving to groups such as:

- the Young Wives and Women's Institutes;
- the Round Table and Ladies' Circle;
- the Rotary and Inner Wheel Clubs.

All you have to do to increase your business and add variety to your work is to carry out a little research to find out information on the above types of company or organisation in your area.

Vocational Training

With the many changes taking place to driving licence categories and the testing procedures for drivers and riders, there is a vast market which is still largely untapped by the ADI.

If you have the appropriate licences, you should consider training in the following areas:

Motorcycling: This is an increasing market involving motorcyclists and moped riders at various levels:

- compulsory basic training;
- pre-test instruction;
- 'Direct Access'.

Special instructional qualifications are needed for the different elements of training. The DSA conducts courses at the Training Establishment, Cardington, as follows:

- CBT – two-day course;
- Direct Access – one-day course.

Minibuses: Drivers with a full licence issued after January 1997 are only allowed to drive vehicles with up to eight seats. Many schools and voluntary organisations require training in vehicles with more than eight seats for both their experienced and new drivers.

Lorries: With staged testing now starting at vehicles of 3.5 tonnes, and the voluntary register of LGV instructors, this is another growing market for training in medium-sized goods vehicles. Although there is, under the voluntary register scheme, a test for LGV instructors, there is no specific instructional qualification as long as you hold the appropriate driving entitlement.

More information on vocational training is included in Chapter 10.

Career Development

Although about 94 per cent of ADIs only conduct L driver training, the above are just a few of the opportunities now open to the instructor who is looking for a wider variety of career development.

DRIVING INSTRUCTOR ASSOCIATIONS

When you have qualified as an ADI, it will be necessary, for your own as well as your pupils' benefit, to keep up to date with the changes taking place in the industry.

Most of the 30,000 driving instructors in the ADI Register work on a 'one-car driving school' basis and often find themselves isolated from their colleagues, with very little idea of where to look for help or information.

Although all instructors now receive the DSA's *Despatch* magazine, this contains only a limited amount of news. To be kept more informed, and also to be able to take advantage of some of the professional and commercial services

Are you an ADI or thinking of becoming one?

The Driving Instructors Association can:-

- Help you qualify for the ADI Register.
- Help steer you on the correct road and avoid the many pitfalls that will be put in your way.
- Advise you on the best training car to use, and whether to purchase or rent.
- Protect you if your car is involved in an accident - in most circumstances we will provide and deliver a dual controlled replacement car absolutely free.
- Supply you with a wide range of publications and instructional material from our Mail Order catalogue.

We take most major credit and charge cards and we even have our own - the DIA MasterCard. Membership is available for trainees prior to getting their ADI licences.

We are only a telephone call away!

Write or call for our no-obligation joining pack

The DIA operates an independent Directory of Recommended Training Establishments (DIA-RTE) in co-operation with the Driving Standards Agency (DSA). All prospective driving instructors should take advantage to avoid unscrupulous training schools.

DIA, Safety House, Beddington Farm Road, Croydon CR0 4XZ.
Tel. 0181 665 5151 - Fax 0181 665 5565

required by ADIs, you should seriously consider joining one of the major national associations.

Two main organisations are open to individual membership:

- *The Driving Instructors' Association (DIA);*
- *The Motor Schools Association (MSA).*

The Approved Driving Instructors' National Joint Council (ADINJC)

This is a national association founded in 1973 whose membership is made up of an individual ADI Group and associations with varying numbers of members.

The ADINJC has consultative status with the DSA and was originally set up to bring unity to the driving instructor industry by amalgamating all the major organisations in one body. It convened the first meetings which led to the ADITE Directory (now ORDIT) and has played an important role in the establishment of the NVQ in Driving Instruction.

A national conference is normally held in October. As well as providing a forum for both its individual and association members, it is also open to non-member ADIs. Voting is open to all delegates.

For further information on the ADINJC contact:
Peter Edwards, General Secretary – ADINJC, 41 Edinburgh Road, Cambridge CB4 1QR. (Tel: 01223 359070).

For information about the individual Driving Instructors' Group (DIG) contact:
Barry Goodison, Group Secretary – 89 Chaucer Road, Parsons Cross, Sheffield S5 9QL (Tel: 0114 233 3566 or e-mail: barrygoodison@activemail.co.uk).

The Driving Instructors' Association (DIA)

The DIA was founded in 1978 and is now the largest trade association in the UK for professional driving instructors and road safety specialists. Membership is open to Approved Driving Instructors, those training for the ADI qualification and anyone with a professional interest in road safety. The DIA has founded the Driving Instructors' Accident and Disability Fund, a registered charity set up to provide benefits for driving instructors and their families in need. In 1995, the Driving Instructors' Association also became a registered charity. The DIA remains a proprietary association, the proprietors being DIA (Int.) Limited, a trading company and publishers of *The Driving Instructors' Manual*. Individual members are therefore fully protected from any financial liability to the DIA. The DIA is guided by a General Purposes Committee, elected from the membership at its Annual General Meeting. It is committed to improving standards of driver education and promoting road safety, while working to promote the welfare and business interests of professional driving instructors.

The DIA has consultative status with the DETR, the Driving Standards Agency, its theory testing organisation and is represented on the Pass Plus Board. It is also represented on the Parliamentary Advisory Committee on Transport Safety (PACTS) and other Government advisory committees. The DIA maintains extensive links with similar trade associations internationally and has consultative status with the European Parliament and United Nations through its membership of the International Association for Driver Education (IVV).

The work of the DIA is comprehensive on behalf of its membership and is carried out by a small dedicated staff. Each member receives regular copies of *Driving Magazine* and *Driving Instructor*, leading high quality publications for road safety specialists and driving instructors. Members also receive free professional indemnity and public liability insurance. Services provided for members vary from DIA Mail Order at preferential rates, training courses, conferences, exhibitions, DIA Quality Assurance (an ISO 9000 Quality programme), DIA Recovery service, medical and hospital plans, discounted car rental and branded advertising schemes to professional accounting services and legal advice. The DIA promotes *DIA Direct Insurance*, a direct insurance scheme set up to provide the very best service to the industry. The DIA has instituted a higher education programme including the *Diploma in Driving Instruction* and *DIAmond Advanced Instructor* qualifications and degree courses at Middlesex University. It promotes the *DIAmond Advanced Motorist Test* scheme to improve driving skills and also consults with the DSA on LGV/PCV, motorcycle, advanced and fleet driver training issues. The DIA administered the *DIA-RTE (DIA-Recommended Training Establishments) Directory* from 1992 and continues this work on the Steering Committee of the new industry register of ADI trainers, *ORDIT*, for the benefit of those seeking to train as ADIs.

A free membership information pack and complimentary copy of *Driving Magazine* and *Driving Instructor* can be obtained by telephoning, faxing or writing to: The DIA, Safety House, Beddington Farm Road, Croydon CR0 4XZ (tel: 020 8665 5151; fax: 020 8665 5565; e-mail: driving@atlas.co.uk).

The Motor Schools Association of Great Britain (MSA)

About the MSA

History

The Motor Schools Association of Great Britain (MSA) was formed on 31 March 1935, just before the driving test was introduced. The association's principal aims, then as now, are to keep members informed of any matters of interest to them; to represent the views of members to Government, its departments and agencies; to provide services which will be of benefit to members; and to set standards of professional and ethical behaviour for teachers of driving.

Membership

Full MSA membership is only available to Driving Standards Agency Approved Driving Instructors. However, those training to become DSA ADIs may join as temporary members and when qualified will be converted at no extra charge to full membership of the association. (Tel: 0161 429 9669; Fax: 0161 429 9779; e-mail: mail@msagb.co.uk).

How it is run

The MSA is a company limited by the guarantee of its members and is run on behalf of members by the Board of Management. Board members, who are all working driving instructors, are democratically elected at local elections held in each of the association's 10 regions. They are paid no salary for the work they do.

Information

The MSA prides itself on the information available to its members. Most of the information passed on to members is contained in the MSA's national publication, *MSA Newslink*. Published monthly, it is sent to all members, who also receive a copy of the regional *MSA Instructor* newspaper every month and a copy of the association's annual report and yearbook.

Representation

The MSA represents driver training interests to all relevant government departments and agencies. The association is also a member of the Parliamentary Advisory Committee on Transport Safety (PACTS); the European Secure Vehicle Alliance (ESVA) and the Royal Society for the Prevention of Accidents (RoSPA). European involvement is as the UK representative to the European Driving Schools Association (EFA).

Services

The MSA is always seeking to expand the services available to members. Over the past 12 months it has introduced a number of new services including £1 million professional indemnity cover for all members. Other services have been improved including an increase to £2 million for third party liability claims.

The future

The MSA is a forward-looking organisation always open to new ideas and improved methods. It plans to offer further services and benefits to members over the coming year.

The ADI Business Club

This is a national organisation set up in January 1994 and is open to individual ADIs and anyone currently training to become a driving instructor. Although a commercial organisation, the ADIBC has consultative status with the DSA.

A wide range of professional and commercial services is offered in areas of driving instruction and driving school management. A nationwide corporate advertising programme is also available which is designed to create work and project a professional image for ADIs.

The ADIBC has its own Code of Practice and has developed its own higher qualifications for ADIs. Information regarding the industry is provided through its magazine *The ADI Business Club News* and there is an online Web Site for ADIs and consumers.

The club has a unique consultation process which provides individual members with an equal say on its policies. By serving on Government Advisory Panels on road safety with regular consultation taking place, members' interests are represented at the highest level both in Britain and Europe. All sectors of the industry are represented.

For information contact: the ADI Business Club, 3 Greenacre Close, Wyke, Bradford BD12 9DQ (tel: 01274 672850).

Whether you:

- are considering driving instruction as a new career;
- are already a trainee instructor; or
- have been involved with driver training for a number of years

THERE IS ALWAYS SOMETHING TO LEARN!

Make it a habit to regularly check on changes to driver licensing and traffic rules and regulations.

The continual changes taking place to our road systems, together with the ever-increasing volume of traffic, mean your teaching methods may also need to be adapted from time to time. Be prepared to keep yourself up to date and to adapt, not only your own style of driving, but also your teaching style.

Remember, the future safety of your pupils could be in your hands!

Principal D. Kenny COAD,
RAC Registered Instructor

MEMBER

Suppliers of a full range of
ADIs' and Road Safety
Requisites
Agent for AA and
National Breakdown

REGISTERED
DRIVING
INSTRUCTOR

Fully Adjustable Dual Controls (Rod or Cable)
• Magnetic Roof Signs • All Adhesive Backed
Stickers (Also Magnetic Sheet) • Adhesive Faced
Stickers • Wide Range of L-Plates (Reflective)
• Wide Range of Books and Stationery
• Cut Out Vinyl Print • Highway Code and
Theory Test Books in Asian Dialects

WE ALSO STOCK A WIDE RANGE OF
"NEW DRIVER" GREEN L-PLATES

34 Peel Street, Denton, Manchester M34 3JY
Tel/Fax: 0161 336 8635
Mobile Tel: 0802 611138
Also Tel: 0161 336 3012 (24 hours)

2

The ADI Register and the Qualifying Examination

This chapter deals with the Department of Transport Approved Driving Instructor Register and the examination to qualify. It includes information on:

- the ADI Register;
- registered and licensed instructors;
- qualifications for registration;
- applications for registration;
- licence to give instruction;
- the Check Test;
- the ADI examination.

The Motor Cars (Driving Instruction Amendment) Regulations 2000 SI No 1805 are available from the Stationery Office (ISBN 0 11 099521 X) or on the HMSO Web site at www.hmso.gov.uk/si/si20001805.htm.

THE ADI REGISTER

In compliance with the Road Traffic Act 1988, anyone giving driving instruction for money or money's worth must be registered with the Driving Standards Agency, or hold a current licence to give instruction.

The first voluntary register was introduced in 1964. Anyone qualifying for registration at that time was known as a 'Ministry of Transport Approved Driving Instructor'.

Many changes have taken place over recent years, which have resulted in candidates having to demonstrate a much higher standard of personal driving and instructional skills in order to qualify.

The official title of a registered driving instructor is *'Driving Standards Agency Approved Driving Instructor (Car)'*. (In Northern Ireland it is Department of the Environment Approved Driving Instructor.)

REGISTERED AND LICENSED INSTRUCTORS

To give driving tuition for money, or money's worth, you must:

- have passed all three parts of the qualifying examination and be a Driving Standards Agency Approved Driving Instructor (Car). The examination consists of:
  - Part 1 Test of Theory;
  - Part 2 Test of Driving Ability;
  - Part 3 Test of Ability to Instruct; and:
- have paid the current registration fee;
- agree to take a test of 'continued ability and fitness to give instruction' (Check Test) when required to do so by the Registrar.

Or:

- hold a *Trainee Licence*. This allows you to gain experience before you take the Part 3 Test of Ability to Instruct. To qualify for this six-month licence you must:
  - have passed Parts 1 and 2 of the qualifying examination; and be sponsored by an ADI.

(In Northern Ireland this may be applied for at the same time as applying for the written test.)

Exemptions

Section 123 of the Road Traffic Act only applies to instruction in the driving of cars. It does not apply to those giving instruction in:

- riding motorcycles;
- driving large goods vehicles;
- driving passenger-carrying vehicles.

Under Section 124, police officers are exempted from Section 123 when giving driving instruction as part of their official duties, providing this is with the authority of the Chief Constable.

Under Section 39 and in relation to the responsibilities of local authorities to provide 'traffic education', Road Safety Officers are exempt from the ADI regulations while carrying out their official duties.

These exemptions do not apply where police or road safety officers are giving instruction in cars outside of their official duties.

Teaching Friends or Relatives Before You Qualify

You do not necessarily have to have a trainee licence to gain experience. It is permissible to teach friends or relatives while training for the ADI examination. However, you must not make any charge or receive payment of any kind, for example in petrol or goods.

QUALIFICATIONS FOR REGISTRATION

To become a Driving Standards Agency Approved Driving Instructor (Car) you must:

- hold a full British or Northern Ireland unrestricted car driving licence;
- have held it for a total of four out of the past six years prior to entering the Register after qualifying, but:
  - a foreign driving licence, an automatic car driving licence or a provisional licence held after passing the driving test, all count towards the four years;
- not have been disqualified from driving at any time in the four years prior to being entered in the Register;
- be a fit and proper person to have your name entered in the Register; and pass the Register qualifying exam.

In addition, you should be aware that you cannot accompany a person learning to drive unless you are 21 or over and have held a full UK driving licence for three years. A foreign full licence will count towards this three-year period as long as it is accepted under the 'exchange' scheme.

Candidates with Disabilities

The Road Traffic (Driving Instruction by Disabled Persons) Act 1993 came into effect in 1996. This created a new category of ADI who can teach in cars with automatic transmission only. It is only open to drivers whose driving licence is limited to automatics because of a disability.

The ADI qualifying examination is exactly the same as that for any other ADI except that the candidate takes the two practical tests in a car with automatic transmission. (For more information refer to the ADI 14 booklet *Your Road to Becoming an Approved Driving Instructor*.)

Application for Registration

The initial application to have your name in the ADI Register is made at the same time as applying for the Part 1 Test of Theory. The forms are included with the ADI 14 (current cost £3.00) and can be obtained from the DSA in Notting-ham. (You will find the address in the section entitled 'Useful Addresses' at the back of this book.)

Examination and registration fees are reviewed from time to time. For details of the current fees you should ask your tutor or enquire with the DSA when you apply for the ADI 14.

THE STRUCTURE OF THE EXAMINATION

You must take and pass all three parts of the examination in the following sequence:

- Part 1 – a test of theory;
- Part 2 – a practical test of your driving ability;
- Part 3 – a practical test of your ability to instruct.

From the date of passing Part 1, you have a period of two years in which to pass Parts 2 and 3. You may sit the test of theory as many times as it takes you to pass. However, you may only have three attempts at Parts 2 and 3.

PART 1 TEST OF THEORY

The application for this part of the ADI exam in included with the ADI.14 starter pack – *Your Road to Becoming an Approved Driving Instructor*.

The test covers a wide range of subjects, including the rules and regulations for driving on our roads; mechanical principles; teaching techniques and dealing with disabilities. A lot of study time is involved. Before you apply for the test, it is sensible to start studying so that you can estimate how long it may take before you have a thorough understanding of all the principles involved.

Tests are conducted, in English only, at 'L' test theory centres throughout the UK. If you are dyslexic it may be possible for special arrangements to be made. However, you must remember to state this condition on your application form and you will need to supply corroboration.

Applications must be sent to the DSA in Nottingham, together with the current fee (£50 at October 2001). If you live in Northern Ireland, send your application with the current fee (£72 at October 2001) to the DVTA in Belfast.

The Syllabus

The test consists of 100 questions. There is one correct answer from a choice of three. Candidates have 90 minutes to complete the test.

The subjects covered in Part 1 are:

- the principles of road safety in general and their application in specified circumstances;
- correct and courteous driving techniques:

- – car control;
- – road procedure;
- – hazard recognition and proper response;
- – dealing safely with other road users and pedestrians;
- – the use of safety equipment;
- the theory and practice of learning, teaching and assessment;
- the tuition required to instruct a pupil in driving a car, and, as well as the above:
    - – identification, analysis and correction of errors;
    - – your manner and the relationship between instructor and pupil;
- simple vehicle adaptations for disabled drivers;
- a knowledge of the Highway Code;
- a knowledge of the DSA book for 'L' Test candidates, *The Driving Test*;
- how to interpret the 'Driving Test Report' (Form DL25C). You will find this reproduced in Chapter 9 of this book;
- a knowledge of basic mechanics and the design of cars adequate for the needs of driving instruction;
- a knowledge of the book *The Driving Manual*.

The Banding System

The questions are banded into four subject groups. These are:

- road procedure;
- traffic signs and signals; car control; pedestrians; mechanical knowledge;
- driving test; disabilities; law;
- publications; instructional techniques.

The Pass Mark

There is an overall pass mark of 85 per cent. However, to ensure candidates have an adequate knowledge in all of the subject areas, they must attain a mark of 80 per cent in each of the four bands. For example, if you attain 100 per cent in three of the bands but only 79 per cent in the fourth – you will fail.

You can see, therefore, the importance of thorough study if you don't want to throw away your test fee!

The Test Format

This part of the ADI exam is a 'Touch Screen' test.

You will be allowed to work through a practice session lasting up to 15 minutes to get used to the system before starting their actual test. Staff will be on hand to help if you have difficulty in using the system.

The screens are easy to read and only one question at a time will appear on the screen. You will be able to move backwards and forwards through them and also go back to any questions you want to look at again. It is easy to change your answer if you wish and the system will alert you if you have not answered a question.

The following is an illustration of how the screen will look. Although this is an example of a question from the learner driver theory test, the screen layout will be the same. The main difference is that for the ADI test, there will always be a choice of three answers and you only have to select one as correct.

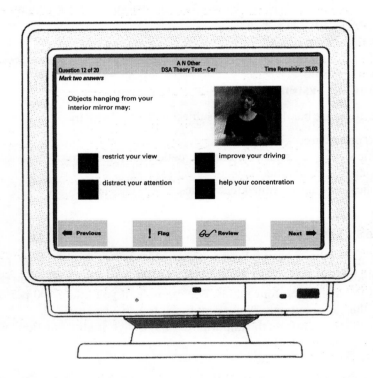

You will receive the result before leaving the test centre. If you pass, you will receive information about applying for the Part 2 Eyesight and Driving Ability test.

PART 2 TEST OF DRIVING ABILITY

You may only apply for this test after you have passed Part 1 and you may take it at the centre of your choice. A list of these is given on the application form. Send your appointment with the current fee (£62 at October 2001) to the DSA in Nottingham. (If you live in Northern Ireland, the fee at October 2001 is £130.) Your appointment will be confirmed by letter – take this with you when you attend for the test, along with your driving licence and some photographic identification.

The Car You Use for Part 2

You must provide a suitable vehicle, which:
- is properly taxed and insured;
- is a saloon or estate car in proper working condition with seatbelts in working order;
- is capable of the normal performance of vehicles of its type, with manual transmission;
- has right-hand steering;
- has a readily adjustable seat for a forward-facing front-seat passenger;
- is not displaying 'L' plates;
- has a seat belt, head restraint and additional rear-view mirror.

The Test

Part 2 lasts for about one hour and is conducted by an SEADI. Occasionally the examiner's supervisor may wish to come along. Don't worry – he or she is watching the examiner, not you. Your trainer may accompany you, if you wish.

The test consists of a test of eyesight and driving technique.

Eyesight

You must be able to read a number plate from a distance of 27.5 metres with glasses or contact lenses if you normally wear these for driving. Where the plate has the new style font with a reduced width of character, this distance is shortened to 26.5 metres.

If you fail this test, you will not be able to take the test of driving technique.

Driving Technique

This test is of an advanced nature and a very high standard of competence is expected. It is not just a slightly more difficult 'L' test. You must drive in a brisk and 'business-like' manner, demonstrating that you have a thorough knowledge of the principles of good driving and road safety. The routes used will include roads which may carry heavy and/or fast moving traffic, for example motorways or dual carriageways, and will include areas in and outside of built-up areas.

You must satisfy the examiner on the following:
- expert handling of the controls;
- application of correct road procedure;
- anticipation of the actions of other road users and taking the appropriate action;
- sound judgement of speed, distance and timing; and
- consideration for the convenience and safety of other road users.

To Pass

You must demonstrate that you can carry out any or all of the following manoeuvres:
- move away, straight ahead or at an angle;
- overtake, meet and cross the path of other vehicles, taking an appropriate course and without undue hesitancy;
- turn left- and right-hand corners correctly without undue hesitancy;
- stop the vehicle as in an emergency;
- reverse into openings to the right and left;
- reverse park into a space behind a parked vehicle;
- turn the car to face in the opposite direction using forward and reverse gears;
- reverse into a parking bay.

Some Common Causes for Failing

Your driving should be natural, safe and within the legal limits. Try to drive as you would normally. Don't try to put on an act for the examiner as this will affect your performance as well as your concentration.

Some of the more common causes of failure are:
- lack of progress, particularly on dual carriageways and motorways;
- not avoiding, or properly correcting, skids in the emergency stop exercise;
- not making the correct observations in the manoeuvre exercises;
- not getting the timing correct in the manoeuvre exercises;
- inconveniencing other road users;
- using excessive, unnecessary or misleading signals; and
- not making effective observations at junctions, including at traffic lights.

At the End of the Test

The examiner will tell you at the end of the test whether you have passed or failed. If you pass, you will be given an application form for Part 3 Test of Ability to Instruct.

The Advanced Driving Test

If you are thinking about becoming a driving instructor, a good first step is to take the DIAmond Advanced Motorist test. We use the DSA standard marking system (six minor faults). It makes for excellent preparation for the ADI Part II test. Successful candidates can subsequently join the MasterDriver Club and use the title for personal publicity. Once ADI qualified, you too can teach your clientele to advanced standards in readiness for admission into membership. The test only costs £30.

Many benefits are available:-

- Discounted insurance for MasterDriver members.
- Free helpline service (domestic, tax and legal).
- Membership regalia and personalised certificate.
- DIAmond Visa card available to members.

Contact your nearest professional instructor for more information. Alternatively, write or telephone direct for further details and an application form.

DIAmond Advanced Motorists, P.O. BOX 3333, Croydon CR9 4ZN. Tel. 0181 660 3333 - Fax 0181 665 5565

Tests 1 and 2
Eyesight and Driving Technique

Register of
Approved Driving
Instructors
Cert

Declaration

- I declare that my use of the test vehicle for the purpose of the test is covered by a valid policy of insurance which satisfies the requirements of the relevant legislation.
- I do/do not have to wear seat belts under the Motor Vehicles (Wearing of Seat Belts) Regulations 1982.

Signed

Date

Centre

Date

Make & model

Reg Mark

Dual Controls   Fitted   Not Fitted

Candidate's Name

Ref . No

Eyesight test

1. **Compliance with the requirements of the eyesight test**

Control

2. **Take proper precautions before starting the engine**

3. **Make proper use of:-**

accelerator   clutch   gears

footbrake   handbrake   steering

4. **Move away:-**
   safely   under control

5. **Stop vehicle in an emergency promptly and under control**

6. **Reverse left into a limited opening:-**
   under control   with proper observation   reasonably accurately

7. **Reverse right into a limited opening:-**
   under control   with proper observation   reasonably accurately

8. **Reverse parking:-**
   under control   with proper observation   reasonably accurately

9. **Turn in the road:-**
   under control   with proper observation   reasonably accurately

Road Procedure

10. **Make effective use of mirror(s) well before:-**

Signalling   changing direction   overtaking

slowing down / stopping

11. **Give signals by direction indicators/arm:-**
   where necessary   correctly   properly timed

Road Procedure (cont)

12. **Take prompt and appropriate action on all:-**
   traffic signs   road markings   traffic lights

   signals by traffic controllers   other road users

13. **Exercise proper care in the use of speed**

14. **Make progress by driving at a speed appropriate to the road and traffic conditions avoiding undue hesitancy**

15. **Keep a safe distance behind vehicles**

16. **Act properly at road junctions with regard to:-**
   speed on approach   observation

   approaching traffic   position before turning right

   position before turning left   right corner cutting

17. **Deal with other vehicles safely when:-**
   overtaking   meeting   crossing their path

18. **Position the vehicle correctly:-**
   during normal driving   exercise lane discipline

19. **Allow adequate clearance to stationary vehicles and obstructions**

20. **Take appropriate action at pedestrian crossings**

21. **Select a safe position for normal stops**

22. **Show awareness and anticipation of the actions of:-**
   pedestrians   cyclists   drivers

23. **Use of ancillary controls**

Examiner took action: verbal   physical

Test terminated at request of candidate

Supervising Examiner:

Oral debrief	*Offered	*Given	*Delete as applicable
	*Yes *No	*Yes *No	

ADI 25 (Rev 7/00)

Weather Conditions

Brief Description of Candidate

Remarks

Result

Supervising Examiner's Signature

Disability

Adaptations

If You Fail

You will fail this test if you commit one serious or dangerous fault, or more than six *driving faults*. The following are a few examples of driving faults:

Mirrors – an experienced driver would be expected to make regular use of the external mirrors.

Gears – if you change down through the gears unnecessarily you will be penalised, whereas a learner driver doing this safely would not fail the 'L' test.

Manoeuvres – late observations and excessively slow reversing may be penalised as being hesitant.

If you fail, the examiner will mark the relevant items on the ADI 25. A brief oral explanation of the errors will be given. You will also be given an application form for a further test.

If you fail this test three times, you will not be allowed to take Part 3. Should you wish to continue the process of qualifying, you will have to take the theory test again. However, you will have to wait until a two-year period has expired from the date you first passed Part 1.

PART 3 THE INSTRUCTIONAL TEST

You will be given an application form for this test when you pass Part 2. Tests are conducted at the centres listed on the application form and can be taken at the centre of your choice. Send your application to the DSA with the current fee (£62 at October 2001). (If you live in Northern Ireland, the fee at October 2001 is £138.) The appointment will be confirmed by letter – take this with you when you attend for the test along with your driving licence and some photographic identification.

The Car You Use for Part 3

You must provide a suitable vehicle, which:

- is properly taxed and insured, including any liability of the examiner as a driver:
  - the insurance should cover any Department of Transport examiner and not name a specific one, as the DSA cannot guarantee that the test will be conducted by a specific examiner;
- is a saloon or estate car in proper condition with seatbelts in proper working order;
- has manual transmission and right-hand drive;
- has a readily adjustable driving seat and a seat for a forward-facing front passenger;
- displays 'L' plates which comply with Regulation 9 (Schedule 2) of the Motor Vehicles (Driving Licences) Regulations 1987.

If You Hold a Trainee Licence to Instruct

If you are working under the Trainee Licence scheme and have signed for the training option, you will have to produce your ADI 21T if you are attending for your first attempt at Part 3 within the first three months of the licence. This should be completed by both yourself and your trainer to confirm that you have had a minimum of 20 hours' additional training. (More information on the trainee licence is included in Chapter 3.)

If you have to take the test for a second or third time, you will need to provide a declaration, signed by both yourself and your trainer, to confirm that a minimum additional five hours' training has been received. If you fail to produce any of the training declarations your test will be cancelled and you will lose the fee.

The Test

The test lasts for about an hour and is conducted by an SEADI. Occasionally the examiner's supervisor sits in on tests to ensure consistency. Your trainer may accompany you if you wish.

To Pass This Test

You have to demonstrate to your examiner that you can pass on your knowledge through your practical teaching ability. The test is in two parts, each lasting about 30 minutes and you must pass both parts. It is conducted as follows:

Phase 1 – the examiner will play the role of a beginner or a learner with limited driving skills;

Phase 2 – the examiner will play the role of a pupil who is at about test standard.

Structuring the Lesson at the Correct Level

At the beginning of each phase, the examiner will give you a brief description of the pupil with an outline of the current standard of his or her driving. You must:

- listen very carefully to this information;
- ask the examiner to repeat anything you have not understood;
- structure your tuition at an appropriate level to suit the pupil described.

You must make every effort to add realism to the lesson. You can do this by:

- trying to treat the examiner as a real pupil;
- getting into your 'driving instructor role' by asking questions to establish prior knowledge;
- listening very carefully and giving extra useful information.

Lesson Format

Each phase should be tailored to suit the time available and the standard of the pupil described. How much instruction you give while stationary should be dictated by the pupil's prior knowledge. Remember, however, that this is a test of your practical ability to instruct – not one of your knowledge. Do not waffle and try to focus on the key elements of the subject.

You may refer to brief notes or subject headings. However, you should remember that you need to look professional – do not quote lengthy paragraphs from books. Training aids should be used where appropriate, particularly if the subject is a new one for the pupil and an illustration would be helpful.

Keep the pupil involved by asking the occasional question where appropriate. Do not, however, completely bombard the pupil with complicated questions that he or she is unlikely to be able to answer. Remember, you are supposed to be building up confidence, not destroying it!

Recognising Faults

You must watch what the pupil is doing all of the time. Mistakes can be made at any time – particularly during Phase 1. A few of the basic mistakes which might be made are:

doors – not properly closed;

seat – not adjusted properly;

seatbelt – forgotten or twisted;

mirrors – not adjusted properly;

safety checks – handbrake and neutral checks omitted before switching on;

observations – no shoulder checks prior to moving away;

control – jerky use of clutch (could be caused by lapse between lessons; practice in a different car; incorrect seat adjustment, etc);

signals – over-use.

Try to make learning a positive experience by watching for these errors and correcting them by asking:

- *are all the doors closed properly?*
- *can you reach and operate the controls comfortably?*
- *what do you need to put on before you drive?*
- *can you see to the rear and sides?*
- *do you need to check anything before you turn the key?*
- *what should you be looking for before moving away?*
- *the clutch may feel strange at first, take your time until you get used to it.*

Recognising Faults on the Move

Do not assume that correct procedures will be followed, even if the pupil has covered the subject before. You should also remember that mistakes may not necessarily relate to the subject being dealt with.

Recognise faults and give some advice on how to improve. Fault identification and remedy is an important part of this test. Even minor faults are worth a mention and these should be easy to deal with on the move. However, where more serious or repeated errors occur, it may be necessary to stop when convenient to discuss them in more detail.

Examination Topics

The examiner will select one subject out of each of the two lists of topics below:

Subjects specified in Phase 1:

- safety precautions on entering the car and explanation of the controls;
- moving off and stopping;
- turn-in-the-road exercise;

- reversing (to the right or left);
- emergency stop and mirrors;
- dealing with pedestrian crossings and giving signals by indicators/arm as appropriate;
- approaching junctions to turn either right or left;
- dealing with emerging at road junctions;
- dealing with crossroads;
- meet, overtake and cross other traffic, allowing adequate clearance for other road users and anticipation.

Subjects specified in Phase 2:

- dealing with crossroads;
- meet, overtake and cross other traffic, allowing adequate clearance for other road users and anticipation;
- approaching junctions to turn either right or left;
- dealing with emerging at road junctions;
- dealing with pedestrian crossings and giving signals by indicators/arm as appropriate;
- making progress and general road positioning;
- reverse parking.

There are 10 set examination exercises. These are listed on pages 48–57 (ADI 26/1–10).

During the test you will be assessed on each of the following:

1. Core Competencies:
    (a) Identification of faults;
    (b) Fault analysis;
    (c) Remedial action.
2. Instructional Techniques:
    (a) Level of instruction;
    (b) Planning;
    (c) Control of the lesson;
    (d) Communication;
    (e) Question and answer techniques;
    (f) Feedback/encouragement;
    (g) Instructor's use of controls.
3. Instructor Characteristics:
    (a) Attitude;
    (b) Approach to pupil.

Please note that where the word 'pupil' appears, this refers to the examiner playing that role. When the 'pupil' has been described to you and that role is assumed, you must try to treat the examiner as a 'real life' pupil throughout each phase of the test. Remember that a different pupil will be portrayed for each phase and you will have to adapt your instruction to suit each one.

The following is an outline of what you should be doing under each of the above headings.

1. Core Competencies

(a) Identification of faults

You have to clearly identify faults committed by the pupil which may or will require correction as part of an effective instructing/learning process. You should note and identify any errors committed by the pupil relating to control of the car and road procedure.

When you have identified a fault, you have to ask yourself whether it is a 'one-off' minor error not really worth mentioning, or whether it needs to be addressed. If worthy of mentioning, you then have to decide whether it is appropriate to draw the pupil's attention to the problem at the time it occurs, or whether you should delay an explanation until a more appropriate time arises.

Key elements in the identification of faults:

- recognise all faults which require correction;
- identify, and bring to the pupil's attention, any significant number of repeated or serious faults.

(b) Fault analysis

When you have identified an error, you have to accurately analyse the cause of it. All faults worthy of noting should be dealt with.

Key elements in the fault analysis process:

- you must accurately analyse faults you have identified;
- the analysis must be complete.

(c) Remedial action

When you have identified and analysed an error, you should then give some constructive advice on how to remedy it. This will also involve deciding on the appropriate time at which to deal with the problem.

You should explain to the pupil what needs to be done in those circumstances and what might have happened because of their actions. You can confirm what you mean by giving an explanation. A demonstration may also be appropriate if you have time. You should then create an opportunity to practise the correct procedure.

Key elements in remedying faults:

- you need to be able to offer solutions for all of the identified problems;
- your corrective advice must be effective;
- you must create the opportunity to practise the correct procedures to help eradicate the problems and improve the pupil's knowledge and skill.

2. Instructional Techniques

(a) Level of instruction

This should include matching your instruction to the level of ability of the pupil described and portrayed in each phase of the test.

You will need to gauge, from the description given by the examiner, and the way the 'pupil' drives, at what level you should be teaching. You should be able to adjust your instruction according to the particular needs of each pupil portrayed, adapting it to suit the strengths and weaknesses, so that you are neither under- nor over-instructing.

Key elements in deciding on the level of your instruction:

- you must ensure that, having matched the level of your teaching to the previous experience and ability of the pupil, your instruction is consistent to that level. This is necessary to avoid confusing the pupil;
- if you recognise the pupil has become confused, you will need to make further adjustment to the level of your instruction to ensure that some learning or improvement in the pupil's driving takes place;
- there should be a complete match of your instruction to the apparent level of competence, experience, knowledge and needs of the pupil. This should ensure that the tasks you set for the inexperienced driver are not too difficult, and those set for a more experienced pupil are not too simple;
- you should make any adjustments necessary to your instruction to match the pupil's apparent strengths and weaknesses.

(b) Planning

This section covers how you plan the lesson and what actually happens. It relates to the sequence of instruction or activity, and the appropriateness and effectiveness of the teaching methods you use. The examiner will also take into account the difficulty and complexity of the lesson content.

Your instruction should be methodically planned and delivered. It must be presented in a clear and logical manner in relation to the subject being covered.

Key elements involved with lesson planning:

- each phase must be well planned and properly structured;
- you must approach each subject logically;
- each lesson must follow a coherent and methodical plan, including an initial allocation of time between theory and practice;

- your presentation of the subject should be well organised and have a clear logical pattern;
- you must demonstrate that you understand the level of complexity of the subject.

(c) Control of the lesson

The SE will be assessing your overall control of the lesson and your interaction with the pupil. An assessment will be made of how you allocate the available time between the theory and practical elements of the lesson. You may even have to change your plan during the lesson according to how the pupil responds.

You will need to demonstrate your ability to anticipate what the pupil may do, taking appropriate action on any potential errors or danger in order to maintain a firm degree of control over the pupil.

Key elements in maintaining proper control:

- you must be alert and show awareness and perception to changes in all-round situations;
- you must judge the pupil's ability to identify and react to different situations;
- there must be a proper balance between the time spent on theory and practice, making sure that enough practical instruction is given to reinforce learning.

(d) Communication

This section relates to the 'pupil's' understanding of the instruction and your use of appropriate language and jargon. Your ability to adapt and to use language and terminology which is likely to be understood by the particular pupil will be assessed.

You should adopt an easy, descriptive and concise approach to which each pupil will be able to relate. Try to ensure that communication is two-way, making use of simple and appropriate terminology. Make sure that the information and directions given are effective and there is no ambiguity or chance of misunderstanding. Your verbal communication should also be fluent and you should be able to adapt and make adjustments to your methods if you can see that the pupil does not understand you.

Key elements involved in the communication process:

- you should demonstrate your ability to give information in an easy-to-understand manner;
- if you use any jargon you must explain its meaning. Avoid using any unnecessary technical jargon;
- you must show an ability to adjust your methods of communication to avoid ambiguities or misunderstandings, or if the pupil appears to be confused.

(e) Question and Answer (Q & A) techniques

This section covers the SE's assessment of your ability to incorporate question and answer techniques as and when this is appropriate.

You have to decide on when Q & A is appropriate and what type of question is relevant to the pupil's current ability and knowledge. You should also be able to answer correctly questions or queries raised by the pupil.

Make sure you allow for pauses in your instruction to give the pupil an opportunity to ask questions. You should make it clear to your pupil that you expect them to ask questions, especially if there is something which they do not quite understand. For example, 'Why must I do that?'

Questions from the pupil should relate to the current topic or lesson. Any irrelevant questions should not be allowed to distract the pupil's attention from the subject in hand. If a totally unrelated question is posed by the pupil, you may need to tactfully delay a discussion to a more appropriate time or set homework which involves the pupil in a discovery exercise.

Questions used should be relevant, posed at the correct time and worded to be thought-provoking. Q & A is a two-way process and can be used to:

- prompt;
- establish knowledge;
- recap a previous lesson; or
- encourage pupil participation.

Your early stage pupil should be made to feel comfortable about the Q & A process, particularly where you feel it is going to assist them in their acquisition of a skill or knowledge and where it will promote better understanding.

Questions which require a simple 'Yes or No' response will not tell you what the pupil thinks or understands. They should be more searching and based on:

- what?
- when?
- where?
- why?
- how?

The 'Why' is the most important. The pupil's response will tell you whether the point under discussion is properly understood.

Key elements involved in the successful application of Q & A:

- you should use Q & A where it is appropriate and it will be of obvious benefit to the pupil;
- you should be able to pose or phrase questions which are suitable for the needs of your pupil;
- make sure the questions are set at an appropriate level according to the current knowledge of the pupil;

- use questions which will not result in confusion;
- use Q & A only when it is the most appropriate method for dealing with the problem in hand;
- only use Q & A when there is sufficient time for the pupil to respond. Make sure it is not too late for the question to be relevant;
- encourage the pupil to ask you questions;
- answer the pupil's questions correctly, giving adequate and relevant information;
- do not ignore the pupil's questions;
- you must be able to recognise when the pupil becomes demoralised because of your use of too many, or the wrong type of, questions.

(f) Feedback/Encouragement

The way in which you provide feedback and encouragement to the pupil in relation to his/her performance will be assessed under this heading.

You should be able to give information which clearly indicates the pupil's level of achievement at any given point during the lesson. You should be able to recognise when the pupil is unsure or uncertain through body language, eye contact or speech and you should be able to respond with appropriate advice and guidance.

You should be able to make use of all opportunities to give praise and encouragement to develop the pupil's confidence. You should also take the time to give credit for improvement in the pupil's car control skills and in their awareness and anticipation of faults committed by other road users.

Your pupil should be encouraged to ask questions so that you can then give more feedback. You should confirm and encourage your pupil to take action as and when required. By asking the pupil what he/she thinks of his/her performance, you should be able to adjust the level of your instruction to suit this perception.

Key elements in giving and gaining feedback:

- you should be able to answer all the pupil's questions, giving correct and complete information;
- you must ensure that your feedback is not ambiguous or confusing;
- when you have obtained feedback from the pupil, you should act positively on it;
- you should give effective acknowledgement and praise of good performance in order to build up the pupil's confidence and avoid them feeling discouraged or perplexed;
- demonstrate your skills as a teacher by promoting questions from your pupil;
- you should be aware of your pupil's uncertainties and address them, providing information on what their achievements are and whether the aims and objectives have been achieved.

(g) Instructor's use of controls

This covers the examiner's assessment of your use of all of the controls. This includes:

- when and how you use the dual clutch and brake;
- covering the gear lever;
- assisting with the handbrake;
- correct use of the steering wheel from the passenger side;
- use of other controls such as indicators, lights, horn, etc.

If you have to use the dual or any other controls in the car, you should make sure your pupil knows the reason why you did so. You could use the dual controls as a positive supplement to your instruction, for example, giving a demonstration where this would be beneficial.

You should try to get your pupil to respond to situations by first of all giving verbal prompts or instructions, avoiding the use of the dual controls until it becomes a necessity. For example:

- Do you think you can get through that space safely?
- Give way to that oncoming car!
- Wait.
- Take some action by either using the dual controls if it is unsafe to proceed, or by assisting with the steering through the space.

Key elements involved in using the controls:

- when any form of control has been used, you must explain when and why you used it;
- avoid taking unnecessary control by means of the dual or other controls. For example: grabbing or pushing the steering wheel; releasing/applying the handbrake; using the indicator, lights, heater, sunvisor, etc; using the dual controls to prevent stalling or move off; or preventing gear changing or reselecting gear;
- avoid taking action yourself if it would be more appropriate to advise and instruct the pupil to do something;
- avoid using the dual controls as a punitive measure.

3. Instructor Characteristics

(a) Attitude

As a driving instructor, the skills which you use to create a relaxed, but supportive, learning environment are extremely important. It is vital that you show a positive attitude towards your job, your pupil and road safety in general.

(b) Approach to pupil

You should be able to establish and maintain rapport and create the right atmosphere for each pupil, striking a balance between being both welcoming and businesslike, blending formality with friendliness.

You should endeavour to put pupils at ease, instil confidence and establish an atmosphere which is conducive to a good instructor/pupil relationship and positive learning.

Key elements in the characteristics of a good instructor:

- try to be natural, avoid any unnatural over-friendliness;
- be approachable so that the pupil remains at ease. This should create a suitable instructor/pupil relationship and a good learning environment;
- your own attitude should show that you are keen for the pupil to learn and you are interested in your work and also road safety. This should be reflected in the pupil's response to you.

After the Examination

Unlike the Test of Driving Ability, the SE cannot give an immediate decision at the end of this test. About 30 minutes will be taken to consider all of the foregoing elements, so that the SE can give a fair assessment of your overall performance. You will also be given an oral debriefing on the result. (If you do not wish to wait, the result will be posted to you.)

Whether you pass or fail, if you would like a fuller explanation, you may ask for an appointment to see the SE – they are normally available on Friday mornings.

You should find the book *Practical Teaching Skills for Driving Instructors* particularly helpful for this part of the examination.

Instructional Test - Part III

The Examiner has marked each aspect of your performance in columns A and B below. Please see overleaf for explanatory notes.

Candidate's Declaration

I certify that

- the vehicle I have provided for the test is properly insured under the Road Traffic Act 1988 and
- I do/do not have to wear seat belts under the Motor Vehicles (Wearing of Seat Belts) Regulations 1982

Signed

Date

Centre

Date

Make & model

Reg Mark

Dual Controls   Fitted [ ]   Not Fitted [ ]

Candidate's Name

Ref. No

Column A

PST No.1 Exercises 1B and 10T

Phase 1-1B Beginner-Controls

	Not Covered	Unsatisfactory	Satisfactory
Doors	[ ]	[ ]	[ ]
Seat/Head Restraint	[ ]	[ ]	[ ]
Seat Belt	[ ]	[ ]	[ ]
Mirrors	[ ]	[ ]	[ ]
Accelerator	[ ]	[ ]	[ ]
Footbrake	[ ]	[ ]	[ ]
Clutch	[ ]	[ ]	[ ]
Handbrake	[ ]	[ ]	[ ]
Gears	[ ]	[ ]	[ ]
Steering	[ ]	[ ]	[ ]
Indicators	[ ]	[ ]	[ ]
Starting	[ ]	[ ]	[ ]
Precautions before moving off	[ ]	[ ]	[ ]
Normal stop position	[ ]	[ ]	[ ]
Normal stop use of MSM	[ ]	[ ]	[ ]
Normal stop control	[ ]	[ ]	[ ]

Phase 2-10T Trained-Crossroads

	Not Covered	Unsatisfactory	Satisfactory
Mirror-Signal-Manoeuvre	[ ]	[ ]	[ ]
Speed	[ ]	[ ]	[ ]
Gears	[ ]	[ ]	[ ]
Coasting	[ ]	[ ]	[ ]
Observation	[ ]	[ ]	[ ]
Emerging	[ ]	[ ]	[ ]
Position right	[ ]	[ ]	[ ]
Position left	[ ]	[ ]	[ ]
Pedestrians	[ ]	[ ]	[ ]
Cross approaching traffic	[ ]	[ ]	[ ]
Right corner cut	[ ]	[ ]	[ ]

The results of your test are:

Phase I Grade [ ]   Phase II Grade [ ]

Supervising Examiner's name

Location [ ]   Section No. [ ]

S E Signature

Column B

In this column the top line of boxes to Phase I and the bottom line of boxes refer to Phase II

1/2/3 = Unsatisfactory   **4/5/6 = Satisfactory**

Core Competencies

	1	2	3	4	5	6
Identification of faults	[ ]	[ ]	[ ]	[ ]	[ ]	[ ]
Fault analysis	[ ]	[ ]	[ ]	[ ]	[ ]	[ ]
Remedial action	[ ]	[ ]	[ ]	[ ]	[ ]	[ ]

Instructional Techniques

	1	2	3	4	5	6
Level of instruction	[ ]	[ ]	[ ]	[ ]	[ ]	[ ]
Planning	[ ]	[ ]	[ ]	[ ]	[ ]	[ ]
Control of lesson	[ ]	[ ]	[ ]	[ ]	[ ]	[ ]
Communication	[ ]	[ ]	[ ]	[ ]	[ ]	[ ]
Q/A Techniques	[ ]	[ ]	[ ]	[ ]	[ ]	[ ]
Feedback/Encouragement	[ ]	[ ]	[ ]	[ ]	[ ]	[ ]
Instructor use of controls	[ ]	[ ]	[ ]	[ ]	[ ]	[ ]

Instructor Characteristics

	1	2	3	4	5	6
Attitude and Approach to Pupil	[ ]	[ ]	[ ]	[ ]	[ ]	[ ]

ADI 26/PT/01 Rev 7/98

FORMS UK plc FCN17651400

**DRIVING
STANDARDS
AGENCY**

Instructional Test - Part III
The Examiner has marked each aspect of your performance in
columns A and B below. Please see overleaf for explanatory notes.

Candidate's Declaration

I certify that
- the vehicle I have provided for the test is properly
  insured under the Road Traffic Act 1988 and
- I do/do not have to wear seat belts under the Motor
  Vehicles (Wearing of Seat Belts) Regulations 1982.

Signed

Date

Centre	
Date	
Make & model	
Reg Mark	
Dual Controls	Fitted ☐ Not Fitted
Candidate's Name	
Ref. No	

Column A
PST No.2 Exercises 2B and 11T
Phase 1-2B Beginner-Moving off / stopping

	Not Covered	Unsatisfactory	Satisfactory
Briefing on moving off/stopping	☐	☐	☐
Mirrors vision and use	☐	☐	☐
Mirrors, direction, overtaking and stopping	☐	☐	☐
Mirror signal manoeuvre	☐	☐	☐
Precautions before moving off	☐	☐	☐
Co-ordination of controls	☐	☐	☐
Normal stop position	☐	☐	☐
Normal stop control	☐	☐	☐

Phase 2-11T Trained-Meet, cross and overtake
other traffic allowing adequate clearance for other
road users and anticipation

Mirror-Signal-Manoeuvre	☐	☐	☐
Meet approaching traffic	☐	☐	☐
Cross approaching traffic	☐	☐	☐
Overtake other traffic	☐	☐	☐
Keep a safe distance	☐	☐	☐
Shaving other vehicles	☐	☐	☐
Anticipation of pedestrians	☐	☐	☐
Anticipation of cyclists	☐	☐	☐
Anticipation of drivers	☐	☐	☐

The results of your test are:

Phase I Grade		Phase II Grade	

Supervising Examiner's name

Location		Section No.	

S E Signature

Column B
In this column the top line of boxes to Phase I and the
bottom line of boxes refer to Phase II

1/2/3 = Unsatisfactory   4/5/6 = Satisfactory

Core Competencies

	1 2 3	4 5 6
Identification of faults	☐☐☐ / ☐☐☐	☐☐☐ / ☐☐☐
Fault analysis	☐☐☐ / ☐☐☐	☐☐☐ / ☐☐☐
Remedial action	☐☐☐ / ☐☐☐	☐☐☐ / ☐☐☐

Instructional Techniques

	1 2 3	4 5 6
Level of instruction	☐☐☐ / ☐☐☐	☐☐☐ / ☐☐☐
Planning	☐☐☐ / ☐☐☐	☐☐☐ / ☐☐☐
Control of lesson	☐☐☐ / ☐☐☐	☐☐☐ / ☐☐☐
Communication	☐☐☐ / ☐☐☐	☐☐☐ / ☐☐☐
Q/A Techniques	☐☐☐ / ☐☐☐	☐☐☐ / ☐☐☐
Feedback/Encouragement	☐☐☐ / ☐☐☐	☐☐☐ / ☐☐☐
Instructor use of controls	☐☐☐ / ☐☐☐	☐☐☐ / ☐☐☐

Instructor Characteristics

	1 2 3	4 5 6
Attitude and Approach to Pupil	☐☐☐ / ☐☐☐	☐☐☐ / ☐☐☐

ADI 26/PT/02 Rev 7/98

FORMS UK plc FCN1765150/0

Instructional Test - Part III

The Examiner has marked each aspect of your performance in columns A and B below. Please see overleaf for explanatory notes.

Candidate's Declaration

I certify that
- the vehicle I have provided for the test is properly insured under the Road Traffic Act 1988 and
- I do/do not have to wear seat belts under the Motor Vehicles (Wearing of Seat Belts) Regulations 1982.

Signed:

Date

Centre

Date

Make & model

Reg Mark

Dual Controls   Fitted ☐   Not Fitted ☐

Candidate's Name

Ref. No

Column A

PST No.3 Exercises 4P and 7T

Phase 1-4P Partly trained-Turn in the road

	Not Covered	Unsatisfactory	Satisfactory
Briefing on turn in the road	☐	☐	☐
Co-ordination of controls	☐	☐	☐
Observation	☐	☐	☐
Accuracy	☐	☐	☐

Phase 2-7T Trained-Approaching junctions to turn either right or left

	Not Covered	Unsatisfactory	Satisfactory
Mirrors	☐	☐	☐
Signal	☐	☐	☐
Brakes	☐	☐	☐
Gears	☐	☐	☐
Coasting	☐	☐	☐
Too fast on approach	☐	☐	☐
Too slow on approach	☐	☐	☐
Position	☐	☐	☐
Pedestrians	☐	☐	☐
Cross approaching traffic	☐	☐	☐
Right corner cut	☐	☐	☐

The results of your test are:

Phase I Grade

Phase II Grade

Supervising Examiner's name

Location

Section No.

S E Signature

Column B

In this column the top line of boxes to Phase I and the bottom line of boxes refer to Phase II

1/2/3 = Unsatisfactory   **4/5/6 = Satisfactory**

Core Competencies

	1	2	3	4	5	6
Identification of faults	☐	☐	☐	☐	☐	☐
Fault analysis	☐	☐	☐	☐	☐	☐
Remedial action	☐	☐	☐	☐	☐	☐

Instructional Techniques

	1	2	3	4	5	6
Level of instruction	☐	☐	☐	☐	☐	☐
Planning	☐	☐	☐	☐	☐	☐
Control of lesson	☐	☐	☐	☐	☐	☐
Communication	☐	☐	☐	☐	☐	☐
Q/A Techniques	☐	☐	☐	☐	☐	☐
Feedback/Encouragement	☐	☐	☐	☐	☐	☐
Instructor use of controls	☐	☐	☐	☐	☐	☐

Instructor Characteristics

	1	2	3	4	5	6
Attitude and Approach to Pupil	☐	☐	☐	☐	☐	☐

ADI 26/PT/03 Rev 7/98

FORMS UK plc FCN176537400

Instructional Test - Part III

The Examiner has marked each aspect of your performance in columns A and B below. Please see overleaf for explanatory notes.

Candidate's Declaration

I certify that
- the vehicle I have provided for the test is properly insured under the Road Traffic Act 1988 and
- I do/do not have to wear seat belts under the Motor Vehicles (Wearing of Seat Belts) Regulations 1982.

Signed

Date

Centre

Date

Make & model

Reg Mark

Dual Controls   Fitted [ ]   Not Fitted [ ]

Candidate's Name

Ref. No

Column A

PST No.4 Exercises 3P and 9T

Phase 1-3P Partly trained-Reversing

Left Reverse [ ]   Right Reverse [ ]

	Not Covered	Unsatisfactory	Satisfactory
Briefing on reversing	[ ]	[ ]	[ ]
Co-ordination of controls	[ ]	[ ]	[ ]
Observation	[ ]	[ ]	[ ]
Accuracy	[ ]	[ ]	[ ]

Phase 2-9T Trained-T Junctions-Emerging

	Not Covered	Unsatisfactory	Satisfactory
Mirror-Signal-Manoeuvre	[ ]	[ ]	[ ]
Speed	[ ]	[ ]	[ ]
Gears	[ ]	[ ]	[ ]
Coasting	[ ]	[ ]	[ ]
Observation	[ ]	[ ]	[ ]
Emerging	[ ]	[ ]	[ ]
Position right	[ ]	[ ]	[ ]
Position left	[ ]	[ ]	[ ]
Pedestrians	[ ]	[ ]	[ ]

The results of your test are:

Phase I Grade [   ]   Phase II Grade [   ]

Supervising Examiner's name

Location   Section No.

S E Signature

Column B

In this column the top line of boxes to Phase I and the bottom line of boxes refer to Phase II

1/2/3 = Unsatisfactory   **4/5/6 = Satisfactory**

Core Competencies

	1	2	3	4	5	6
Identification of faults						
Fault analysis						
Remedial action						

Instructional Techniques

	1	2	3	4	5	6
Level of instruction						
Planning						
Control of lesson						
Communication						
Q/A Techniques						
Feedback/Encouragement						
Instructor use of controls						

Instructor Characteristics

	1	2	3	4	5	6
Attitude and Approach to Pupil						

ADI 26/PT/04 Rev 7/98

FORMS UK plc FCN176512/00

Instructional Test - Part III

The Examiner has marked each aspect of your performance in columns A and B below. Please see overleaf for explanatory notes.

Candidate's Declaration

I certify that
- the vehicle I have provided for the test is properly insured under the Road Traffic Act 1988 and
- I do/do not have to wear seat belts under the Motor Vehicles (Wearing of Seat Belts) Regulations 1982.

Signed

Date

Centre
Date
Make & model
Reg Mark

Dual Controls   Fitted [ ]   Not Fitted [ ]

Candidate's Name
Ref. No

Column A

PST No.5 Exercises 6P and 8T

Phase 1-6P Partly trained-Emergency stop/Mirrors

	Not Covered	Unsatisfactory	Satisfactory
Briefing on emergency stop/mirrors	[ ]	[ ]	[ ]
Quick reaction	[ ]	[ ]	[ ]
Use of footbrake/clutch	[ ]	[ ]	[ ]
Skidding	[ ]	[ ]	[ ]
Mirrors vision and use	[ ]	[ ]	[ ]
Mirrors, direction, overtaking and stopping	[ ]	[ ]	[ ]
Mirror-signal-manoeuvre	[ ]	[ ]	[ ]

Phase 2-8T Trained-Progress / Hesitancy - Normal position

	Not Covered	Unsatisfactory	Satisfactory
Progress to fast	[ ]	[ ]	[ ]
Progress too slow	[ ]	[ ]	[ ]
Hesitancy	[ ]	[ ]	[ ]
Normal position too wide from the left	[ ]	[ ]	[ ]
Normal position too close to the left	[ ]	[ ]	[ ]

The results of your test are:

Phase I Grade [ ]   Phase II Grade [ ]

Supervising Examiner's name

Location [ ]   Section No. [ ]

S E Signature

Column B

In this column the top line of boxes refer to Phase I and the bottom line of boxes refer to Phase II

1/2/3 = Unsatisfactory   4/5/6 = Satisfactory

Core Competencies

	1 2 3	4 5 6
Identification of faults	[ ][ ][ ]	[ ][ ][ ]
Fault analysis	[ ][ ][ ]	[ ][ ][ ]
Remedial action	[ ][ ][ ]	[ ][ ][ ]

Instructional Techniques

	1 2 3	4 5 6
Level of instruction	[ ][ ][ ]	[ ][ ][ ]
Planning	[ ][ ][ ]	[ ][ ][ ]
Control of lesson	[ ][ ][ ]	[ ][ ][ ]
Communication	[ ][ ][ ]	[ ][ ][ ]
Q/A Techniques	[ ][ ][ ]	[ ][ ][ ]
Feedback/Encouragement	[ ][ ][ ]	[ ][ ][ ]
Instructor use of controls	[ ][ ][ ]	[ ][ ][ ]

Instructor Characteristics

	1 2 3	4 5 6
Attitude and Approach to Pupil	[ ][ ][ ]	[ ][ ][ ]

ADI 26/PT/05 Rev 7/98

FORMS UK plc FCN176518/00

Instructional Test - Part III

The Examiner has marked each aspect of your performance in columns A and B below. Please see overleaf for explanatory notes.

Candidate's Declaration

I certify that:
- the vehicle I have provided for the test is properly insured under the Road Traffic Act 1988 and
- I do/do not have to wear seat belts under the Motor Vehicles (Wearing of Seat Belts) Regulations 1982.

Signed

Date

Centre

Date

Make & model

Reg Mark

Dual Controls ... Fitted [ ]   Not Fitted [ ]

Candidate's Name

Ref. No

Column A

PST No.6 Exercises 12P and 5T

Phase I-12P Partly trained-Pedestrian crossings and the use of signals

	Not Covered	Unsatisfactory	Satisfactory
Briefing on pedestrian crossings/signals			
Mirror-signal-manoeuvre			
Speed on approach			
Stop when necessary			
Overtaking on approach			
Inviting pedestrians to cross			
Signals by indicator			
Signals by arm			
Signals – timing			
Unnecessary signals			

Phase 2-5T Trained-Reverse parking

	Not Covered	Unsatisfactory	Satisfactory
Briefing on reverse parking			
Co-ordination of controls			
Observation			
Accuracy			

The results of your test are:

Phase I Grade [ ]   Phase II Grade [ ]

Supervising Examiner's name

Location [ ]   Section No. [ ]

S E Signature

Column B

In this column the top line of boxes to Phase I and the bottom line of boxes refer to Phase II

1/2/3 = Unsatisfactory   4/5/6 = Satisfactory

Core Competencies

	1	2	3	4	5	6
Identification of faults						
Fault analysis						
Remedial action						

Instructional Techniques

	1	2	3	4	5	6
Level of instruction						
Planning						
Control of lesson						
Communication						
Q/A Techniques						
Feedback/Encouragement						
Instructor use of controls						

Instructor Characteristics

	1	2	3	4	5	6
Attitude and Approach to Pupil						

ADI 26/PT/06 Rev 7/98

FORMS UK plc FCN17651900

Instructional Test - Part III

The Examiner has marked each aspect of your performance in columns A and B below. Please see overleaf for explanatory notes.

Candidate's Declaration

I certify that
- the vehicle I have provided for the test is properly insured under the Road Traffic Act 1988 and
- I do/do not have to wear seat belts under the Motor Vehicles (Wearing of Seat Belts) Regulations 1982.

Signed:

Date

Centre	
Date	
Make & model	
Reg Mark	
Dual Controls	Fitted ☐ Not Fitted ☐
Candidate's Name	
Ref. No	

Column A

PST No.7 Exercises 7P and 12T

Phase 1-7P Partly trained-Approaching junctions to turn either right or left

	Not Covered	Inadequately Covered	Adequately Covered
Briefing on approaching junctions	☐	☐	☐
Mirrors	☐	☐	☐
Signal	☐	☐	☐
Brakes	☐	☐	☐
Gears	☐	☐	☐
Coasting	☐	☐	☐
Too fast on approach	☐	☐	☐
Too slow on approach	☐	☐	☐
Position	☐	☐	☐
Pedestrians	☐	☐	☐
Cross approaching traffic	☐	☐	☐
Right corner cut	☐	☐	☐

Phase 2-12T Trained-Pedestrians crossings and the use of signals

	Not Covered	Inadequately Covered	Adequately Covered
Mirror-Signal-Manoeuvre	☐	☐	☐
Speed on approach	☐	☐	☐
Stop when necessary	☐	☐	☐
Overtaking on approach	☐	☐	☐
Inviting pedestrians to cross	☐	☐	☐
Signals by indicator	☐	☐	☐
Signals by arm	☐	☐	☐
Signals timing	☐	☐	☐
Unnecessary signals	☐	☐	☐

The results of your test are:

Phase I Grade	Phase II Grade
Supervising Examiner's name	
Location	Section No.
S E Signature	

Column B

In this column the top line of boxes refer to Phase I and the bottom line of boxes refer to Phase II

1/2/3 = Unsatisfactory   4/5/6 = Satisfactory

Core Competencies

	1 2 3	4 5 6
Identification of faults	☐☐☐	☐☐☐
Fault analysis	☐☐☐	☐☐☐
Remedial action	☐☐☐	☐☐☐

Instructional Techniques

	1 2 3	4 5 6
Level of instruction	☐☐☐	☐☐☐
Planning	☐☐☐	☐☐☐
Control of lesson	☐☐☐	☐☐☐
Communication	☐☐☐	☐☐☐
Q/A Techniques	☐☐☐	☐☐☐
Feedback/Encouragement	☐☐☐	☐☐☐
Instructor use of controls	☐☐☐	☐☐☐

Instructor Characteristics

	1 2 3	4 5 6
Attitude and Approach to Pupil	☐☐☐	☐☐☐

ADI 26/PT/07 Rev 7/98

FORMS UK plc FCN17652000

DRIVING STANDARDS AGENCY

Instructional Test - Part III

The Examiner has marked each aspect of your performance in columns A and B below. Please see overleaf for explanatory notes.

Register of Approved Driving Instructors Cars

Candidate's Declaration

I certify that
- the vehicle I have provided for the test is properly insured under the Road Traffic Act 1988 and
- I do/do not have to wear seat belts under the Motor Vehicles (Wearing of Seat Belts) Regulations 1982.

Signed

Date

Centre	
Date	
Make & model	
Reg Mark	
Dual Controls	Fitted [ ] Not Fitted [ ]
Candidate's Name	
Ref. No	

Column A

PST No.8 Exercises 9P and 11T

Phase 1- 9P Partly trained-T Junctions-Emerging

	Not Covered	Unsatisfactory	Satisfactory
Briefing on T junctions	[ ]	[ ]	[ ]
Mirror-signal-manoeuvre	[ ]	[ ]	[ ]
Speed	[ ]	[ ]	[ ]
Gears	[ ]	[ ]	[ ]
Coasting	[ ]	[ ]	[ ]
Observation	[ ]	[ ]	[ ]
Emerging	[ ]	[ ]	[ ]
Position right	[ ]	[ ]	[ ]
Position left	[ ]	[ ]	[ ]
Pedestrians	[ ]	[ ]	[ ]

Phase 2-11T Trained-Meet, cross and overtake other traffic allowing adequate clearance for other road users and anticipation

	Not Covered	Unsatisfactory	Satisfactory
Mirror-Signal-Manoeuvre	[ ]	[ ]	[ ]
Meet approaching traffic	[ ]	[ ]	[ ]
Cross approaching traffic	[ ]	[ ]	[ ]
Overtake other traffic	[ ]	[ ]	[ ]
Keep a safe distance	[ ]	[ ]	[ ]
Shaving other vehicles	[ ]	[ ]	[ ]
Anticipation of pedestrians	[ ]	[ ]	[ ]
Anticipation of cyclists	[ ]	[ ]	[ ]
Anticipation of drivers	[ ]	[ ]	[ ]

The results of your test are:

Phase I Grade		Phase II Grade	
Supervising Examiner's name			
Location		Section No.	
S E Signature			

Column B

In this column the top line of boxes refer to Phase I and the bottom line of boxes refer to Phase II

1/2/3 = Unsatisfactory   4/5/6 = Satisfactory

Core Competencies

	1 2 3	4 5 6
Identification of faults		
Fault analysis		
Remedial action		

Instructional Techniques

	1 2 3	4 5 6
Level of instruction		
Planning		
Control of lesson		
Communication		
Q/A Techniques		
Feedback/Encouragement		
Instructor use of controls		

Instructor Characteristics

	1 2 3	4 5 6
Attitude and Approach to Pupil		

ADI 26/PT/08 Rev 7/98

FORMS UK plc FCN170652J/00

**DRIVING
STANDARDS
AGENCY**

Instructional Test - Part III

The Examiner has marked each aspect of your performance in
columns A and B below. Please see overleaf for explanatory notes.

Register of
Approved Driving
Instructors
(Car)

Candidate's Declaration

I certify that
- the vehicle I have provided for the test is properly
  insured under the Road Traffic Act 1988 and
- I do/do not have to wear seat belts under the Motor
  Vehicles (Wearing of Seat Belts) Regulations 1982.

Signed

Date

Centre	
Date	
Make & model	
Reg Mark	
Dual Controls	Fitted ☐ Not Fitted ☐
Candidate's Name	
Ref. No	

Column A

PST No.9 Exercises 10P and 12T

Phase 1-10P Partly trained-Crossroads

	Not Covered	Unsatisfactory	Satisfactory
Briefing on crossroads	☐	☐	☐
Mirror-signal-manoeuvre	☐	☐	☐
Speed	☐	☐	☐
Gears	☐	☐	☐
Coasting	☐	☐	☐
Observation	☐	☐	☐
Emerging	☐	☐	☐
Position right	☐	☐	☐
Position left	☐	☐	☐
Pedestrians	☐	☐	☐
Cross approaching traffic	☐	☐	☐
Right corner cut	☐	☐	☐

Phase 2-12T Trained-Pedestrian crossings and signals

	Not Covered	Unsatisfactory	Satisfactory
Mirror-Signal-Manoeuvre	☐	☐	☐
Speed on approach	☐	☐	☐
Stop when necessary	☐	☐	☐
Overtaking on approach	☐	☐	☐
Inviting pedestrians to cross	☐	☐	☐
Signals by indicator	☐	☐	☐
Signals by arm	☐	☐	☐
Signals timing	☐	☐	☐
Unnecessary signals	☐	☐	☐

The results of your test are:

Phase I Grade		Phase II Grade	

Supervising Examiner's name

Location   Section No.

S E Signature

Column B

In this column the top line of boxes to Phase I and the
bottom line of boxes refer to Phase II

1/2/3 = Unsatisfactory   4/5/6 = Satisfactory

Core Competencies

	1 2 3	4 5 6
Identification of faults	☐☐☐ ☐☐☐	
Fault analysis	☐☐☐ ☐☐☐	
Remedial action	☐☐☐ ☐☐☐	

Instructional Techniques

	1 2 3	4 5 6
Level of instruction	☐☐☐ ☐☐☐	
Planning	☐☐☐ ☐☐☐	
Control of lesson	☐☐☐ ☐☐☐	
Communication	☐☐☐ ☐☐☐	
Q/A Techniques	☐☐☐ ☐☐☐	
Feedback/Encouragement	☐☐☐ ☐☐☐	
Instructor use of controls	☐☐☐ ☐☐☐	

Instructor Characteristics

	1 2 3	4 5 6
Attitude and Approach to Pupil	☐☐☐ ☐☐☐	

ADI 26/PT/09 Rev 7/98

FORMS UK plc FCN17652200

Instructional Test - Part III

The Examiner has marked each aspect of your performance in columns A and B below. Please see overleaf for explanatory notes.

Candidate's Declaration

I certify that
- the vehicle I have provided for the test is properly insured under the Road Traffic Act 1988 and
- I do/do not have to wear seat belts under the Motor Vehicles (Wearing of Seat Belts) Regulations 1982.

Signed

Date

Centre	
Date	
Make & model	
Reg Mark	
Dual Controls	Fitted ☐ Not Fitted ☐
Candidate's Name	
Ref. No	

Column A

PST No.10 Exercises 11P and 8T

Phase 1-11P Partly trained-Meet, cross and overtake other traffic allowing adequate clearance for other road users and anticipation

	Not Covered/ Incorrect	Unsatisfactory	Satisfactory
Briefing	☐	☐	☐
Mirror-signal-manoeuvre	☐	☐	☐
Meet approaching traffic	☐	☐	☐
Cross other traffic	☐	☐	☐
Overtaking other traffic	☐	☐	☐
Keep a safe distance	☐	☐	☐
Shaving other vehicles	☐	☐	☐
Anticipation of pedestrians	☐	☐	☐
Anticipation of cyclists	☐	☐	☐
Anticipation of drivers	☐	☐	☐

Phase 2-8T Trained-Progress / hesitancy - normal position

Progress too fast	☐	☐	☐
Progress too slow	☐	☐	☐
Hesitancy	☐	☐	☐
Normal position too wide from the left	☐	☐	☐
Normal position too close to the left	☐	☐	☐

The results of your test are:

Phase I Grade		Phase II Grade	

Supervising Examiner's name

Location _____ Section No. _____

S E Signature

Column B

In this column the top line of boxes to Phase I and the bottom line of boxes refer to Phase II

1/2/3 = Unsatisfactory   4/5/6 = Satisfactory

Core Competencies

	1 2 3	4 5 6
Identification of faults	☐☐☐	☐☐☐
Fault analysis	☐☐☐	☐☐☐
Remedial action	☐☐☐	☐☐☐

Instructional Techniques

	1 2 3	4 5 6
Level of instruction	☐☐☐	☐☐☐
Planning	☐☐☐	☐☐☐
Control of lesson	☐☐☐	☐☐☐
Communication	☐☐☐	☐☐☐
Q/A Techniques	☐☐☐	☐☐☐
Feedback/Encouragement	☐☐☐	☐☐☐
Instructor use of controls	☐☐☐	☐☐☐

Instructor Characteristics

	1 2 3	4 5 6
Attitude and Approach to Pupil	☐☐☐	☐☐☐

ADI 26/PT/10 Rev 7/98

FORMS UK plc FCN17652400

Interpreting the Marking Sheet

The examiner has to assess your overall performance in general and in particular all of the topics listed previously under the following three headings:

- Core Competencies;
- Instructional Techniques;
- Instructor Characteristics.

To pass, you need to attain the minimum grade of four in each phase. However, an overall assessment is made, and a grading given, by taking the markings of both columns A and B into consideration. For example:

> A candidate fails to identify a serious error. Because of this failure, nothing is done to correct the problem. Then the examiner would mark the appropriate box in column A under 'not covered' or 'unsatisfactory'. This would then be transferred to column B under the heading 'identification of faults'.

You must remember that because of this overall assessment of what actually happens on the day, no two tests can ever be the same. Even manoeuvre exercises cannot be rehearsed and you will need to be able to adapt to what is happening in different circumstances. This is all part of the test of your potential ability.

If You Fail

Using the application form on the reverse of the letter, you may apply for a further test if: 1) you are still within the two-year qualifying period; and 2) the test was your first or second attempt.

Otherwise, if you wish to continue, you will have to wait until the two-year period has elapsed before you can apply for Part 1 again. For a fuller explanation, SEs are normally in their office on Friday mornings, when they are only too happy to give further advice to help you improve your instruction.

When You Pass

You will be given a letter confirming the result and you may apply for entry onto the Register of Approved Driving Instructors (Car). Complete the application form on the reverse of the letter and send it with the current fee (£200 at October 2001 and £240 in Northern Ireland).

Registration Declaration

When you apply for registration, you must sign a declaration to the effect that you will:

- notify the Registrar of any change of name, address or place of employment;
- notify the Registrar if convicted of any offence;
- return the certificate if your registration lapses or is revoked;
- agree to undergo, when requested by the Registrar, a Check Test conducted by DSA staff.

The ADI Certificate

You should receive your official green ADI Certificate of Registration within a week. This will incorporate:

- your name;
- your photograph;
- your ADI number;
- the date of issue; and
- the date of expiry of the certificate.

Displaying Your ADI Certificate

As a qualified instructor, whenever you are giving tuition, you must:

- display the official green certificate on the left-hand side of the car's windscreen;
- produce your certificate if requested by a police officer or any person authorised by the Secretary of State. Failure to do so constitutes an offence. If you can satisfy the Registrar that your certificate has been lost, damaged or destroyed, a duplicate can be issued on payment of the current fee.

Records will be kept of the test results of all the pupils you present for test and a printout of these will be sent to you. You should use this information to monitor your tuition. For example, if pupils are failing for the same faults, it could be your teaching methods that may need adjusting. If you wish to discuss any subjects relating to driving tuition, your SEADI will normally be available on a Friday morning.

The Check Test

As a condition of continued registration, all ADIs must, when requested by the Registrar, take a Check Test with their Supervising Examiner (SEADI). The main objective of this is for the SEADI to assess whether your teaching methods and lesson content are up to the minimum standard required to remain in the Register. (More information on the Check Test is given in Chapter 3.)

Full information on the ADI Register and the qualifying examination is given:

- in the ADI.14 starter pack; and
- on the DSA web site: www.driving-tests.co.uk

Detailed advice on preparing for the examination and also the Check Test is given in the next chapter.

3

Training for the ADI Examination and Preparing for the Check Test

This chapter contains information on:

- the examination structure;
- how to select a tutor;
- the types of course available:
  - what the syllabus should include;
  - useful training materials;
  - how long it may take to qualify;
- preparing for the:
  - Part 1 Test of Theory;
  - Part 2 Test of Driving Ability;
- the Licence to Instruct;
- preparing for the Part 3 Test of Ability to Instruct;
- preparing for the Check Test;
- instructor grading.

THE EXAMINATION STRUCTURE

As you have already read in Chapter 2, this exam is conducted in three parts:

- Part 1 Test of Theory;
- Part 2 Test of Driving Ability;
- Part 3 Test of Ability to Instruct.

You should decide on the method of training that can best be fitted in with your other commitments and that also takes the exam structure into consideration.

Your Tutor

Statistics show that only about a third of those beginning the process of training will eventually qualify as ADIs. Before you commit yourself to training, therefore, it is sensible to arrange for an assessment with a tutor and ask for an honest opinion of your potential. This can avoid lots of heartache and bitterness later on.

Most failures occur in the Part 3 Test of Ability to Instruct. It is vital therefore that the practical training you receive for this test is effective. Make sure that your tutor is experienced in the training of new instructors. Training to teach requires skills that are totally different from those needed to teach people to drive.

The tutor's role is to:

- train new instructors;
- re-train experienced instructors;
- prepare instructors for the Check Test.

It is widely accepted that good drivers don't necessarily make good instructors. It is also very true that not all ADIs, although they are very good at teaching people to drive, may have the complex skills required to train new instructors. Training to teach is totally different from teaching to drive. The local ADI may have an extremely good reputation with learner drivers; however, you may have to look further afield for a tutor who is fully up to date and conversant with the exam requirements and who trains new instructors on a regular basis.

A list of training establishments is included with the ADI 14, which you should already have applied for. These ORDIT establishments (Official Register of Driving Instructor Trainers) have been inspected by specially trained DSA staff and recommended to the ORDIT Management Committee as being suitable for inclusion in the Directory.

The ADINJC also have a Register of Tutors. For details contact: John Milne MBE, Head of Training – ADINJC, 121 Marshalswick Lane, St Albans, Herts AL1 4UX (tel: 01727 858068).

The MSA (tel: 0161 429 9669) and the DIA (tel: 020 8665 5151) may also be able to put you in contact with a suitably qualified tutor.

As this change of career will entail a great deal of investment in terms of time, commitment and cost, before enrolling on any course you will need to seriously consider the following aspects:

- Do I have the potential to become an ADI?
- Can I really afford the expense, given that there are no guarantees of qualifying?
- Does the course allow for training to be tailored to the structure of the exam?
- Will I be getting sufficient individual training in preparation for Parts 2 and 3?
- Will the course be structured to suit my own needs?
- Does my tutor have plenty of experience in the training of new instructors?

The Types of Course Available

Before paying out large sums of money for 'complete' or 'intensive' courses, you should bear in mind that you have to apply for, and pass, each test in sequence. To be realistic, the qualifying procedure is likely to take a minimum of around seven to eight months (if you pass each element first time and there are no delays with test appointments).

You should also remember that, should you fail Part 2 three times, you will not be eligible to take Part 3. Make sure that you will not be paying for what you can't have!

Courses vary a great deal in content, duration and cost. Before deciding on the one that most suits your needs, you should make every effort to find out what you will be getting for your money! Ask for a full description of the syllabus and the format of the training in relation to each element of the exam. Remember, everyone has different rates of learning – training to develop practical teaching skills should, therefore, be adapted to suit the individual candidate.

The following list gives examples of the types of training available:

- distance learning programmes for candidates to study privately for Part 1, with practical training for Parts 2 and 3;
- combined classroom and practical courses to cover all three tests;
- intensive courses to prepare candidates for all three tests;
- intensive courses where the majority of the training is conducted in the classroom with very little emphasis on practical in-car work;
- courses to prepare candidates initially for Parts 1 and 2 with a view to obtaining a trainee licence and working for a driving school while preparing for Part 3.

Before committing yourself, you should clarify some of the following points:

- If you opt for working under the Trainee Licence Scheme, will you be receiving proper training and support – particularly prior to being sent out with learners?
- Will your training consist of sitting in the back of an instructor's car merely observing, without receiving any individual training?
- Will your training be conducted by someone with the appropriate experience and not someone who has only recently passed that particular element of the exam?
- Is the course set up by an agency that gets funding and sub-contracts the work out to local ADIs who may not have tutoring skills?

Whichever course you opt for, remember to ask about your tutor's special qualifications, how much of the training is conducted in the classroom and how much individual in-car training you will receive.

Course Syllabus

Having considered all of the above, you must compare the syllabus of the course you have selected with the examination format and syllabus. A good ADI training course should prepare you properly for each of the three tests. It should include:

- up-to-date books, materials and questions and answers for the Test of Theory;
- sufficient training, preferably on an individual basis for the Part 2 Driving Ability test;
- plenty of training, preferably on an individual basis (certainly no more than a ratio of two trainees to one tutor) for the Part 3 Instructional test. (If you opt to take up a trainee licence certain criteria must be met. These are dealt with later in this chapter.)

Course material

To prepare yourself properly for the examination, you will need the following materials, which are recommended by the DSA:

- *The Driving Instructor's Handbook* by John Miller & Margaret Stacey, published by Kogan Page;
- *The Official DSA Guide for Driving Instructors*, published by the Stationery Office;
- The Driving Standards Agency publication *The Driving Manual*;
- *The Highway Code*
- *The Driving Test* (the DSA guide published by HMSO);
- DL25A/B Driving Test Report form;
- *The Motor Vehicles (Driving Licences) Regulations 1996*, ISBN 0–11–063309–1, available from HMSO;
- *Know Your Traffic Signs*, published by the Stationery Office.

Other useful material, available from the authors, includes:

- *Instructor Home Study Programme*, written and published by Margaret Stacey;
- *Practical Teaching Skills for Driving Instructors* by John Miller, Tony Scriven & Margaret Stacey, published by Kogan Page;
- *The Advanced Driver's Handbook* by Margaret Stacey, published by Kogan Page;
- *Learn to Drive in 10 Easy Stages* by Margaret Stacey, published by Kogan Page;
- *Visual Teaching System* published by Margaret Stacey (helpful for practical in-car training).

Driving Instruction Car Hire

At Conway's we offer you an unbeatable package to make your life easier

- **New dual controlled car every 18 months delivered to your door**

- **No big capital outlay**

- **No car tax to pay**

- **No insurance to pay**

- **No repair bills to pay**

- **Replacement car for accident/repair**

We have probably the largest and most varied fleet of dual control cars in the UK. So, telephone 01254 682880 now for an information pack

CONWAY CONTRACT HIRE LTD

How Long Will it Take to Qualify?

Because of the structure of the exam, and the time it may take to get appointments for the three tests, the process of qualifying is likely to take seven or eight months. It can take considerably longer than this if tests are postponed or if you fail any of them. You should take all of this into consideration if you opt for an intensive course. It is highly likely that you will have to return for 'top-up' training for Part 3, which may also mean additional training fees.

PREPARING FOR THE TEST OF THEORY

As you know by now, this 'touch screen' test consists of 100 multiple-choice questions, each question having one correct answer from the three given.

Some of the questions require you to know the exact wording in *The Driving Manual* and *The Highway Code*. It is therefore not enough just to know what the basic principles and rules for driving are! Many of the questions are worded negatively. You therefore need a full understanding of the meaning of the rules and regulations in both of these publications as well as a thorough knowledge of the other recommended reading materials.

Because of the high standard of knowledge required, you must exercise a degree of self-discipline and be prepared to set aside a lot of time for private study. Even if you opt for a classroom course to prepare for this test, there is still a lot of reading to do!

Methods of Study

There are different ways in which you may study for this test, including:

- purchasing all of the books and studying at home in your own time;
- home study programmes – properly organised and structured courses which you work through and mark yourself. A programme banded similarly to Part 1 is available from Margaret Stacey, who can also supply the textbooks;
- correspondence courses – you are supplied with papers which need to be sent to your training establishment for marking and then returned;
- classroom courses – where you have contact with a tutor and other students (remember – you will also have to do a lot of studying at home).

Only apply for the test when you are confident that you have an adequate knowledge and understanding of all the subjects listed in the ADI 14. Remember it is better to delay taking the test than to throw away the examination fee if you're not quite ready.

PREPARING FOR THE TEST OF DRIVING ABILITY

To be able to drive skilfully and safely, you need a thorough working knowledge of the Highway Code and *The Driving Manual*. It is not enough merely to be able to recite the rules, you must be able to show that you can apply them sensibly and correctly.

The following is a quote by the Driving Standards Agency on the Part 2 Test of Driving Ability:

> This test is not just a slightly more difficult 'L' test. It is of an advanced nature and a very high standard of competence is required. You must show that you have a thorough knowledge of the principles of good driving and road safety and that you can apply them in practice.

Guidance for the Experienced Driver

All candidates, including those who are members of any of the advanced driving organisations, are advised to obtain guidance from a recognised tutor before taking this test. Experienced tutors know what the Supervising Examiner will be looking for, and are skilled at assessing and advising on any adjustments required to improve style and efficiency.

Streamlining your performance

Even if you have been driving for many years, modifications may be needed to streamline your performance. It is often said that 'unlearning' something which has been practised for years is far more difficult than learning something new. You may have developed habits over the years which need correcting.

A good tutor will be able to guide you along the route to improvement and explain why any changes need to be made. You should remember that you may have only three attempts at this test. If you are not up to the required standard, not only will failure be expensive, but there will be more pressure on you to pass at your next attempt.

Reasons for Seeking Proper Training

- Candidates who have been driving for many years may have been practising inefficient methods.
- The standard of performance required by the Driving Standards Agency is much higher than that of the advanced driving organisations.
- It is vital that any false assumptions about the test and its content are removed – a good tutor will put you straight on these matters.
- Candidates generally require training to give them some experience in being assessed under test conditions.

- Although candidates have passed the Part 1 Test of Theory, there may still be deficiencies in some areas of their knowledge which could result in failure. The trained tutor will be able to identify and give guidance in these.
- Because of the foregoing, candidates who do not take any special training, and manage merely to 'scrape through' this test, may well be at a disadvantage when they attend for practical training for Part 3.
- Time spent receiving corrective tuition with a trained tutor provides a first-hand demonstration of the teaching techniques you will have to learn to put into practice later.
- Failure is expensive and increases pressure.

What Your Examiner Will be Looking For

When you take the Test of Driving Ability, you must remember that you are not expected to be driving like a 'good learner'. Your examiner wants to see you drive with skill and confidence. It will be obvious to the trained eye if you are trying to put on a show of being 'extra careful'. Doing this will only be a distraction and may cause you to make incorrect decisions and to fail to make proper progress.

To prepare for this test, you should:

- take some advice from your tutor on those aspects of your driving which need improvement;
- continue referring to your books on driving;
- get as much practice as possible on different types of road and in differing conditions;
- apply the correct procedures whenever you are driving;
- try to maintain progress in relation to the conditions, the law and the type and performance of your car.

As well as making progress, you should also take into consideration vehicle sympathy and the comfort of your passengers. To maximise this, you should:

- make sure you can reach all of the controls properly;
- use the controls smoothly and progressively;
- hold, turn and straighten the steering wheel properly;
- demonstrate vehicle sympathy by selecting gears at the correct time and in accordance with power requirements;
- plan well ahead so that you can use 'accelerator sense' to avoid excessive use of the brakes;
- maximise fuel economy by keeping the engine revs at the correct level.

To maintain progress and demonstrate your personal driving skills, you should:

- look and plan well ahead, preparing for hazards before you reach them;
- adjust your speed to avoid any unnecessary stops;
- start looking early at junctions so that you can take opportunities to proceed, as soon as you are sure it is safe;
- be aware of the speed limit wherever you are and make progress by driving up to the limit according to the conditions and your vehicle.

To protect yourself, your passengers and road users all around, you should:

- be aware of what is happening all around your car at all times by using all of the mirrors on a regular basis;
- respond properly to what you see in your mirrors;
- anticipate and make allowances for the mistakes of other road users;
- exercise self-discipline when threatened by other road users;
- show courtesy and consideration to anyone else using the road;
- always be prepared to give way, even if it is your priority.

Show that you can handle your car efficiently in all of the manoeuvre exercises by:

- maintaining absolute control on all gradients, using the handbrake when necessary;
- making effective observations throughout, and responding correctly to any other road users;

- demonstrating accurate steering skills to complete each exercise effectively;
- keeping full control during the emergency stop, avoiding skidding; but if you skid, correcting it properly.

Try not to be influenced by the person sitting beside you. If you are putting into practice those principles of safe driving which you have learnt for Part 1, then your decisions should only be influenced by what is happening all around you. Remember, your decision should be based only on what you know is safe for the circumstances. Examiners are highly skilled and specially trained and should know what you are basing your decisions on.

It is sensible to have a couple of 'mock test' sessions with your tutor prior to taking Part 2, just in case you have any last-minute doubts or queries, and need any advice or reassurance.

If you put all of these principles into practice, passing the Test of Driving Ability at your first attempt should not be a problem.

PREPARING FOR THE INSTRUCTIONAL TEST

When studying for the Test of Theory you should gain a lot of the background knowledge you will need for teaching new drivers.

While training you for the Test of Driving Ability, your tutor will be demonstrating the teaching skills which you will have to learn to put into practice as a driving instructor. A good tutor should teach you how to:

- establish prior knowledge by using a question and answer technique – this is even more relevant now, with the establishment of the Theory Test;
- break down subjects into their key elements;
- adopt the teaching principle of explanation – demonstration – practice;
- use a question-and-answer technique to maximise understanding and obtain feedback;
- give full talk-through instruction;
- give more responsibility to learners by decreasing the level of instruction at the appropriate time;
- improve learners' awareness and understanding by encouraging commentaries;
- supervise and assess more experienced learners;
- use visual aids to assist the learner's understanding;
- identify, analyse and correct errors made by drivers of differing abilities;
- avoid problems on the road by early verbal intervention;
- explain about the use of the dual and ancillary controls.

Training and Practice

Although practice with real learners can be beneficial in the later stages of your training, it can sometimes be very frightening if it is attempted before you have

HE-MAN DUAL CONTROLS

- HE-MAN Dual Controls are Precision made

- Dedicated for the Vehicle

- Positive action on instructor's side

- Most controls have the option of instructor's pedals remaining
stationary or moving in unison with driver's pedals

Order Direct

HE-MAN EQUIPMENT LTD, Cable Street, Southampton, SO14 5AR
Telephone: (023) 8022 6952 or 8022 7309 Fax: (023) 8033 0132

MAIL ORDER
EXPRESS SERVICE

had some professional training yourself. It is absolutely essential, therefore, that you get some properly structured training from your tutor before you practise with learners.

To teach you most of the aspects listed above, a good trainer needs the ability to role-play realistically drivers with different abilities and learning aptitudes so that you can learn how to teach in safety.

Your tutor should teach you how to:

- plan the instruction to suit the level of ability of each pupil;
- organise routes so that pupils can cope;
- avoid inconveniencing other road users;
- maintain safety for your pupils, yourself and others.

Practice under the Trainee Licence Scheme

When you have passed Parts 1 and 2, you may wish to gain practice with real learners by working for a driving school under this scheme. If you decide that this is a good way of earning while you are preparing for the test, you must ensure that your sponsoring ADI is prepared to give you adequate training and the support you will need for passing the Test of Ability to Instruct.

It is sensible to get written confirmation from your sponsor that you will be given training in all of the topics listed below and which are specified by the DSA as the 'core curriculum' subjects:

- explaining the controls of the vehicle, including use of the dual controls;
- moving off and making normal stops;
- reversing into openings to the left and the right;
- turning the car round, using forward and reverse gears;
- parking close to the kerb, using forward and reverse gears;
- using the mirrors and making emergency stops;
- approaching and turning corners;
- judging speed and making normal progress;
- road positioning,
- dealing with junctions and crossroads;
- dealing with pedestrian crossings;
- meeting, crossing the path of, overtaking and allowing adequate clearance for other vehicles and anticipating other road users;
- giving correct signals;
- understanding traffic signs, including road markings and traffic lights;
- method, clarity, adequacy and correctness of instruction;
- the general manner of the driving instructor.

Records must be kept of the training and supervision you receive. As you have to sign to say that you have received adequate training in the above subjects, and that you have been supervised while giving driving lessons, *it is in your own interest to make sure that your sponsor carries out these responsibilities*.

Should you fail Part 3 because you have not had adequate training, there will be no recourse for complaint afterwards. If you gave up other employment to work under this scheme, you will also find yourself out of work.

Qualifying Independently

You can prepare for Part 3 totally independently of a driving school. This will then give you the freedom when you qualify of either working for yourself or seeking employment with a driving school.

In any case, you should bear in mind that this is the most difficult element of the exam. You will need plenty of good quality training. This may be quite expensive, but remember – *you are investing in your future career*! This initial investment will be more beneficial than skimping and failing. Remember you are allowed only three attempts at this test. If you fail, you will be increasing the stress factor.

You need to seek out a tutor with plenty of experience who will advise you on when and how to practise with friends or relatives, and when to apply for the test.

The Trainee Licence

You may opt to work for a driving school while preparing for your Part 3. Under the provisions of the Road Traffic Act 1972 and the Road Traffic (Driving Instruction) Act 1988, a six-month licence to give instruction (fee at April 2001 is £100.00) can be issued to suitable applicants wishing to gain practice during the final stages of their training. If you wish to take up this option, you can apply for a licence after passing the Part 2 Test of Driving Ability.

Only one licence will normally be granted. The registrar will exercise discretion over whether to issue a further licence. Refunds are not normally granted for any period when a licence is not used, or for any period after the Test of Ability to Instruct has been passed.

In Northern Ireland, a trainee licence can be applied for at the same time as making an application for a written test (the fee at April 2001 is £120.00). A maximum of two will be issued; each is valid for six months.

Conditions Under Which a Trainee Licence is Granted

The following explains the conditions under which licences are granted:

- You are only authorised to give instruction for the school whose address is shown on the licence. If you change your school, you must apply to have your licence reissued.
- There must be at least one ADI working at the supervisor's address for every trainee licence holder.
- You must receive 40 hours practical training from an ADI. This period of training must start no earlier than 12 months before, and be completed by, the date of issue of the licence. You must receive training in all of the following subjects:
  - explaining the controls of the vehicle, including use of the dual controls;
  - moving off and making normal stops;
  - reversing into openings to the left and the right;
  - turning the car around using forward and reverse gears;
  - parking close to the kerb, using forward and reverse gears;
  - using the mirrors and making emergency stops;
  - approaching and turning corners;
  - judging speed and making normal progress;
  - road positioning;
  - dealing with junctions and crossroads;
  - dealing with pedestrian crossings;
  - meeting, crossing the path of, overtaking and allowing adequate clearance for other vehicles and anticipating other road users;
  - giving correct signals;
  - understanding traffic signs, including road markings and traffic lights;

- – method, clarity, adequacy and correctness of instruction;
- – the general manner of the driving instructor;
- – manner, patience and tact in dealing with pupils;
- – ability to inspire confidence in pupils.
- You must not advertise yourself as a fully qualified instructor.
- You must abide by one of the following conditions:
  a) sponsoring ADI must supervise 20% of all the lessons you give. A record of all lessons given, along with the supervision received, must be kept on form ADI 21S, which is issued with the licence. This must be signed by both you and your sponsor and must be returned to the DSA as soon as the licence expires.

Or

  b) You must receive a minimum additional 20 hours training covering all the above topics. This extra training must take place within the first three months of the licence or before you take your first attempt at Part 3, whichever is the soonest.

  A record of this training must be kept on form ADI 21AT and must be sent to the DSA before the end of the three-month period, or presented to the examiner who conducts your Part 3 test, whichever is the earliest. At least 25% of the period of training has to be practical training, under-taken in a car at a maximum instructor-to-trainee ratio of no more than two trainees to one ADI.

  If the training option is selected and you subsequently fail either your first or second Part 3 test, you must take a further five hours training before being allowed to take another test. You have to provide the examiner on the day with a declaration signed by both you and your ADI. Failure to do so will result in your test being cancelled.

Displaying Your Trainee Licence

Whenever you are giving driving lessons under this scheme you must:

- display the red licence in the left-hand side of the car's windscreen;
- produce your licence if requested by a police officer or any person authorised by the Secretary of State. Failure to do so constitutes an offence. If you can satisfy the registrar that your licence has been lost, damaged or destroyed, a duplicate can be issued on payment of the current fee.

What Your Examiner Will be Looking For

The Part 3 is not a test of your knowledge – that is assessed in the Test of Theory. Neither is it a test of your driving skills – they are tested in the Test of Driving Ability. It is, in fact, a test of your *practical ability to give driving instruction*.

Your SE will be assessing whether you can transmit your knowledge and skills effectively, in a way which will result in understanding and good driving practices being learnt by the pupil.

The test is conducted in two parts or 'phases':

- *Phase 1* – the SE plays the role of a beginner or partly trained learner.
- *Phase 2* – the SE plays the role of a learner at about Driving Test standard.

Because of the time constraints placed on you and your examiner, you may not be able to cover every essential detail of the topics to be taught. However, you must ensure that all the key elements, and the basic routines and procedures, are included, whether this is during the explanation at the beginning of each 'lesson', or during the practice time while the 'pupil' is driving.

During this test you should demonstrate your ability to:

- explain clearly the key elements of the topic;
- give the necessary help and talk-through instruction to develop and improve the 'pupil's' skill;
- use questions and answers to help the 'pupil' to understand why certain rules and procedures must be followed;
- develop the pupil's confidence by transferring responsibility when skills improve;
- identify, analyse and correct errors by explaining how you would have dealt with situations;
- give feedback and encouragement when improvement takes place.

To encourage effective observations at junctions, you could ask the following questions:

- Keep looking both ways – can you see both ways?
- How far can you see?
- Is it clear all around?

Fault Assessment

Emphasis during this test is placed on fault assessment. Although you should not nit-pick at every minor error, you will be expected to deal with any mistakes which could develop into bad habits, and any which are potentially serious or which could result in danger.

The easiest way to recognise and deal with any faults made by the examiner is to ask yourself: 'Would I be doing this if I were driving?' You can then transfer your thoughts by asking the SE for a reason and explanation. How you then deal with the matter will depend on the response you get.

Remember, the major faults are normally associated with the lesson topic. However, other faults will be introduced and these need to be dealt with effectively. When you recognise something as deviating from the driving norm, you should:

- query the fault;
- ask the 'pupil' if they understand the correct procedure for dealing with such a situation;
- explain how you would have dealt with it;
- give the reason why;
- practise the correct procedure to reinforce the point.

The Structure of the Part 3

Phase 1 – key elements

- establish the base-line for the lesson by using questions and answers;
- explain the routines and procedures to be learnt;
- give talk-through instruction until skills begin to develop;
- decrease instruction and use questions and answers to develop independence;
- do not restrict yourself to the topic but use other opportunities as they arise to teach awareness;
- identify and analyse faults when they arise and give advice on how to improve;
- give the 'pupil' plenty of encouragement and feedback.

The SE will assess your ability to:

- teach a new subject to the pupil, or to
- reinforce and practise a subject where the pupil has some prior knowledge.

Listen carefully to the SE. How you establish the base-line for your lesson should depend on the description of the 'pupil' and what experience they already have.

Your first task, therefore, is to find out what the 'pupil' already knows. You can do this by asking a few questions that are relevant to the subject. Remember, now that new drivers have to prepare for the Theory Test, using questions and answers is even more relevant in establishing whether they are studying or not.

Depending on the response, either you may have to go through all of the key elements, or you may only need to reinforce anything the 'pupil' omitted.

Visual aids   If the 'pupil' appears to be having difficulty in understanding, you should use *visual or other in-car aids*. Not only will these help the pupil because he or she can 'see' what you mean, but they will also serve as a memory-jogger for you.

Demonstrations   These may be offered where appropriate.

Practice   If the subject is relatively new, you should be prepared to give full 'talk-through' instruction to build up the 'pupil's' confidence. Lots of help is necessary in the early stages of a learner's career; you have to be prepared, therefore, to repeat procedures and to give as much assistance as is necessary.

Remember, your instruction should not be confined to the lesson topic. Any situation that arises during the drive which needs to be dealt with should be mentioned. For example, if you are dealing with junctions, you should not ignore parked vehicles and the possibility that there may be oncoming traffic.

Using the question-and-answer technique on the move   You should avoid over-instruction and be ready to decrease the instruction when you can see skills beginning to develop. Asking a few simple questions early enough can encourage the pupils to take a little responsibility for carrying out routine procedures. For example, to encourage the 'pupil' to make effective safety checks before moving off, you could ask: *'Is there anyone behind?'*, or *'Is there anyone in your blind area?'*

Developing the pupil's understanding   Whatever the type of error committed, you must give a valid reason for dealing with the situation in the manner you want to deal with it. Remember, when you make a correction you should always finish with the *'because'* element. This does not mean saying: 'Because I say so!' or 'If you don't, you'll fail your test!' Your reasoning should be based on the correct application of the rules, regulations and procedures for driving safely and considerately – in other words, *in order to survive*.

Positive correction   You must maintain control of the lesson. Sometimes this means preventing a potentially serious situation from arising. A positive instruction to *'wait'* may sometimes be all that is required – for example, if you feel that the pupil is going to emerge from a junction without taking effective observations all around.

Retrospective correction   If the 'pupil' is allowed to emerge unsafely and is reprimanded afterwards, it could be too late! It is no consolation to anyone involved in a near-miss situation to confirm after the event that *'You shouldn't have pulled out without looking properly!'* Learning is more likely to take place if the pupil is made to deal with the situation correctly in the first place.

Giving feedback and encouragement   These are both important aspects of the instructor's job, no matter what the standard and ability of the pupil. At the end of each practice element, within each phase, let the pupil know what progress has been made and where improvement and more practice are needed. Encourage the pupil to ask if they don't understand something you have been working on.

Confirm that you will record any items necessary for the pupil to refer to before the next lesson. Encourage them to study for the *theory test* or to revise any relevant aspects of the current subject which are not clearly understood.

Remember to finish on a 'high'. Give praise for those areas where improvement took place.

Phase 2

The SE will assess your ability to:

- assess what the pupil already knows and can do;
- identify and analyse errors or weaknesses;
- give remedial instruction to achieve improvement.

Establish any underlying problems   Listen very carefully to the SE's description and driving experience of the 'pupil' – there may be hints of an underlying problem. Ask a few questions to confirm whether or not the key elements of the topic are understood and confirm correct procedures where any weakness is evident.

Practice   You should aim to 'get the car moving' as soon as possible. Remember, your job with the pupil is to make an assessment of his or her strengths and weaknesses, and to give any advice which may be necessary to improve their understanding of the skills involved.

Over-instruction   This should be avoided by allowing the pupil to demonstrate his or her skill at making decisions and putting the correct procedures into practice.

Correcting faults   Although you have a specific subject to deal with, you should remember that faults will occur in other areas. These must also be dealt with.

Try to avoid 'nit-picking'. Where mistakes occur on a very minor, one-off basis, they may not even be worth a mention. However, if similar errors are committed more than once, or if you are unsure, then query them. You may be able to deal with these minor errors on the move by asking a simple question or making a positive comment.

Where errors of a more serious or potentially dangerous nature occur, then you must deal with these in more detail. It may be appropriate to stop the car when it is safe to avoid distracting the pupil's attention from the driving task.

Key Learning Points

Each of the 'pre-set test' subjects is made up of a number of key elements. You may only have time to cover some of these briefly during your explanation. However, *you must ensure that the correct procedures and routines are put into practice during the driving part of each phase*. The following pages give an outline of each of the pre-set test subjects, with a list of the key learning points which should be covered in either the explanation or the practice part of the lesson.

Controls Lesson (Phase 1 – ADI 26/PT/01)

The main purposes of this first practical driving lesson are:

- for the instructor and pupil to get to know each other;
- to reassure the pupil and to gain their confidence;
- to explain the use and functions of the main driving controls;
- to ensure that some learning takes place.

Lesson structure

First, you must introduce yourself and establish how you will address each other. When it has been confirmed that the pupil has not driven before, you will have to drive to the training area. You should also confirm that the 'pupil' has a valid driving licence and can read a number plate from the prescribed distance.

During this journey, you should use the time to find out a little about the 'pupil' and their reasons for learning to drive. You can ask if you were recommended by another pupil.

Ask whether the 'pupil' has taken, or has applied for, his or her Theory Test yet and, while driving, you can explain some of the routines you are putting into practice and how these relate to what they are learning.

Lesson content

Remember, this is not a test of your knowledge. You should take into consideration how much information the pupil is likely to absorb. Avoid overloading your lesson with irrelevancies. For example, at 9 am on a sunny morning, do you really need to include information about all the lights, gauges, dials and other equipment? You can confirm that this information will be covered in a future lesson, or as the need arises to use the wipers and explain about other equipment.

Timing your explanation

You will probably spend more time parked up giving an explanation of the controls than you will with any other topic. The time you spend on each of the key points should depend on whether the 'pupil' has any prior knowledge or understanding. For example, most people have been car passengers and will probably know about seatbelts; or a trained mechanic will probably be able to tell you a thing or two about how the clutch works and the relationship between power requirements and gears.

Remember to ask questions at intervals to confirm what the 'pupil' may already know. *Learning scripts can be a total waste of time – you must adapt the lesson to take prior knowledge into consideration.*

Key elements

Driver checks:

- an explanation of safety in opening and closing doors should be given (as you will have driven the car to the training area, this explanation should include the passenger and driver doors);
- checking the car is safely secured (handbrake and neutral);
- seating position for reaching hand and foot controls comfortably;
- adjustment of head restraint;
- adjustment of all mirrors;
- how to put on and remove the seatbelt;
- how to start and switch off the engine.

The steering:

- explain how to hold the wheel;
- the importance of looking well ahead when driving along – explain how the hands follow the eyes;
- refer to the pull-push method as described in *The Driving Manual*;
- indicators – relate their operation to the direction of turning the steering wheel. You could ask the question: 'When turning right, if the wheel has to go to the right, which way do you think the indicator will have to go?';
- horn – ask the pupil to refer to the appropriate Highway Code rules so that you can ask them about these on the next lesson.

Use of the wipers, washers and other necessary controls should be covered if weather or light conditions dictate.

Handbrake:

- explain how it operates on the rear wheels;
- explain its purpose;
- give one or two examples of where to use it;
- let the pupil practise releasing and applying it – ask them to apply the footbrake before practising, which should help develop an understanding of the relationship between these two controls.

Gear lever:

- give the pupil plenty of practice at gear selection;
- let them develop a feel for moving the lever through the gear sequences;
- make sure they can find the gears while looking through the windscreen;
- the 'palming' method, and relating the position of the first four forward gears with the road wheels, may help if difficulty is experienced;
- explain simply about the power and speed requirements. For example: first gear is normally used for moving off because it is the most powerful and has

to get the weight of the car moving. Encourage the pupil to ask questions, so that anything which has not been understood can be repeated.

Simple illustrations may help to promote better understanding, as well as helping to develop a sense of vehicle sympathy.

Accelerator, footbrake and clutch:

- get the pupil to position the feet correctly, bearing in mind that it is more important to be able to stop the car than to make it go faster;
- explain the terminology you will be using;
- let the pupil cover and feel for the pedals without looking down;
- explain how to start the engine;
- explain what each control does in simple terms and how they should be used gently and progressively;
- let the pupil practise 'setting the gas';
- introduce the use of the mirror before braking and explain about the brake lights;
- let the pupil listen and feel the range of the clutch.

How the clutch works The main purpose of the clutch is to connect and disconnect the power from the engine to the road wheels. It is needed so that changes can be smoothly made from one gear into another.

Remember, explaining is unlikely to be enough. Practising while stationary will help the pupil to develop confidence. Tell the pupil what to do and let them practise until they feel they can cope.

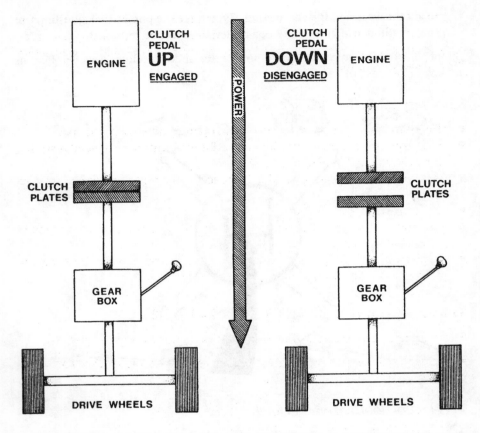

If you still have some time left, continue by explaining how to move off and stop.

Moving off and stopping:

- explain how to put the M-S-M routine into practice for moving off and stopping;
- include the precautions to be taken before moving away, ie explain about the blind spots;
- ensure that your instructions for moving off are properly timed to ensure initial success;
- give full talk-through for moving off, changing gear, steering and stopping the car.

Build confidence

Try to ensure that early success is achieved by giving your instructions in the correct sequence and properly timed. By doing this you can assure the pupil that driving is quite easy and dispel any fears that they may have previously had.

These first attempts to follow instructions on the move will show the pupil what effect the controls have on the car. Moving off and changing gear at an early stage will have a beneficial effect on the over-anxious and help to satisfy the expectations of the more able.

Summary of the key points

- Enter and leave the car safely (safety in opening and closing doors).
- Carry out the driver checks (doors, handbrake, neutral, seat, head restraint, mirrors, belt and switching on engine).
- Assume a correct seating position for reaching the foot controls and steering wheel.
- Check handbrake and neutral, and start the engine.
- Identify the function of, and locate, the main driving controls (steering/indicators/handbrake/gear lever/accelerator/footbrake/clutch).
- Explain the MSM routine and give simple instructions for moving off, changing gear, steering, and stopping in a safe position.

Moving off/Stopping (Phase 1 – ADI 26/PT/02)

The main purposes of this lesson are for the instructor to help the pupil to:

- understand the principles behind the Mirror–Signal–Manoeuvre routine;
- develop basic car control skills in order to:
  - move off smoothly under reasonable control;
  - stop smoothly and parallel with the kerb;
- understand the need to stop in safe places.

Lesson structure

Following the initial introductions, you will have to drive to the training area. Establish any prior knowledge by asking a few simple questions, such as:

- Are you familiar with this type of car?
- Do you know what 'Set the gas' and 'Find the biting point' mean?
- Have you moved off and stopped before?
- Are you studying for the Theory Test?
- Do you understand the MSM routine? Can you explain it to me?

The lesson should then follow a simple pattern. You should:

- state the purpose of the lesson;
- explain about the MSM routine;
- practise using the foot controls as necessary while stationary;
- give a full talk-through and practice for:
  - moving off and stopping (level, uphill and downhill, if appropriate);

- – moving off, building up speed and changing gear;
- – driving along and checking the mirrors;
- – slowing down and changing down;
- stopping smoothly in safe places;
- give feedback and encouragement.

Explanation of the M-S-M routine

Mirrors:

- Explain about the MSM routine including: the purpose and use of mirrors before moving off; signalling; changing direction; braking and stopping.

Signals:

- Explain the purpose and use of signals and relate this to the Highway Code. Discrimination should be introduced, even at this stage, in order to develop the pupil's 'look, assess and decide' processes. Before moving away you could ask: 'Is there anyone about to benefit from a signal?'

Mirror-signal-manoeuvre routine:

- Explain how and why this sequence should be followed for every change of speed or direction, including: moving off, overtaking and stopping.

Precautions before moving off: Explain about the blind spots and why these should be checked before moving off. For example: if parked at the side of the road, pick out an object on the offside pavement which will be in the pupil's blind spot. Ask if they can see it without turning round to check.

Another way of emphasising the need to look round is to get the pupil to watch for a vehicle approaching from behind. Ask them to watch it in the interior mirror and then the off-side mirror and keep watching until it disappears into the blind spot. It is important that the pupil develops an understanding of what might happen if blind spots are not checked.

Co-ordination of the controls

In order to build the pupil's confidence, try to ensure that first-time success is achieved. Do this by giving full 'talk-through' instruction for moving the car a few yards and then stopping.

Recognising and avoiding problems

In the early stages, pupils will only do what they are told to do; no more and no less. You must ensure that you tell them everything in the correct sequence to enable them to control the car smoothly and build their confidence.

During initial practice at moving off, and so that problems can be avoided, you must ensure that you respond immediately should things start to go wrong. For example, if the pupil eases pressure from the accelerator, you could say: 'Keep the gas set.' If the clutch is allowed to come up too far, you could say: 'Clutch down a little.'

Try to imagine how your pupil would feel if, when moving off for the first time, the engine stalled – hardly the best way to build up confidence!

Be ready to correct any steering errors. If the pupil is steering in towards the kerb or out towards the centre of the road, ask where they are looking and explain how 'The hands follow the eyes. Look well ahead at where you want to go.'

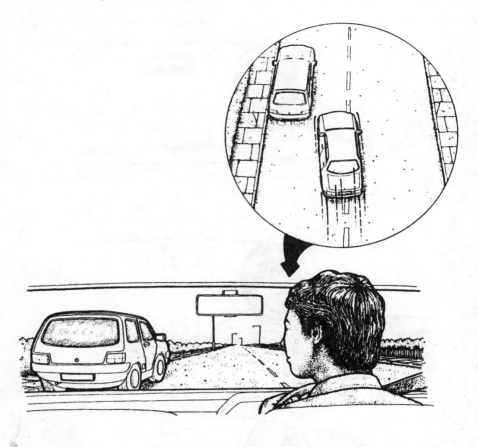

Normal stop control

- Explain the MSM routine for stopping.
- After moving off for the first time, prepare the pupil for stopping.
- To encourage early development of mirror use, ask if there is anyone following.
- Give the instruction to apply the left signal if it is needed.
- Give full talk-through instruction to ensure a smooth and safe stop is attained, ie 'Cover the brake and the clutch. Brake gently. Clutch down, brake gently to a stop.'
- Give the instruction: 'Keep both feet still. Put the handbrake on and the gear lever into neutral. Now, rest your feet.' This will ensure that the engine is kept running and build the pupil's confidence in their ability. (Sometimes a feeling of relief at stopping can cause pupils to release the foot controls before the car has been secured, resulting in a stalled engine. This can result in a sense of inability and disappointment.)

Carry out the moving off and stopping exercise a couple of times and, if the pupil begins to respond favourably, encourage them to try the procedure without your assistance. You should, however, continue giving assistance if required.

Normal stop position: Introduce the Highway Code rules relating to stopping. Ask the pupil for a couple of examples of where it would not be safe or legal to stop. Try to time your initial instructions to coincide with safe stopping places. If, however, the pupil stops where unsafe or inconvenient, ask: 'Why do you think this is not a safe place for stopping?'

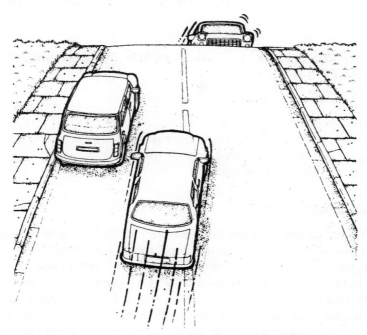

Making progress by building up speed and using the gears

Practice should now be given at moving off, building up speed, changing through the gears to make progress, and then stopping.

Remember to time your instructions so that the car responds smoothly to the pupil's actions.

Encourage use of the mirror while driving along. This will get them into the habit of regularly checking on the situation to the rear.

Summary of the key points

● briefing; confirm what the pupil knows, explain the objectives of the lesson, ie to learn to move off, change up the gears and stop the car, applying the mirror-signal-manoeuvre routine;

- mirrors: explain the need to use them well before changing speed or direction, and stopping;
- mirror-signal-manoeuvre: explain the system of car control as defined in *The Highway Code, The Driving Test* and *The Driving Manual*;
- precautions before moving off: explain about blind spots;
- co-ordination of the controls: explain and practise using the controls smoothly;
- normal stop: explain and practise how to stop smoothly;
- normal stop position: explain about the importance of selecting safe places for stopping.

Turn in the Road (Phase 1 – ADI 26/PT/03) and Reversing (Phase 1 – ADI 26/PT/04)

The main purposes of the manoeuvre exercises are to:

- develop the pupil's car control skills;
- make the pupil aware of the importance of observations throughout;
- teach the pupil how to respond to other road users;
- improve the general driving skills.

Lesson structure

Introduce yourself and establish the 'base-line' for the lesson by asking a few questions that are relevant to what the 'pupil' should have learnt.

Before you explain a manoeuvre exercise, you will need to make the 'pupil' aware of the need to find somewhere that is Safe – Legal – Convenient.

Use the time spent driving to the training area to assess the 'pupil's' ability to put into practice what should have been learnt so far. Particularly check for co-ordination of the foot controls. Use simple questions to confirm knowledge of the usual routine procedures for driving along, and for dealing with junctions and other hazards. Give any remedial advice for minor errors, where relevant, while on the move.

If any errors of a more serious nature are committed, deal with them when you stop at the training area. When you give remedial advice, remember that you must give a reason.

Lesson content

Put into practice the general teaching principle of Explanation – Demonstration – Practice.

Confirm that the site is safe, legal and convenient. Referring to *The Highway Code*, a few questions should suffice. For example:

- Are there any signs or road markings which would make this manoeuvre illegal?
- Do you think we will be inconveniencing other road users?
- Are there any parked vehicles or obstructions nearby?

When reversing round a left or right corner, ensure that the 'pupil' looks into the side road to check for any obstructions.

Transferring previously learnt skills

Find out whether the 'pupil' has carried out the manoeuvre previously and, if so, ask for the procedures to be explained to you. Listen carefully, adding any comments or clarification you feel necessary. Continue by allowing the 'pupil' to practise the exercise and be ready to give help if the pupil experiences difficulty.

If the 'pupil' has no previous experience, give reassurance by stating that the manoeuvre only involves using all the co-ordination skills learnt on previous lessons – that is, combining the use of the accelerator, clutch and footbrake to keep the speed low in order to give more time to work on the steering.

Ask the 'pupil' to explain how to control the clutch at low speed. For example:

- How do you creep forwards to get a better view at junctions?
- How do you hold the car steady on a hill?

Explanation

Use visual aids to help the 'pupil' to understand the main principles. Your explanation should include:

- making sure of vision by adjusting the seating position for reversing;
- breaking down the exercise into each element;
- showing when to make the observations, where to look and how to respond;
- confirming that control is of major importance and accuracy will come with practice.

Demonstration

If you feel that it is appropriate, offer to give a demonstration. Remember, however, that the time you have available is limited. You could consider combining a demonstration with your explanation by changing seats and talking yourself through the exercise. This could benefit you in two ways. First, the more anxious pupil will see that the manoeuvre looks easier than it sounds and, secondly, it will save you time.

Practice

Remember, when you teach a new topic, one of your main aims should be for the 'pupil' to achieve a degree of success. You should ensure, therefore, that your talk-through is effective and that you respond promptly if the 'pupil' is having difficulty in co-ordinating the controls.

Try to imagine how the 'pupil' may be feeling. Although he or she has probably carried out all the essential skills required, they now have to combine them and, at the same time, they have to look for other road users. Expect a little 'loss of memory' and give as much help as possible to encourage success and confidence.

If, after a couple of attempts at the exercise, you can see the 'pupil's' skill developing, allow them to try again with less help from you. Be ready, however, to give more help if necessary.

Responsibility for all-round safety lies with you

As the 'pupil's' observations are likely to be very superficial, you must remain fully aware of what is happening all around, all of the time. If you see anyone approaching, you can draw the 'pupil's' attention to the problem by instructing them to pause and then ask: 'Have you seen that other car? Let's wait and let it pass.'

At this point, the 'pupil' does not need the extra pressure of knowing that they are holding someone up. As long as it is safe and you have checked all around, avoid this pressure by allowing the other driver to proceed.

Giving feedback

Confirm the 'pupil's' progress and give praise where the co-ordination skills have improved. Explain any weaknesses where more practice is needed. Encourage the 'pupil' to read about the principles before the next lesson.

Summary of the key points

- Set the base-line for the lesson by confirming previous knowledge.
- Assess the pupil's control skills and general driving, giving remedial advice as necessary.
- Explain the manoeuvre, including observations and how to respond to others.
- Give full talk-through and decrease the help as skill improves.
- Ensure the pupil is given feedback of progress.

Emergency Stop/Mirrors (ADI 26/PT/05)

The main purposes of this lesson are to:

- confirm what the pupil knows about the adjustment and use of mirrors;
- improve the pupil's general driving skills and all-round awareness;
- teach the pupil how to stop quickly and under control;
- advise on how to correct a simple skid.

Lesson structure

As there are two topics to be dealt with, this Phase 1 exercise can be split into two sections. Discuss mirrors first, so that during the drive to the training area you can check that all the correct routines and procedures are being put into practice.

Introduce yourself in the usual manner and establish the base-line for the lesson by confirming the 'pupil's' previous knowledge. This means that you should:

- check that the pupil is in the correct seating position and has adjusted all the mirrors so that they can be checked without an exaggerated head movement;
- confirm the reason for checking blind areas and make sure that these are checked;
- ask a few questions about when mirrors should be checked in relation to moving off/speeding up and slowing down/changing direction/passing parked cars/overtaking/MSM routine.

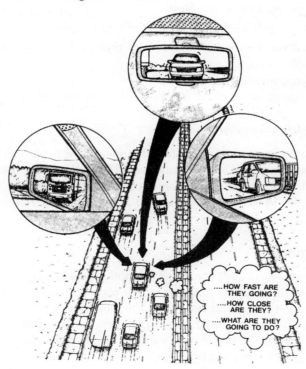

Fault analysis

During the drive to the training area you must watch the 'pupil' carefully to ensure that regular checks are being made of the appropriate mirrors. You must ensure that the 'pupil' understands the importance of:

- checking the mirrors regularly;
- reacting properly to what is seen in the mirrors – ie, by putting into practice the MSM routine by:
  - deciding how actions may affect any following driver;
  - delaying signals if necessary;
  - signalling earlier and braking more gently if appropriate when stopping;
  - deciding whether or not a signal is required;
- keeping a safe distance from the vehicle ahead if someone is following too closely.

Avoiding conflict No matter how good an instructor you may be, it is humanly impossible to check every time a driver uses a mirror. In order to avoid arguments, if you are not quite sure whether a mirror check was carried out, simply ask, 'Did you check the mirrors before signalling?' Then follow this up with, 'Why is it important to check the mirrors before you do anything else?' The response will tell you whether or not the pupil understands the principles behind the MSM routine, and if you need to give more information when you reach the training area for the Emergency Stop.

You can now link the two subjects by confirming that:

- the good driver is using all the mirrors regularly and is aware of the all-round traffic situation;
- emergencies can arise at any time;
- if an emergency arises, there may be no time for another mirror check.

How to avoid emergencies

Emphasis should be placed on the fact that good drivers plan well ahead and take into consideration what is happening. They also anticipate what might happen where they can see a situation developing, or where they cannot see at all. For example, no one can see around a bend, so how can a driver know what may be there?

Quick reactions

In an emergency, the priority is to react promptly and to stop the car quickly and safely. Refer to the stopping distances in *The Highway Code* and relate these to the road and weather conditions, and to the amount of pressure which can be applied safely to the brakes. Explain that firm but progressive pressure is required. Harsh braking may result in a skid, which creates further risk. Allow the 'pupil' to practise pivoting between the accelerator and footbrake.

Confirm, by asking, where the driver's hands should be when braking. A firm hold is necessary since more than normal braking pressure is being applied; this should also help to keep the car travelling in a straight line.

Let the 'pupil' explain to you what the clutch is used for when stopping, and whether there will be any difference in an emergency situation. Remember, engine braking can help to slow down the car more quickly and this can be more useful than keeping the engine running. Stopping the car is a priority, not keeping the engine running. Reassure the 'pupil' that stalling the engine is not a 'deadly sin', as long as the necessary precautions are taken before re-starting it.

Ask the 'pupil' about securing the car after stopping and confirm that this is even more important in an emergency situation. Also confirm that, because the car was stopped in an unusual position, checks of all the blind areas will need to be made prior to moving off again.

Skidding

The information required here is merely to reassure the 'pupil' if they brake too harshly and the car skids.

Ask the 'pupil' about the causes of skidding and confirm that these normally only occur when a driver is not responding properly in relation to the road and weather conditions. Harsh braking can cause a skid and the most common type is the rear-wheel skid. Explain that if a skid occurs he or she will need to:

- remove the cause by:
  - releasing the brake pedal;
  - pumping it on and off until the brakes take effect again;
- steer into the skid by straightening up the front of the car.

So that the 'pupil' can 'see' what you mean, you can either use a model car or show an illustration to clarify the principle.

Maintaining safety

Explain the signal you will be giving when you want the 'pupil' to stop. Sit still and try not to make any movements which may distract the 'pupil' into stopping prematurely.

Remember, as a driving instructor, you are responsible for the safety of yourself, your passenger, your vehicle and other road users around you. Make sure that this exercise is carried out in complete safety. Only give the signal for stopping when you are clear of parked vehicles, pedestrians and junctions. After stopping, ensure that the car is secured. Ask the 'pupil' where they are in the road and where they will be checking before they move away.

Practise the exercise two or three times, giving remedial advice as necessary in relation to how the 'pupil' reacted and used the controls.

Summary of the key points

- Establish what the pupil knows about mirror adjustment and use.
- Identify and analyse faults, giving remedial advice as necessary.
- Explain how to avoid emergencies by planning ahead.
- Describe how to use the controls to stop quickly and under control.
- Explain about skids and how to correct them.
- Practise the emergency stop and give feedback and advice.

Pedestrian Crossings and the Use of Signals (ADI 26/PT/06 – Phase 1); (ADI 26/PT – Phase 2); (ADI 26/PT/09 – Phase 2)

The main purposes of this lesson are to:

- establish what the pupil knows about the use of different methods of signalling;
- assess whether the pupil is correctly applying the MSM routine;
- teach the pupil how to approach and deal safely with pedestrian crossings;
- identify and analyse faults and give remedial advice.

Lesson structure

Introduce yourself and establish the base-line for the lesson. How the lesson is structured will depend on whether you are dealing with the subject at Phase 1 or Phase 2.

Using signals

Whichever phase you are dealing with, the 'pupil' should have previously learnt how to:

- check the mirrors and the all-round situation to decide whether or not a signal is required;
- use the signals correctly, when necessary and at the correct time.

Confirm the routine by asking a few relevant questions and also that there are other methods of signalling, including using the brake lights, positioning in good time and using arm signals. Explain that, when approaching zebra crossings, although following drivers should see the brake lights, oncoming drivers will have no indication of the intention to stop. Therefore an arm signal could be helpful if there is time and it is convenient. Confirm that the Highway Code rules are understood and check by asking the 'pupil' to demonstrate arm signals.

Dealing with pedestrian crossings

Bearing in mind that new drivers will have experienced using crossings as pedestrians, you should be able to confirm the basic rules which apply by asking a few relevant questions. This process will probably take a little longer with the Phase 1 pupil who has no previous experience of approaching crossings as a driver. However, bearing in mind that generally pupils are now studying for the Theory Test in parallel with their driving lessons, they should have some knowledge.

See how many types of crossing the 'pupil' can identify. It may be particularly relevant to mention school crossings if the lesson is at a time when children may be on their way to or from school. Because of the number of different crossings, you will probably only have time to deal with the main types – ie, zebra and pelicans. If you are asked specific questions, or there are any other types of crossing peculiar to the area in which you are working, obviously you will need to cover these.

The main elements to be emphasised are:

- looking ahead for pedestrian activity;
- the application of the MSM routine on the approach;
- approaching at the correct speed to stop if necessary;
- planning the approach in relation to the colour of the light showing;
- the rules relating to overtaking and inviting pedestrians across.

Phase 1

If the 'pupil' has no previous experience, you will need to give some talk-through instruction to encourage forward planning and to develop the 'pupil's' confidence. As skill improves, you can then decrease the level of tuition and transfer the responsibility by asking the 'pupil' to tell you how far ahead they are looking and what they will be doing.

Phase 2

As the 'pupil' will have previous experience, you should allow them to drive unaided for a few minutes. This should give you time to assess the level of their skill and understanding. Where any problems arise, you should identify and analyse them. Whether you can do this on the move or whether you will need to find somewhere to stop will depend on the degree of the error and to what depth you will need to go into the subject.

Fault assessment

Remember, no matter what the standard of the 'pupil', *positive* correction is better than *negative* or *retrospective* correction. If you can see a problem developing ahead, it is sensible to give some positive prompt to encourage the 'pupil' to take action. This is far safer and more effective than allowing a potentially dangerous situation to arise, particularly where pedestrians are involved.

During the drive you should assess whether the 'pupil' is putting all the established routines into practice. Identify and analyse problems. Give advice on how to improve, and when you make a correction, remember to give a good reason for it.

Common faults

The following is a list of some of the common faults you should be looking for:

- ineffective application of the MSM routine;
- wrong, unnecessary or incorrectly timed signals;
- inviting pedestrians or other road users;
- approaching crossings too fast;
- failing to stop when necessary;
- not securing the car when stationary at crossings;
- failing to respond to the traffic lights;
- moving off from crossings prematurely.

Summary of the key points

- Establish what the pupil knows about the different methods of signalling.
- Confirm the use of the MSM routines in all situations.
- Confirm the rules relating to the different types of pedestrian crossing.
- Emphasise the importance of approaching crossings at the correct speed.
- Identify, analyse and give remedial advice on where to improve, and give valid reasons.
- Give feedback on where learning or improvement has taken place.

Approaching Junctions to Turn Left and Right (ADI 26 PT/07 – Phase 1); (ADI 26/PT/03 – Phase 2)

The main purposes of this lesson are to:

- establish what the pupil already knows about the MSM routine and how this system is applied to junctions;
- teach the Phase 1 pupil how to deal safely with junctions;
- assess how the Phase 2 pupil deals with junctions;
- identify and analyse faults and give remedial advice.

Introduce yourself and establish the base-line for the lesson by assessing what the 'pupil' already knows and can do.

The main elements of the lesson are:

- the correct application of the Mirror – Signal – Manoeuvre routine, breaking this down and analysing:
- Mirror:
  - checking early to see what is happening;
  - working out how any other road user may be affected by the manoeuvre;
  - deciding when to signal.
- Signal:
  - to warn or inform other road users at the correct time, so as not to confuse.
- Manoeuvre – position:
  - early to confirm the signal;
  - appropriately for:
    - the direction;
    - the width of the road;
    - any obstructions;
    - vision.
- Speed:
  - appropriate for:
    - vision;
    - the required gear;
    - obstructions;
    - oncoming traffic;
    - pedestrians.
- Look:
  - all around prior to turning for:
    - obstructions;
    - other road users;
    - pedestrians.

Phase 1

Where you set the base-line will depend on whether the 'pupil' has any previous knowledge or experience at dealing with turning left and right. Remember, most pupils are now studying for the Theory Test in conjunction with their practical driving lessons. They should be able, therefore, to answer some simple questions on the correct MSM routine. However, assume nothing. Asking these questions will give you feedback of the 'pupil's' level of knowledge and understanding.

Where the pupil has previous experience

Listen carefully to the 'pupil'. If they have already practised turning left and right, it may be boring and unnecessary to give them an absolute and thorough explanation of how to turn left and right. You can just confirm their knowledge and get on the move to assess whether they understand and can carry out the routines correctly. Where the 'pupil' experiences difficulty, or lack of understanding, you must be ready to help as much as is necessary until their skills improve.

Where the pupil has no previous experience

If the 'pupil' has not experienced turning left or right, you will need to give a more detailed explanation of the routines. Use visual aids to assist the pupil's understanding and keep him or her involved by asking a few questions, such as 'What routine do you use when you are moving off and stopping?', 'Why is it important to check the mirror and what are you looking for?', 'When does the Highway Code tell you to use signals?'

You will need to give full talk-through instruction to confirm the correct routines. Decrease the level of help as the 'pupil's' skill and understanding improve, but be ready to help when necessary.

Remember, every situation can be used as a teaching opportunity. Do not restrict your teaching to the topic in hand, but be ready to deal with other problems which may arise. For example, if there are parked vehicles or obstructions, encourage the 'pupil' to think about the possibility of oncoming traffic.

Phase 2

As the 'pupil' will have previous experience, ask a few questions to confirm their knowledge and understanding. Listen carefully – something may be quoted out of sequence or some other element may be omitted altogether. Re-affirm any points that you think are necessary and get on the move so that you can make a practical assessment.

Not all errors committed will relate directly to the subject in hand. Any potentially serious error must be dealt with. The degree of error will dictate whether it can be dealt with on the move or whether you will need to find somewhere safe to stop and discuss it in more detail.

Fault assessment

Remember, no matter what the standard of the pupil, *positive* correction is better than *negative* or *retrospective* correction. If you can see a problem developing ahead, it is sensible to give some positive prompt to encourage the pupil to take action. This is far safer and more effective than allowing a potentially dangerous situation to arise, particularly where other road users are involved.

During the drive you should assess whether the 'pupil' is putting all the established routines into practice. Identify and analyse problems. Give advice on how to improve, and when you make a correction, remember to give a good reason for it.

Common faults

- Lack of understanding of the MSM routine.
- Not checking the mirrors effectively or signalling at the same time.
- Signalling too early or too late.
- Not using the brakes effectively to slow down in good time.
- Making unnecessary gear changes or changing down too late.
- Coasting round corners.
- Not positioning correctly according to the circumstances.
- Approaching too fast and swinging out on left turns.
- Lack of awareness of pedestrians and the need to give priority.
- Crossing approaching traffic.
- Not looking effectively into the new road.
- Cutting corners.

Summary of the key points

- Establish what the pupil already knows about approaching junctions.
- Confirm the correct application of the MSM–PSL routine.
- Identify, analyse and give remedial advice on weaknesses, and allow practice to improve.
- Give feedback on where improvement has taken place and where more work is needed.

Emerging from T-junctions (ADI 26/PT/08 – Phase 1); (ADI 26/PT/04 – Phase 2)

The main purposes of this lesson are to:
- establish what the pupil already knows about the MSM routine and its application at junctions;
- teach the Phase 1 pupil how to approach and emerge from T-junctions safely;
- assess how the Phase 2 pupil deals with junctions;
- identify and analyse faults and give remedial advice.

Introduce yourself and establish the base-line for the lesson by finding out what the 'pupil' already knows and understands about junctions.

The main elements of this lesson are:

- confirmation of the application of the MSM routine;
- explaining about 'Give Way' and 'Stop' junctions;
- observation and decisions to proceed according to sightlines;

- positioning correctly according to circumstances:
- wide or narrow roads;
  - obstructions;
  - one-way streets;
  - responding to pedestrian activity.

Phase 1

To set the base-line for the lesson, confirm previous experience by asking a few questions on the MSM routine for dealing with turning left and right into side roads, and ask what the 'pupil' knows about 'emerging' from junctions.

Where the pupil has some previous experience

Confirm that the 'pupil' knows the correct routines. Listen carefully and give advice or information where anything is omitted or given in the wrong sequence. Get on the move as soon as possible so that you can assess whether or not the pupil understands the principles involved. Remember, be ready to give assistance where necessary, and if you can see a potential problem arising, try to give some positive prompt to keep the 'pupil' out of trouble.

If the pupil has no previous experience

Although 'emerging' may be a new topic, the 'pupil' will have already dealt with turning left and right into side roads. You will need to build on this knowledge and explain the different aspects involved when emerging from junctions.

Emphasis should be placed on:

- the type of junction:
  - 'Give Way' or 'Stop',
- position on the approach;
- vision:
  - restricted sightlines in one or both directions;
  - good vision in one direction only;
  - good vision all around;
  - obstructions to sightlines.
- emerging safely without affecting others, including pedestrians.

Practice

You will need to give full talk-through instruction until the 'pupil's' understanding and control skills begin to develop. Decrease the instruction when you feel the 'pupil' can cope. However, be ready to give more help if necessary.

Be ready to intervene and prevent the 'pupil' from emerging unsafely if necessary.

Phase 2

This 'pupil' will have had plenty of experience at emerging but will have weaknesses. You must establish what these are. If they are not obvious from your short question-and-answer discovery session, you will need to get on the move and watch the 'pupil' carefully.

You must ensure that the correct routines and procedures are being put into practice and watch to see how the 'pupil' responds to the all-round traffic situation. You should not allow a potentially unsafe situation to arise. For example, if you feel the 'pupil' is about to emerge unsafely from a junction before an adequate view is available, you should give some positive command, such as *'Wait!'* Follow this up with *'How far can you see?'* or *'What if something is approaching out of the blind area at 40 mph?'*

It may be appropriate, when convenient, to pull in and give more information on sightlines and the importance of being able to see properly before emerging.

Fault assessment

As previously stated, remember that positive correction is better than negative or retrospective correction. Preventing a potentially dangerous situation, such as the one just described, should result in:

- a greater degree of safety for everyone;
- more positive learning and understanding taking place.

Common faults

- Lack of understanding of the MSM routine.
- Ineffective application of the MSM routine.
- Not identifying or responding to the type of junction, ie 'Give Way' or 'Stop'.
- Not taking into consideration restrictions to sightlines.
- Not looking early enough at 'open' junctions.
- Not responding to pedestrians.
- Emerging unsafely.

Summary of the key points

- Establish prior knowledge and understanding of the MSM–PSL routines.
- Confirm the correct application of the routines.
- Ensure that the pupil has a good understanding of sightlines and vision.
- Identify, analyse and give remedial advice.
- Give feedback where improvement has been made.

Dealing with Crossroads (ADI 26/PT/09 – Phase 1); (ADI 26/PT/01 – Phase 2)

The main purposes of this lesson are to:

- establish what the pupil understands about the MSM routine and the different types of junction;
- teach the Phase 1 pupil how to adapt the procedures to deal safely with crossroads;
- assess how the Phase 2 pupil deals with crossroads;
- identify and analyse faults and give remedial advice.

Introduce yourself and establish the base-line for the lesson by finding out what the 'pupil' already knows and understands about different types of junction. Confirm that the MSM routine applies at crossroads, but emphasise that there are more observations to be made in all directions.

The main elements of the lesson are to explain or confirm:

- the application of the MSM routine;
- its application at crossroads;
- priorities at junctions with different markings;
- the extra observations when turning or going straight ahead;
- positioning for turning right, ie offside and nearside;
- the observations and priorities when turning right.

Phase 1

Confirm the 'pupil's' previous experience by asking a few questions on the MSM routine for dealing with turning into and out of T-junctions. Ask if he or she has dealt with crossroads before and, if so, what they can tell you about it.

Where the pupil has no previous experience

In order to build up the 'pupil's' confidence, it is sensible to keep new topics as simple as possible. If the 'pupil' has no experience and there are quiet crossroads nearby, this will give you the opportunity of establishing the different aspects to be introduced. Use visual aids where these will assist the 'pupil's' understanding. Point out the different observations to be made and what the 'pupil' should be looking for. Explain how the 'pupil' should respond to other road users and be willing to give way if he or she is unsure, particularly when turning right.

Allowing the 'pupil' to drive and put into practice what he or she knows about junctions, you should be ready to help with talk-through instruction when approaching, driving through and emerging from crossroads. Watch carefully and make sure that the 'pupil' is making the necessary observations. Remember also to comment on any other situations which may arise during the drive.

Where the pupil has some previous experience

Confirm that the 'pupil' knows the correct routines. Ask a few questions and listen carefully. Give any extra advice or information if the 'pupil' seems unsure of the procedures. Normally, if the 'pupil' has only limited experience, quieter crossroads should be used until the routines become established. Assess how the 'pupil' is responding to the all-round situation. Watch carefully to ensure that observations are being made in all directions at crossroads, no matter who has priority. Confirm that the 'pupil' is looking for anyone who may be emerging across their path.

If the local road layout dictates that you will have to deal with traffic-light controlled or busier junctions, you may need to explain how to turn nearside and offside. Remember the level of ability of your 'pupil' – you will probably have to give lots of help until confidence is built up.

Phase 2

By this stage, the 'pupil' should have experienced driving on most types of urban roads. The procedures for dealing with crossroads should therefore merely need confirming with a few relevant questions. Confirm what the main dangers are when turning right at crossroads and what the 'pupil' should be looking for.

Once on the move, you should assess how the 'pupil' is responding in all situations. Look and plan well ahead. Should you feel that the 'pupil' is not reacting early enough to any situation, try to instigate the correct action by prompting with a question or suggestion, particularly where lane changes are necessary. Be careful, however, not to over-instruct. Avoid giving definite instructions unless you can see a potentially serious situation developing.

Minor or 'one-off' errors can usually be dealt with on the move, as long as this will not distract the 'pupil.' However, where necessary, stop to discuss any serious faults.

Fault assessment and feedback

Whatever the level of the 'pupil', you must be constantly looking for:

- weaknesses in his or her knowledge;
- their application of the rules;
- their response to the all round-traffic situation.

Let the 'pupil' know when improvement has taken place and confirm where more work has to be done.

Common faults at crossroads

Driving along the main road:

- proceeding through without making observations;

- turning left and/or right without checking in all directions;
- turning left and/or right without following the correct MSM routine.

Approaching 'Give Way' or 'Stop' controlled crossroads:

- not applying the correct routine on the approach;
- being unaware of the type of junction being approached;
- not making all-round observations before emerging;
- not responding correctly to other road users.

Traffic-light controlled junctions:

- lack of forward planning and anticipation;
- incorrect application of the MSM routine on the approach;
- not positioning according to the type of junction/road markings/other drivers;
- making decisions to proceed before the way ahead is clear;
- crossing approaching traffic;
- not looking all around before turning.

Summary of the key points of this lesson

- Establish prior knowledge and understanding for dealing with junctions.
- Confirm extra observations required at crossroads.
- Ensure that all the correct routines are being put into practice.
- Identify, analyse and give remedial advice on any weaknesses.
- Give feedback where improvement has been made and where more practice is needed.

Meet, Cross and Overtake Other Traffic, Allowing Adequate Clearance for Other Road Users (ADI 26/PT/10 – Phase 1); (ADI 26/PT/02 – Phase 2); (ADI 26/PT/08 – Phase 2)

The main purposes of this lesson are to:

- establish how much experience the pupil has in dealing with other traffic;
- teach the Phase 1 pupil about priorities when:
  - dealing with parked vehicles;
  - turning right;
  - dealing with pedestrians and cyclists;
- assess the Phase 2 pupil on all of the above;
- explain how to overtake safely;
- identify and analyse faults, and give remedial advice.

As there are a number of different elements involved in this Pre-set Test, your examiner will identify those topics which you must concentrate on. You must therefore listen very carefully so that you can plan the lesson around the selected topics and not try to cover everything.

Introduce yourself and establish the base-line for the lesson by finding out what the 'pupil' already knows about the topics. Confirm the MSM routine for approaching all hazards and then focus on those subjects which need either teaching or reinforcing.

Meeting other traffic, allowing adequate clearances

The key elements are:

- Looking and planning ahead for parked vehicles.
- Deciding on priorities by acting on available information:
  - obstruction on own side of road;
  - obstruction on other side of road;
  - speed, position and size of oncoming traffic;
  - uphill or downhill situation.
- MSM routine and holdback position:
  - to maintain the view ahead;
  - to be able to steer through in a straight line when safe.
- Clearances for parked vehicles relative to:
  - volume of traffic;
  - time of day;
  - pedestrian activity.
- Speed relative to available space:
  - the narrower the gap, the lower the speed to give more time to respond.
- Clearances for cyclists.

Crossing other traffic

The key elements are:

- Priorities when turning right:
  - speed and distance of oncoming traffic;
  - if there is time to walk across, there should be time to turn safely;
  - is it safe to turn? what is happening in the new road?
  - is there time to turn without cutting the corner?
- Selecting lanes in good time to avoid cutting across the path of others.

Overtaking

The key elements are:

- *Safe:*
  Is there an adequate view of the road ahead?:
  - consider bends/brows of hills/dead ground.
  Are there any junctions ahead?

- *Legal – refer to the Highway Code:*
  Are there any pedestrian crossings ahead?
  What road markings are there?
  Are there any signs which would make overtaking illegal or dangerous?
  What is the speed limit? Will it have to be exceeded to complete the manoeuvre?
  Necessary:
  What speed is the vehicle ahead travelling at in relation to the speed limit?
  Will we be turning off soon?
  Do we need to get by to make progress?
- Following at a safe distance to give a better view of the road ahead.
- MPSL, MSM:
  - mirror;
  - position – to get a view to the nearside;
  - mirror – position to get a view ahead;
  - speed – select a lower gear to give sustained power;
  - look – check all around again;
  - mirror – check to ensure that the manoeuvre will be safe;
  - signal to let other drivers know of your intended manoeuvre;
  - manoeuvre – quickly and efficiently;
  - mirrors – check before returning to the left and accelerating away.

Anticipation

Teaching anticipation is an ongoing process which should start from day one of a pupil's driving career. The key elements are:

- looking for other vehicles whose drivers may:
  - emerge from junctions;
  - open doors or move off without warning;
  - take priority when they should be giving way;
- looking and planning ahead for any pedestrian activity:
  - expecting them to walk into the road;
  - at junctions between parked cars/behind buses/at crossings – in fact, any-where!
- looking and planning ahead for the actions of cyclists:
  - expecting them to ride into the road without warning;
  - change position or turn at junctions without signals;
  - cycle around obstructions without checking;
  - ride alongside near crossings, at junctions and in laned traffic.

Phase 1

Establish the 'pupil's' previous knowledge and driving experience. Using your visual aids where appropriate, explain how to approach and deal with the different types of hazard, confirming the use of the MSM routine.

If the 'pupil' has very little experience at driving in busier areas, you must give sufficient talk-through to ensure both safety and confidence. Look and plan well ahead and describe what you can see happening and encourage the 'pupil' to respond early enough to avoid problems.

Even where the 'pupil' has previously driven in busier areas, you must be ready to assist when necessary to avoid uncomfortable situations developing. Remember that you are responsible for the safety of your 'pupil' and all other road users around you.

Identify any weaknesses in the 'pupil's' general driving and explain how improvements can be made. When you suggest alternative action, remember that you will need to give a valid reason. Give encouragement where routines are carried out correctly and safely.

Phase 2

At this stage, the 'pupil' will have had experience at driving in traffic and you may only need to confirm prior knowledge by asking a few questions on how to approach and deal with the different types of hazard.

If overtaking is to be included in the lesson, you will need to know whether or not the 'pupil' is familiar with the routine. You may need to give an explanation and, should an opportunity to overtake arise during the drive, talk the 'pupil' through the procedure.

At this stage, you should be constantly monitoring the 'pupil's' performance in relation to correct driving procedures and hazard recognition. Anything which deviates from the driving 'norm' needs to be addressed, either briefly if the error is minor, or by stopping somewhere safe if it is of a more serious nature.

Common faults

- Failing to anticipate hazards or potential risk situations.
- Not applying the correct MSM routine when approaching hazards.
- Shaving parked vehicles on the left.
- Going out too far and meeting oncoming traffic dangerously.
- Not allowing for the actions of pedestrians, cyclists or other drivers.
- Turning right across the path of approaching traffic.

Summary of the key points

- Establish prior knowledge and experience.
- Give adequate information on any new subject, particularly when meeting other traffic/passing parked vehicles/driving in busy areas/overtaking;
- Ensure that all the correct routines are put into practice;
- Identify, analyse and give remedial advice on any weaknesses;
- Give feedback where improvement has taken place and where more practice is needed.

Progress/Hesitancy – Normal Position (ADI 26/PT/05 – Phase 2); (ADI 26/PT/10 – Phase 2)

The main purposes of this lesson are to:

- ensure that the pupil is aware of the need to make progress when safe;
- encourage the pupil to have the confidence to take all safe opportunities to proceed at junctions;
- check that the pupil is aware of the need to drive in the correct position in relation to the:
  - type of road;
  - width of the road;
  - vision and safety margin.

This subject is only dealt with at the Phase 2 level. You are therefore dealing with a 'pupil' who has plenty of experience and should be aware of all the correct routines and procedures for driving in different road and traffic situations.

The main elements of the lesson are to:

- confirm prior knowledge of the speed limits for different types of road;
- check knowledge of braking and stopping distances/two-second rule;
- check that the pupil is aware of factors which should influence the speed – ie type of road/surface/weather conditions/volume of traffic/pedestrian activity;
- confirm the need to make progress when safe and what effect driving too slowly for the conditions can have on other drivers;
- ensure that the pupil is looking early for gaps when emerging from junctions and that the car is prepared for moving promptly;
- check the pupil's knowledge and skill at judging their position on different types of road.

Lesson content

Introduce yourself and explain the objectives of the lesson – ie, to encourage the 'pupil' to have the confidence to drive effectively and safely, taking all suitable opportunities to proceed, while maintaining the correct position according to the type and width of the road.

Establish the 'pupil's' previous experience and confirm his or her knowledge on the elements listed above by asking a few relevant questions.

Fault assessment

Once you are on the move, you will need to assess how the 'pupil' is driving in relation to the all-round traffic situation. Remember to query anything which deviates from the driving norm. If the 'pupil' is driving too slowly for the conditions, or is missing opportunities at junctions, you must encourage them to make progress, even if it means talking them through a few situations to demonstrate what you mean. This will not be classed as over-instruction! After all, if the pupil is not driving appropriately, he or she will need to be taught and encouraged to do so.

If the 'pupil' is driving too fast for the conditions, not taking into account the possible dangers, you must be firm and get the speed under control. Wherever this is necessary, you must give valid reasons. For example, if the road has a 30 mph speed limit and is busy with pedestrians along its pavements, confirm what speed you would be driving at and explain what you would be looking for.

Check that the correct position is maintained for the type of road. Ensure that the 'pupil' is planning ahead and selecting the correct lane in good time. Confirm the positioning for turning right on one-way streets and narrow roads.

Common faults

- Moving off slowly and not changing up through the gears efficiently.
- Driving too slowly on faster roads.
- Breaking the speed limit.
- Driving too fast where conditions are unsafe.
- Missing opportunities to proceed at junctions.
- Not looking in all directions at junctions and getting out of position, particularly at roundabouts.
- Positioning incorrectly on narrow roads or one-way streets.
- Driving too close to, or too far out from the kerb.
- Incorrect positioning on bends.
- Not maintaining lane discipline.

Summary of the key points

- Establish prior experience.
- Confirm the importance of making progress where safe.
- Ensure that safety margins are maintained according to the conditions.
- Confirm the importance of being in the correct place on the road at all times.
- Identify and analyse faults and give remedial advice with reasons.
- Give feedback on improvement and emphasise where more practice is needed.

Reverse/Parking (ADI 26/PT/06 – Phase 2)

The aims of this lesson are to:

- develop the pupil's ability to manoeuvre into parking spaces;
- identify and analyse driving faults and give remedial advice.

This manoeuvre is taught to pupils whose car control skills should be well developed. The reverse and turn-in-the-road should have been taught earlier, and this exercise involves transferring all those previously learnt skills to parking in more challenging conditions.

The main elements of the lesson are to:

- confirm the site for practice: *safe – legal – convenient*;
- assess the pupil's general driving;
- teach or reinforce the manoeuvre – ie *co-ordination of controls/accuracy/ observations*;
- identify and analyse any problems.

Lesson content

Introduce yourself and establish the 'pupil's' previous experience. Confirm what the 'pupil' already knows about manoeuvring and the control skills required. Ask the 'pupil' to drive away, putting all previously learnt routines and procedures into practice.

Use the drive to identify any weaknesses. Analyse these and give remedial advice. Remember, you should be able to deal with most of the minor errors on the move. If any serious errors are committed, comment on these and, if necessary, deal with them in more detail when you stop.

Confirm that the site chosen is safe, legal and convenient. Explain that this exercise sometimes has to be carried out where there are other road users and that the traffic flow must be taken into consideration.

Where the pupil has previous experience

If the 'pupil' has practised the exercise previously, ask questions on the different elements and then allow him or her to demonstrate their skill. Should problems arise, you must be ready to help in order to encourage improvement.

Where the pupil has no previous experience

Prior to starting the exercise, get the 'pupil' to work out whether the reversing is going to be on the level, uphill or downhill. Also, look around for pedestrians and other road users.

A full talk-through for the first attempt should encourage success and build confidence. Depending on progress, you can then either give more help or encourage the 'pupil' to try the exercise unaided. However, should the pupil still experience difficulty, you must be ready to help.

The manoeuvre

- check MSM to get into position alongside the other vehicle: the signal element will depend on the presence of other road users – ie indicator, confirming arm signal, brake lights, reversing lights;
- co-ordinating the controls according to the gradient;

- relate the point of turning the wheel to reversing around a corner to the left, but explain that the wheel has to be straightened earlier and then turned to the right;
- emphasise the need for regular observations and how to respond to others;
- get the pupil to check their position in relation to clearing the other vehicle;
- confirm looking through the rear window well down the road to straighten;
- complete the manoeuvre with wheels straight.

Practising the reverse park

Although the 'pupil' may benefit from more practice at this exercise, it is sensible from the point of view of good public relations not to reverse around the same vehicle more than twice. It will be of greater benefit to drive somewhere else so that the exercise can be carried out under different circumstances – for example, on a different gradient or a narrower road.

Common faults

- Not putting into practice the MSM routine prior to the exercise.
- Lack of awareness of the gradient, resulting in the incorrect use of the controls.
- Lack of co-ordination of the controls.
- Not looking in the direction of steering.
- Under-/over-steering.
- Not keeping a check on the all-round traffic situation.
- Not responding to other road users.

Summary of the key points

- Confirm the pupil's previous experience.
- Assess driving and give remedial advice where necessary.
- Confirm the elements involved – ie, control/accuracy/observations and response.
- Practise the exercise and encourage confidence.
- Give feedback of improvement and confirm where more practice is needed.

OVERVIEW OF INSTRUCTOR TRAINING

While the emphasis in this chapter is on the content of the ADI examinations, your tutor should, first and foremost, teach you how to become an effective ADI. Your skills will then need to be honed to fit in with the requirements of the exam – particularly where the Part 3 Test of Ability to Instruct is concerned.

Do not fall into the trap of trying to learn set scripts for each of the pre-set tests. Neither you, nor your examiner, have any control over what may happen on the road around you. Neither do you know how your examiner, in the role of the learner, will react or what will be said to you. You need a thorough understanding of the key elements for the different topics and the practical ability to teach them in different circumstances.

The fact that much emphasis is placed on the core competencies should tell you that you need to be able to:

- identify faults;
- analyse them;
- give advice on how to put them right;
- create opportunities to practice correct procedures;
- use Q & A to encourage pupils' understanding;
- give praise when deserved.

If you can do all these things effectively then not only should you pass the examination, but you should be well prepared to teach your future pupils 'safe driving for life'.

When you have passed the qualifying examination and your name has been entered onto the ADI Register, you must, as part of the regulations, undergo a periodic 'test of continued ability and fitness to give instruction'.

PREPARING FOR YOUR CHECK TEST

The DSA provides instructors with a breakdown of their pupils' driving test results. All instructors, whether newly qualified or with years of experience, should use the Check Test as an opportunity to discuss with their SEADI any queries they may have relating to these statistics, or any other matters relating to driving tuition. This applies particularly if:

- a lower grading is achieved than was expected;
- you would like to attain a higher grade;
- pupils are consistently failing for similar errors.

The Invitation to Attend For a Check Test

Tests are conducted during the SEADI's normal working hours and the invitation to attend will specify:

- the date and time;
- the place – normally local to the area you work in and often the local driving test centre.

You must acknowledge receipt of this invitation as soon as possible, particularly if the appointment is not convenient.

DRIVING STANDARDS AGENCY

WORKING SHEET

Cert. Expiry Date [ ]   SOM [ ]   Vehicle [ ]

Dual Controls: Yes [ ] No [ ]   Pupil: Male [ ] Female [ ]   Practising Privately: Yes [ ] No [ ]

Hours tuition with this ADI [ ]   Hours tuition with another ADI [ ]

Please circle main content of lesson: 1 2 3 4 5 6 7 8 9 10 11 12 13 14 15 16 17 18 19

- -

DRIVING STANDARDS AGENCY

Test of continued ability and fitness to give instruction (Check Test)

The examiner has marked each aspect of your performance in columns A and B below. See overleaf for explanatory notes.

COLUMN A	1	2	3		Fault Assessment	COLUMN B 1	2	3	4	5	6
1. Controls					Identification						
2. Move away/stopping					Analysis						
3. Emergency stop					Remedy						
4. Reverse Left/Right											
5. Turn in the road					**Instructional Techniques**						
6. Reverse park					Recap at start						
7. Mirrors					Aims/Objectives						
8. Signals					Level of instruction						
9. Planning					Planning						
10. Use of speed					Control of lesson						
11. Junctions					Communication						
12. Roundabouts					Q & A Technique						
13. Meet/Cross/Overtake					Feedback/Encouragement						
14. Positioning					Instructor's use of controls						
15. Adequate clearance					Recap at end						
16. Pedestrian crossings											
17. Anticipation/Awareness					**Instructor Characteristics**						
18. Dual C'way/Motorway											
19. Pass Plus Module					Attitude & approach to pupil						

Instructor [ ]   PRN [ ]

Supervising Examiner's Name [ ]   Date [ ]

S E Signature [ ]   Grade [ ]

ADI 26CT (A) (Rev 9/97)

The Pupil You Select to Teach on Your Check Test

Although the driver you choose need not necessarily be a provisional licence holder, it must not be another ADI. The most important thing to remember is that the SE is assessing your ability to instruct and not the pupil's ability to drive. You must therefore ensure that, whatever standard the driver has attained, your instruction is pitched at the correct level. If you do not have a client available, it may be possible for the SE to 'act' as your pupil.

The Car You Use For Your Check Test

A driving school car should always be kept in a roadworthy condition and display 'L' plates if the driver is a provisional licence holder. It should go without saying that a clean and tidy car will create a professional image.

If the lesson is to be conducted in a pupil's car, then it is sensible for you to check on its condition beforehand. Your ADI Certificate must be displayed if you are charging for the lesson.

Preparing your lesson for the Check Test is much the same as the lesson structure for each of the pre-set tests. The following is a list of the elements assessed by your SEADI:

- lesson structure;
- setting objectives;
- flexibility to deviate from objectives if necessary;
- level of instruction suitable to the ability of your pupil;
- method, clarity, adequacy and correctness of your instruction;
- your identification, analysis and correction of errors – with reasons;
- effectiveness of your question and answer technique;
- your manner, patience, tact and your ability to inspire confidence;
- your recap at the end giving feedback on progress.

Instructor Grading

The examiner will be marking your instruction on the working sheet shown on page 113. You will be assessed on all aspects of your performance and the lowest grade you attain during the lesson will normally be the final grade given at the end of the lesson.

The following gives the DSA's description of the six grades:

Grade 6

Overall performance to a very high standard with no significant instructional weaknesses. Concise accurate recap given on the previous lesson and realistic, attainable objectives set for the current lesson. There was dialogue, with pupil involvement. Consistently demonstrated the ability to vary/select the most appropriate instructional techniques as necessary to suit the needs, aptitude and ability of the pupil. Quick to recognise and address all important driving faults and provided thoroughly sound analysis, with clear, prompt and appropriate remedial action. An appropriate route chosen for the pupil's ability and experience and took every opportunity to develop the pupil's driving skills and awareness using the problems presented *en route*. Structured an appropriate learning environment that positively encouraged the pupil to further develop their skills and good driving practice. The lesson concluded with a concise recap, which was an accurate overview of the lesson. The strengths and weaknesses in the pupil's performance identified and discussed constructively. Realistic and appropriate objectives set for the next lesson. Professional attitude and approach to the pupil throughout the lesson.

Grade 5

A good overall standard of instruction with some minor weakness in instructional technique. A recap given on the previous lesson and objectives set for the current lesson, with pupil involvement. Demonstrated the ability to vary/select the most appropriate instructional techniques as necessary to suit the needs, aptitude and ability of the pupil, with only minor weaknesses. Recognised and addressed all important driving faults and provided sound analysis with appropriate remedial action. An appropriate route chosen for the pupil's ability and experience, taking advantage of most of the opportunities to develop the pupil's driving skills and awareness using the problems presented *en route*. Structured an appropriate learning environment in which the pupil could readily further develop their skills and good driving practice. The lesson concluded with a concise recap, which was an accurate overview of the lesson. The strengths and weaknesses in the pupil's performance identified and discussed. Objectives set for the next lesson. Attitude and approach to the pupil was good throughout the lesson.

Grade 4

A competent overall performance with some minor deficiencies in instructional technique. Acceptable recap with limited pupil involvement and objectives for the current lesson outlined. Demonstrated the ability to vary/select the most appropriate instructional techniques as necessary to suit most of the needs, aptitude and ability of the pupil. Recognised and addressed the important driving faults, providing generally sound analysis and remedial action. An acceptable route chosen for the pupil's ability and experience, taking advantage of most of the opportunities to develop the pupil's driving skills and awareness using the problems presented *en route*. Structured a generally appropriate learning environment that provided opportunities for the pupil to develop their skills and good driving practice. The lesson concluded with a general summary, giving an accurate overview of the lesson. The main strengths and weaknesses in the pupil's performance identified. Attitude and approach to the pupil was acceptable throughout the lesson.

Grade 3

An inadequate overall performance with some deficiencies in instructional technique. Inadequate or sketchy recap on the previous lesson. Did not adequately set out/explain the objectives for the current lesson, and did not involve the pupil. Demonstrated only a limited ability to vary/select the most appropriate instructional techniques as necessary to suit the needs, aptitude and ability of the pupil. Inconsistent identification, analysis and remedial action of driving faults. Some unnecessary retrospective instruction. A poor route chosen for the pupil's ability and experience and missed opportunities to develop the pupil's driving skills and awareness using the problems presented *en route*. Failed to structure a learning environment to enable the pupil to develop their skills and good driving practice. Inaccurate or incomplete summary at the end of the lesson. Many of the strengths and weaknesses in the pupil's performance not identified, or treated superficially. Shortcomings in attitude and approach to the pupil.

Grade 2

A poor overall performance with numerous deficiencies in instructional technique. Little or no recap on previous lesson, failed to set objectives for the current lesson. Unable to vary/select instructional techniques as necessary to suit the needs, aptitude and ability of the pupil. Many problems with correct identification of driving faults and analysis, very late remedial action. An unsuitable route chosen for the pupil's ability and experience and missed numerous opportunities to develop the pupil's driving skills and awareness using the problems presented *en route*. A poor learning environment from which the pupil would not be able to develop their skills and good driving practice. Superficial summary at the end of the lesson. Main strengths and weaknesses in the pupil's performance not mentioned. Serious shortcomings in attitude and approach to the pupil.

Grade 1

Overall standard of instruction extremely poor or dangerous with incorrect or even dangerous instruction. No recap on previous lesson, no objectives set for the current lesson. Unable to even recognise the need to vary/select the most appropriate instructional techniques as necessary to suit the needs, aptitude and

INSTRUCTOR TRAINING SPECIALISTS LTD

DO YOU FIND PART 3 DIFFICULT?
DO YOU FEEL LET DOWN?
CHECK TEST PROBLEMS?
DO YOU NEED HELP?

CALL NOW!

Call Barry Jones for *QUALITY PERSONAL TRAINING AND ADVICE*

25 YEARS COMBINED EXPERIENCE AS:

- DSA Assistant Chief Driving Examiner
- DSA Cardington Instructor and Examiner (all categories)
- Edexcel Advanced Driving Instructor
- Trainer of Police Driving Instructors
- Approved Driving Instructor Grade 6

Registered with DSA ORDIT and Edexcel/BTEC. The only UK Edexcel/BTEC Training Centre offering BTEC accredited training & qualifications in Driving Instruction (ADI & advanced) plus Advanced Driving

Full Courses for ADI 1–2 & 3 and Advanced • ADI Advice, Development & Check Test Service

Tel: 01530 563 572 • Website: www.itsadi.co.uk

ability of the pupil. Failed to identify, analyse or correct driving faults, many of which were of a serious or dangerous nature. A totally unsuitable route chosen for the pupil's ability and experience and didn't use the opportunities presented *en route* to develop the pupil's driving skills and awareness. No attempt to structure any kind of learning environment. No summary at the end of the lesson. Very serious shortcomings in attitude and approach to the pupil.

Keeping Up To Date

Many instructors who have been on the Register for a number of years are now finding it a struggle to retain their grading, with a higher proportion being graded as 'sub-standard'. In the 12-month period ending 28 February 1999 there were 57 instructors graded as 'sub-standard' and removed from the Register.

Even if you have only been on the Register for a short time it may be beneficial to seek some refresher training prior to attending for your Check Test.

You will find more information on preparing for your Check Test in *Practical Teaching Skills for Driving Instructors*, by John Miller, Tony Scriven and Margaret Stacey, published by Kogan Page.

$\boxed{4}$

The Driver

Professional driving instructors need to have a good working knowledge of the regulations covering the issue of driving licences. Pupils often ask them for advice and assistance with their application for a licence.

This chapter deals with the legal responsibilities of the driver in relation to:

- driving licence regulations;
- licence categories;
- minimum ages for driving;
- health requirements;
- vocational driving licences.

DRIVER LICENSING

All driving licences are issued by the Driver and Vehicle Licensing Authority (DVLA) at Swansea. The licence document shows details of all licence categories which the driver is entitled to drive, including large goods vehicles and passenger carrying vehicles. Any provisional licence entitlement as well as any restrictions are also shown. Driving without a current and valid licence usually means that any insurance cover is invalidated.

Anyone wishing to drive a mechanically propelled vehicle on a public road in the UK must hold a full or provisional driving licence for the type of vehicle being driven.

A provisional licence for motorcycles and mopeds must be supported by a Compulsory Basic Training certificate.

A foreign licence or an international driving permit may be used for a limited period. More details of this are given on page 126 under the heading, 'Visitors and new residents'.

Photocard licences are now issued by the DVLA. To apply for a photo licence you have to use form D750 and, as well as sending a photograph, you must supply original identifying documents. To voluntarily change an existing licence for a photocard, a fee of £17.50 is payable (current at October 2001).

Whereas a paper licence has an extended expiry date, a photo licence has to be renewed after 10 years to keep the photograph up-to-date.

You can obtain a factsheet on photo licence arrangements by calling the DVLA on 01 792 792 792.

Provisional Driving Licences

In order to learn to drive and to take the regulation driving test, a provisional driving licence must be obtained before a vehicle can be taken out on the public roads. The holder of a provisional licence may drive a vehicle only when accompanied by, and under the supervision of, a driver who holds a full licence for that type of vehicle. The supervising driver must be over 21 years of age and have held a full driving licence for the type of vehicle being driven for at least three years. This rule, however, does not apply under certain circumstances and when driving certain vehicles, eg when taking a driving test or when riding a motorcycle. More information on the supervision of learner drivers is covered on page 139 under the heading 'Legal Obligations of a Supervising Driver'.

Note that a provisional motorcycle licence holder must not carry any pillion passenger, even if that passenger is a qualified rider or driver.

In Northern Ireland, a vehicle displaying the prescribed 'L' or 'R' plates is restricted to a maximum speed of 45 mph. This same restriction applies to provisional licence holders.

Licence Entitlement

Your entitlement to a licence depends on your age and the type of vehicle on which you passed the driving test. Passing the test for a particular category may entitle you to drive vehicles of some other categories and may also entitle you to use the licence as a provisional licence for other groups. Full details will be found on the driving licence application forms, but a summary is given on pages 120–21 of some of the main groups.

You will see from the table that there are certain restrictions:

1. A test passed on a moped or motorcycle does not allow the candidate a full motor car licence.
2. A test passed on a moped does not entitle the candidate to a full motorcycle licence.
3. A test passed on an electrically propelled vehicle does not permit the candidate to drive a car or heavy duty motor vehicle.
4. A test passed in a car with automatic transmission does not entitle the candidate to drive vehicles with manual transmission.

Definitions of different types of vehicles will be found in the D100 leaflet, *What You Need To Know About Driver Licensing.*

Driving test group	Additional entitlement
Motor car without automatic transmission	Motor car with automatic transmission Motor tricycle Moped Agricultural tractor Mowing machine Pedestrian-controlled vehicle Electrically-controlled vehicle
Motor car with automatic transmission	Moped Tractor Mowing machine Pedestrian-controlled vehicle Electrically-controlled vehicle
Three- or four-wheeled light vehicle	Moped Mowing machine Pedestrian-controlled vehicle Electrically-controlled vehicle
Motor bicycle (with or without sidecar)	Motor tricycle Moped Two-wheeled electrically propelled vehicle
Moped	None

Driver Licence Categories for Tests Passed After 1 January 1997

Type of Vehicle	Category	Minimum age
Motorcycles up to 25 kW (33 bhp) and a power to weight ratio not exceeding 0.16 kW/kg. Motorcycle combination with a power to weight ratio not exceeding 0.16 kW/kg	A	17
Light motorcycles with a cubic capacity not exceeding 125 cm³ and of a power output not exceeding 11 kW (14.6 bhp)	A1	17
Any size motorcycle with or without a sidecar	A	21 (see note 1)
Mopeds	P	16
Cars: motor vehicles with a MAM not exceeding 3500 kg having not more than eight passenger	B	17 (see note 2)

seats with a trailer up to 750 kg. Combinations of
towing vehicles in category B and a trailer, where
the MAM of the combination does not exceed
3500 kg and the MAM of the trailer does not
exceed the unladen mass of the towing vehicle

Automatic cars: as cars, but with automatic transmission	B Automatic	17 (see note 2)
Cars with trailers: combinations of vehicles consisting of a vehicle in category B and a trailer, where the combination does not come within category B	B+E	17
Three- or four-wheeled light vehicles: Motor tricycles/quadricycles up to 550 kg unladen	B1	17
Medium-sized goods vehicles: Lorries between 3500 kg and 7500 kg with a trailer up to 750 kg	C1	18 (see note 3)
Medium-sized goods vehicles with trailers: Lorries between 3500 kg and 7500 kg with a trailer over 750 kg – total weight not more than 12,000 kg	C1+E	18 (see note 3)
Large goods vehicles: vehicles over 3500 kg with a trailer up to 750 kg	C	21 (see note 4)
Large goods vehicles with trailers: vehicles over 3500 kg with a trailer over 750 kg	C+E	21
Minibuses: vehicles with between 9 and 16 passenger seats with a trailer up to 750 kg	D1	21 (see note 5)
Minibuses with trailers: combinations of vehicles where the towing vehicle is in sub-category D1 and its trailer has a MAM of over 750 kg, provided that the MAM of the combination thus formed does not exceed 12,000 kg, and the MAM of the trailer does not exceed the unladen mass of the towing vehicle	D1+E	21 (see note 5)
Buses: any bus with more than eight passenger seats with a trailer up to 750 kg	D	21 (see note 5)
Buses with trailers: Any bus with more than eight passenger seats with a trailer over 750 kg	D+E	21 (see note 5)
Agricultural tractors	F	17 (see note 6)
Road rollers	G	21 (see note 7)
Tracked vehicles	H	21
Pedestrian-controlled vehicles: up to three wheels and not over 410 kg	K	16

Notes

1. Or two years from the date of passing the standard A test.
2. Or 16 if you are receiving Disability Living Allowance at the higher rate.
3. Or 21 if combined weight is over 7500 kg.
4. 17 if member of Armed Forces; 18 if member of Young Driver Scheme.
5. Age 17 if member of Armed Forces.
   Age 18 while learning to drive or taking Category D Driving Test.
   Age 18 after passing Category D Driving Test when:

   - driving a PCV out of service without passengers;
   - driving on a regular service where the route does not exceed 50 km;
   - driving a PCV constructed to carry no more than 16 passengers within the UK;
   - driving buses with up to 16 passenger seats operated under a permit.

6. Age 16 for tractors less than 2.45 m wide. It must only pull trailers less than 2.45 m wide with two wheels, or four close coupled.
7. Age 17 for small road rollers with metal or hard rollers. They **must not** be steam powered, weigh more than 11,650 kg or be made for carrying goods.

Driving Licence Application

You may apply for a full licence if you have:

- passed the driving test and you exchange the pass certificate for a full licence within two years of the date of the test;
- held a full licence issued in the Channel Islands or the Isle of Man, valid within the last 10 years; or
- held a full British licence or a full licence issued in Northern Ireland granted on or after 1 January 1976.

You may also apply for a full licence if you have been resident in Great Britain for less than one year and you surrender a valid full licence issued in the EC or some other countries (see page 126). Application for a licence should be made at least three weeks before the date of commencement of the licence. Application forms for a licence are available from Post Offices and Local Vehicle Licensing Offices. The completed form should be sent to the Driver and Vehicle Licensing Authority, Swansea SA99 1AB. Application may be made at any time within two months prior to the date from which the licence is required. If you need to make an enquiry about your licence, you are advised to contact the Driver Enquiry Unit, DVLA, Swansea SA6 7JL (tel: 01792 772151) quoting your driver number. It is worth making a note of this number in case your licence is mislaid.

Driving licence fees

The current fees (October 2001) for driving licences are:

First provisional licence   **£27.50**
Car, motorcycle, medium/large goods, mini bus/bus

Changing provisional for first full   **£12.50**

Duplicate   **£17.50**
If your licence is lost, stolen or defaced

Exchange   **£17.50**
This includes adding a test pass to a full licence, adding/surrendering provisional
motorcycle entitlement, removing expired endorsements or exchanging an old
style pink or green licence for a new style one.

Renewing your licence
- Car licence at 70 or over   **£6.00**
- Full – for medium/large, minibus/bus   **£32.50**
- Provisional – for medium/large, minibus/bus   **£27.50**
- For medical reasons   **FREE**

Exchanging licences from other countries
- Full Northern Ireland car licence   **£17.50**
- Full N. Ireland for medium/large, minibus/bus   **£27.50**
- Full EC/EEA or other foreign licence
  (including Channel Islands & Isle of Man)   **£27.50**

New licence after disqualification
- Car licence, motorcycle, medium/large vehicle, minibus/bus   **£28.50**
- Medium/large or minibus/bus with less than 3 months to run   **£32.50**
- If disqualified for some drink/drive offences   **£37.50**

If you are disqualified and have to take another driving test, you normally
have to pay £28.50 for a provisional licence. You also have to pay £17.50 for a
full licence after passing the test. Licences are normally valid until the applicant's 70th birthday, at which time a new licence may be issued for one, two or

three years at a time, depending on health and other factors. Renewal in these circumstances is free of charge.

A duplicate or exchange licence is valid for the period of the original licence. A replacement licence which is issued after a period of disqualification is charged at the same rate as a duplicate licence. An exchange licence may be required by a driver who is adding an extra category to an existing licence, or where motorcycle entitlement is required, or whose licence contains out-of-date endorsements. A Northern Ireland full licence may be exchanged for a GB licence for the appropriate fee.

A duplicate licence is needed to replace a licence which has been lost, mislaid or defaced. Replacement of a licence following a change of address is made free of charge.

Health and Eyesight

When applying for a licence the driver has to make various declarations regarding health and eyesight. You must declare, for example, any disability and any illness which might affect your driving. The law also requires the driver to notify the licensing authority if there is likely to be any worsening of any condition and if there has been a change in any disability since the issue of the licence. Examples of the kind of health conditions in question are listed in the leaflet D100, but if there is any doubt about whether or not the condition should be reported, the driver is advised to consult the family doctor. It is not necessary to report any medical conditions that are not likely to last more than three months.

Epilepsy: under certain circumstances a licence may be issued to someone who has been free of attacks for one year.

Pacemakers: people who are subject to sudden faintings or giddiness have, in the past, not been issued with a licence. The law, however, has been changed, and a licence may now be granted if this disability is corrected by the fitting of a cardiac pacemaker and if other medical conditions are satisfied.

Disabilities: drivers who are physically and mentally capable of driving but are otherwise disabled may be issued with a licence which restricts them to driving a vehicle of special design or construction. This type of licence does not entitle the driver to use it as a provisional licence for other groups of vehicles. If the driver then wishes to learn to drive a vehicle of a different type, he or she must first apply for the appropriate provisional entitlement to be added to the original licence.

Eyesight: in order to conform with the law there is a minimum standard of eyesight which must be reached (with glasses or contact lenses if necessary). The requirement is to read a motor vehicle number plate in good daylight at a distance of 67 feet (20.5 metres) for the old style number plates and 20 metres for the new plates. In the case of the driver of a mowing machine or pedestrian controlled vehicle the relevant distances are 45 feet and 40 feet.

If you need glasses or contact lenses in order to attain these standards, then you must wear them every time you drive. It is an offence to drive if your eyesight does not meet the required standard.

An applicant who declares a disability to the DVLA may be asked for permission to obtain a report from the applicant's doctor. A licence may be issued for a limited period so that the condition can be reviewed or the licence may be restricted to certain types of vehicles.

Procedure for medical assessment

When information about a disability is received, the DVLA may require the applicant or licence-holder to authorise his or her doctor to make available information about the disability to the Medical Adviser at the Centre. If the applicant or licence-holder fails to do so, or if the information available from the doctor is not conclusive in relation to fitness to drive, the Centre may require him or her to have a medical examination by a nominated doctor or doctors.

Motorcycle Licences

A full car licence usually acts as a provisional licence for motorcycles and as a full licence for mopeds. A new provisional motorcycle licence is issued for a maximum of two years. If a full licence is not obtained in this time it is not possible to renew the licence for a period of one year. The provisional licence entitles the rider to use a solo motorcycle with an engine capacity of up to 125 cc. Pillion passengers are not allowed to accompany a learner rider, even if the passenger has a full licence for that type of machine.

All learner motorcyclists and learner moped riders must have a valid Compulsory Basic Training certificate before they can ride on the road. This now applies to all learners, including those who have been riding with 'L' plates, regardless of when the original licence was issued. Many learner motorcyclists and learner moped riders with older licences have not previously had to complete the CBT. This exemption changed on 1 January 1997 and all 'L' riders must now complete the CBT.

The new licence regulations include a change in the categories for small, lightweight motorcycles, and a restriction on the size of the bike which may be ridden during the first two years after passing the test. Provision is made for new riders over the age of 21 to gain direct access to large bikes and for those learners to take specialised training and a separate test on the larger machine. Please note that there is no CBT scheme in Northern Ireland.

More detailed information on motorcycle training and tests is given in Chapter 10.

Vocational Licences

Licences for Large Goods Vehicles (LGVs) and Passenger Carrying Vehicles (PCVs) are issued by the Driver and Vehicle Licensing Agency as extra entitlements to the ordinary licence.

A driver who passes the 'L' Test is now issued with a licence for driving vehicles up 3,500 kg or a maximum of eight passenger seats. For driving anything over these limits, a separate test is needed for each type of vehicle. For example, you need to hold a full licence for cars before obtaining a provisional licence for medium-sized goods vehicles, and a full rigid vehicle licence is required before you can drive an articulated vehicle or draw-bar combinations. There are also restrictions on the type of trailer which can be towed – for example a separate test and licence entitlement would be needed to tow a large trailer behind a heavy motor car if the combined weight was more than 4,250 kg or if the gross weight of the trailer was more than the unladen weight of the towing vehicle.

The rules relating to vocational licences, medicals and test procedures are dealt with in more detail in Chapter 10, which also deals with training and qualifications for vocational licences.

Driving Abroad

Some countries do not accept a British driving licence. Others, such as Italy, will accept a translation of the GB licence. For driving in countries which do not accept the GB licence, an International Driving Permit is required, for which you must be over 18. These can be obtained from the RAC, the AA, the RSAC or the National Breakdown Club. A passport-type photograph must accompany the application.

Visitors and New Residents

Anyone holding a full Northern Ireland licence, or test pass certificate, can exchange it for a GB licence. Alternatively the NI licence can be used in Great Britain until it runs out.

Cars, lorry or bus licences issued in Jersey, Guernsey or the Isle of Man can be exchanged as long as they were valid in the last 10 years.

Anyone who has a valid full licence issued in a European Community country does not need to exchange it immediately for a GB licence. So long as the licence remains valid it can be used until the driver reaches age 70 (or for 3 years if that is longer).

Car, motorcycle and moped licences issued in the following countries may be exchanged for a full GB licence up to 5 years after the driver becomes resident in this country: Australia, Republic of Cyprus, Kenya, British Virgin Islands, Switzerland, New Zealand, Hong Kong, South Africa, Japan, Barbados, Singapore, Malta, Gibraltar, Zimbabwe, Canada.

To take a driving test, however, you need to first exchange the foreign licence for a UK one. The rules for exchanging lorry and bus licences are more strict and the driver should contact DVLA for individual details.

Licences from any other country may not be exchanged. However, it is permissible to drive for up to one year on a current full foreign licence or an International Driving Permit. Anyone becoming resident in GB should apply for a driving test as soon as possible. If the one year ruling expires, a provisional licence will need to be applied for and all the rules relating to learner drivers will apply.

ROAD TRAFFIC LAW

Most people are unsure about the law for motorists although, at any time when driving or using a car, they may find themselves faced with some aspect of it. The purpose of this section is to enable you to find out how the law affects you and your pupils.

The motorist is affected by the *civil* as well as by the *criminal* law, and an offence in a criminal court may well be followed by another case in a civil court. For example, a driver who injures a pedestrian and is found guilty of dangerous driving may then find himself being sued for damages in a civil court.

Most of the criminal law is found in the Road Traffic Act 1991. Apart from the criminal law, the Road Traffic Act gives the Secretary of State for Transport the power to make other regulations regarding various motoring matters. The most important of these regulations are the Motor Vehicles (Construction and Use) Regulations.

Much of the civil law which affects motorists is not contained in special rules relating to the roads. It is a part of the general law of the land. For example, the law of negligence applies to anyone, whether driving or not. The motorist is most likely to encounter the civil law after he has been involved in a road accident in which there has been injury to a person or damage to property. In these cases, the law allows the person injured to claim against the other driver, or the insurance company.

However, the motorist may be guilty of an offence under criminal law even if no accident has taken place. An offence may have been committed even if it was not intended; for example, driving without lights at night is an offence even though the driver may have checked the operation of the lights before starting his journey. There is also a certain amount of confusion regarding the Highway Code. Although the Code is drawn up by the Department of Transport under the specific rules of the Road Traffic Act, a breach of it is not necessarily a punishable offence. However, the Highway Code can be used as a reference in a court when assessing the actions of a driver. A breach of a particular part of the Highway Code may in some cases amount to a breach of a specific part of the Road Traffic Act. Nevertheless, the offence will be found to be against a section of the Road Traffic Act.

Questions of liability may arise when a driver is using a vehicle while carrying out his normal work or when the vehicle is being used for driving instruction. These questions of liability often arise under the Construction and Use Regulations when the driver, supervising driver and the employer may all be equally guilty of an offence.

Driving Offences

The 1991 Road Traffic Act created several new offences including:

- causing death by dangerous driving;
- dangerous driving (replacing reckless driving);
- causing death by careless driving when under the influence of drink or drugs;
- causing danger to other road users.

Offences of driving without a licence, without 'L' plates, without supervision, or under the age when a licence can be obtained, are now dealt with under the offence of 'driving otherwise than in accordance with a licence'. Penalty points for this offence vary from three to six depending on the circumstances and seriousness of the offence.

These offences are based more firmly on the actual standard of driving. 'Dangerous driving' has to have two main features:

- A standard of driving which falls far below that expected of a competent and careful driver.
- The driving must involve actual or potential danger of physical injury or serious damage to property.

The standard of driving is judged in absolute terms and takes no account of factors such as inexperience, age or disability of the driver. It is not intended that the driver who merely makes a careless mistake, of a kind which any driver might make from time to time, should be regarded as falling far below the standard expected of a competent and careful driver.

The danger must be one which a competent and careful driver would have appreciated or observed. It means any danger of injury (however minor) to a person or of serious damage to property.

Careless and inconsiderate driving is defined in the new Act in relation to 'a person driving a mechanically propelled vehicle on a road or other public place'. This means that non-motorised vehicles and offences on private property to which the public have access may now be included. The main ingredients in this offence are referred to in terms of 'driving without due care and attention, or without reasonable consideration for other road users'.

Offences incurring disqualification

The following offences carry automatic disqualification:

- manslaughter caused by the driver of a motor vehicle;
- causing death by dangerous driving;
- causing death by careless driving when unfit through drink;
- dangerous driving;
- motor racing on the highway;
- driving, or attempting to drive, when under the influence of drink or drugs, or with more than the permitted blood/alcohol level;
- failure to provide a blood or urine sample.

Legal alcohol limits

The legal alcohol limits are:

- 35 microgrammes of alcohol per 100 millilitres of breath;
- 80 milligrammes of alcohol per 100 millilitres of blood;
- 107 milligrammes of alcohol per 100 millilitres of urine.

The minimum period of obligatory disqualification for drink-driving and other offences may be reduced by the Court by up to one-quarter, if the defendant at the time of the sentence agrees to participate in a rehabilitation course and completes it successfully.

A second drink-drive offence within 10 years carries a minimum disqualification period of three years.

The extended driving test

Courts now have the power, for some of the more serious offences, to order disqualification until an 'appropriate' driving test is passed. These offences include motor manslaughter, causing death by dangerous driving, and dangerous driving. The test is longer and more rigorous than the normal 'L' test. It therefore provides scope for the driver to be tested in a greater variety of road and traffic conditions.

The courts' existing discretionary power to order offenders to be disqualified until passing an appropriate test is retained. In determining whether to make such an order, the court must have regard to the safety of road users. For offences involving obligatory disqualification, the 'appropriate' test is the new, extended test, and might therefore apply to the driver who has been disqualified under the 'totting up' procedure, and who has been ordered by the court to retake the test. For those offences which involve obligatory endorsement (as opposed to obligatory disqualification), the appropriate test is the ordinary test of competence to drive.

Penalty Points

Offence	Points
Being in charge of a vehicle when unfit to drive	10

Failing to stop after an accident	5–10
Failing to report or to give particulars	5–10
Careless and inconsiderate driving	3–9
Driving while uninsured	6–8
Driving while disqualified by a court	6
Driving other than in accordance with a licence	3–6
Exceeding a speed limit	
– in court proceedings	3–6
– by fixed penalty	3
Contravention of temporary prohibition or restriction	
– in court proceedings	3–6
– by fixed penalty	3
Contravention of motorway regulations	
– in court proceedings	3–6
– by fixed penalty	3
Failure to give identity of driver	3
Unlawful carriage of motorcycle passenger	3
Contravention or failure to comply with C & U Regs.	3
Driving with defective eyesight	3

Penalty points for some offences are graded according to the seriousness of the offence. A driver who is convicted for several offences committed on the same occasion may have the points for each offence added together. This means that it is now possible for the driver to be disqualified from driving for offences committed on the one occasion. An accumulation of 12 points within three years means that the driver will automatically be disqualified from driving, although the courts are given powers not to disqualify in exceptional circumstances. The three-year period is measured backwards from the date of the latest offence.

The period of disqualification as a result of an accumulation of penalty points is:

- six months, if there has been no disqualification in the past three years;
- one year, if there has been one disqualification in the past three years;
- two years, if there has been more than one disqualification in the past three years.

Disqualification may be imposed for a single offence if the court feels that the offence is serious enough.

A penalty points endorsement can be removed after four years from the date of the offence.

An endorsement of disqualification may be removed four years after the date of conviction (11 years for drinking and driving offences).

After a disqualification for a period of more than two years you can apply for the disqualification to be lifted after a period of:

1.   two years if the disqualification period is less than four years;
2.   half the period of disqualification if between 4 and 10 years;
3.   five years if the disqualification was for more than 10 years.

The New Driver Act

This Act affects any newly qualified driver who accumulates six or more penalty points within two years of passing their driving test.

The accumulation of six or more points (whether arising from court convictions or from fixed penalty offences) means that the licence is automatically revoked by the DVLA and the driver has to revert to a provisional licence. Both the theory and practical tests will need to be retaken before a full licence can be issued. After passing the tests a new full licence will generally include all previous licence entitlements, but the points will carry forward, as these could count towards any future 'totting up'.

Disqualification and the ADI

One of the requirements of ADI qualification is: 'will have held a full driving licence for four years'. An important point to be remembered by professional driving instructors is that any period of disqualification from driving will involve a further period of disqualification from the ADI Register. For example, one-year disqualification for a driving offence is followed by a four-year disqualification from the official Register. The instructor would, therefore, be unable to practise his trade for a total period of five years.

Fixed penalties

Traffic wardens and police officers are empowered to enforce the law in connection with various offences by use of the fixed penalty system. The relevant offences include waiting, parking, loading and obstruction as well as offences relating to vehicle tax, lights and reflectors. Driving offences such as making 'U' turns and driving the wrong way in a one-way street are also included.

The ticket is given to the driver or is fixed to the vehicle. Payment must be made within 28 days or alternatively the offender may request a court hearing. If the driver who committed the offence cannot be identified or found, the registered owner of the vehicle is ultimately responsible for payment of the fine. However, in the case of hired vehicles, special rules apply and the person who hires the vehicle will become liable for any fines or excess charges.

The extended fixed penalty scheme covers various moving traffic offences including speeding, failure to comply with traffic directions and vehicle defect offences. The following categories are now included in the scheme and for these offences the issuing of the ticket is normally the responsibility of the police:

Contravening a traffic regulation order

Breach of experimental traffic order

Breach of experimental traffic scheme regulation in Greater London

Using a vehicle in contravention of a temporary prohibition or restriction of traffic on a road, ie where a road is being repaired, etc

Contravening motorway traffic regulations

Driving a vehicle in contravention of order prohibiting or restricting driving vehicles on certain classes of roads

Breach of pedestrian crossing regulations

Contravention of a street playground order

Breach of a parking place order on a road

Breach of a provision of a parking place designation order and other offences committed in relation to it, except failing to pay an excess charge

Contravening a parking place designation order

Breach of a provision of a parking place designation order

Contravention of minimum speed limits

Speeding

Driving or keeping a vehicle without displaying registration mark or hackney carriage sign

Driving or keeping a vehicle with registration mark or hackney carriage sign obscured

Failure to comply with traffic directions or signs

Leaving vehicle in a dangerous position

Failing to wear a seatbelt

Breach of restrictions on carrying children in the front of vehicles

Driving a vehicle elsewhere than on the road

Parking a vehicle on the path or verge

Breach of Construction and Use Regulations

Contravention of lighting restrictions on vehicles

Driving without a licence

Breach of provisional licence provisions

Failure to stop when required by constable in uniform

Obstruction of highway with vehicle

Penalty tickets for endorsable offences are handed to the driver as the driving licence will have to be surrendered for possible endorsement with the appropriate penalty points. If the licence shows an accumulation of points which, together with the current offence, would bring the total to 12 points or more, then the fixed penalty ticket would not be issued. In those circumstances a prosecution for the offence would follow.

If the licence is not immediately available, it must be produced within seven days at a nominated police station. A receipt for the licence is then issued and this is an accepted document if for any reason the licence has to be produced at a later date.

The fixed penalty fines of £20 for non-endorsable and £40 for endorsable offences are payable within 28 days (or as specified in the notice). If payment is not received in time, the charge is increased by 50 per cent to £30 and £60 respectively. A driver may request a court hearing if he considers that the issue of the ticket was wrong or unfair.

A penalty points endorsement can be removed after four years from the date of the offence.

An endorsement of disqualification may be removed four years after the date of conviction (11 years for drinking and driving offences).

After a disqualification for a period of more than two years, you can apply for the disqualification to be lifted after a period of:

1. two years if the disqualification period is less than four years;
2. half the period of disqualification if between 4 and 10 years;
3. five years if the disqualification was for more than 10 years.

Driver Improvement Scheme

Several police forces are now offering this scheme as an alternative to prosecution for drivers committing some less serious or careless driving offences.

The offender is given the opportunity to attend a short (one- or two-day) course at his or her own expense. The aim is to address driver behaviour and to provide remedial instruction tailored to suit the individual's needs. The scheme is not normally used for more serious offences or where there is an element of dangerousness or deliberate recklessness.

Driver Identity

The 1991 Act defines the circumstances in which a person can be required to give information about the identity of a driver who is alleged to be guilty of a road traffic offence. This is particularly important in connection with the identification of drivers involved in speeding or other offences detected by automatic devices, including cameras.

A photograph, showing the registration number, is taken of the offending vehicle. It is not intended that the registered keeper of the vehicle should bear responsibility for the offence detected by the device, if someone else was driving at the time of the offence. It is, therefore, necessary to trace the driver through the registered keeper. The penalty for not providing the information has been increased to three penalty points to provide an incentive to do so.

The existing fixed penalty system requires the vehicle and the person committing the offence to be present at the time the fixed penalty ticket is issued. However, under the provisions of the RTA 1991, a conditional fixed penalty offer is available for all fixed penalty offences, including those detected by automatic cameras and other devices. These provisions allow for the police to issue a notice to the alleged offender by post.

The notice is first issued to the registered keeper of the vehicle, requiring information about the identity of the driver. The conditional offer of a fixed penalty will then be issued to the person identified as the driver of the vehicle when the offence was detected. If the information about the driver is not given, the 'keeper' of the vehicle will have committed an offence, which is now endorsable.

If the driver wishes to take up the offer of the fixed penalty, the driving licence and payment are sent to the Fixed Penalty Office and the payment is accepted, so long as the licence shows that the driver would not be subject to a 'totting up' disqualification. In those circumstances, the payment and licence would be returned and a court summons would then be issued.

Driving Licence Endorsements

Endorsement offences appear on a driving licence in a coded version which includes details of the court, the offence and of the fine and endorsement.

Code	Accident Offences
AC10	Failing to stop and/or give particulars after an accident.
AC20	Failing to report an accident within 24 hours.

	Undefined Accident Offence
AC30	Undefined Accident Offence.
	Driver Banned from Driving (disqualified)
BA10	Driving while disqualified.
BA20	Driving while disqualified by virtue of age.

	Careless Driving
CD10	Driving without due care and attention.
CD20	Driving without reasonable consideration for other road users.
CD30	Driving without due care and attention or without reasonable consideration for other road users.

	Construction and Use Offences
CU10	Using a vehicle with defective brakes.
CU20	Causing or likely to cause danger by reason of use of unsuitable vehicle or using a vehicle with parts or accessories (excluding brakes, steering or tyres) in a dangerous condition.
CU30	Using a vehicle with defective tyres.
CU40	Using a vehicle with defective steering.
CU50	Causing or likely to cause danger by reason of load or passengers.
CU60	Undefined failure to comply with Construction and Use Regulations.

Dangerous Driving

DD10	Driving in a dangerous manner.
DD20	Driving at a dangerous speed.
DD30	Reckless driving.
DD40	Driving in a dangerous or reckless manner, etc.
DD50	Causing death by dangerous driving.
DD60	Culpable homicide while driving a vehicle.
DD70	Causing death by reckless driving.

Drink or Drugs

DR10	Driving or attempting to drive with blood alcohol level above limit.
DR20	Driving or attempting to drive while unfit through drink or drugs.
DR30	Driving or attempting to drive then refusing to supply a specimen of blood or urine for laboratory testing.
DR40	In charge of a vehicle while blood alcohol level above limit.
DR50	In charge of a vehicle while unfit through drink or drugs.
DR60	In charge of a vehicle then refusing to supply a specimen of blood or urine for laboratory testing.

Insurance Offences

IN10	Using a vehicle uninsured against third party risks.

Licence Offences

LC10	Driving without a licence.
LC20	Driving when under age.

Miscellaneous Offences

MS10	Leaving a vehicle in a dangerous position.
MS20	Unlawful pillion riding.
MS30	Playstreet offences.
MS40	Driving with uncorrected or defective eyesight or refusing to submit to eyesight test.
MS50	Motor racing on the highway.
MS60	Offences not covered by other codes.
MS70	Driving with uncorrected defective eyesight.
MS80	Refusing to submit to an eyesight test.

Motorway Offences

MW10	Contravention of Special Roads Regulations (excluding speed limits).

Pedestrian Crossing

PC10	Undefined contravention of Pedestrian Crossing Regulations.
PC20	Contravention of Pedestrian Crossing Regulations with moving vehicle.
PC30	Contravention of Pedestrian Crossing Regulations with stationary vehicle.

Provisional Licence Offences

PL10	Driving without 'L' plates.
PL20	Driving while not accompanied by a qualified person.
PL30	Carrying a person not qualified
PL40	Drawing an unauthorised trailer.
PL50	Undefined failure to comply with conditions of a Provisional Licence.

Speed Limits

SP10	Exceeding goods vehicle speed limit.
SP20	Exceeding speed limit for type of vehicle (excluding goods or passenger vehicles).
SP30	Exceeding statutory speed limit on a public road.
SP40	Exceeding passenger vehicle speed limit.
SP50	Exceeding speed limit on a motorway.
SP60	Undefined speed limit offence.

Traffic Directions and Signs

TS10	Failing to comply with traffic light signals.
TS20	Failing to comply with double white lines.
TS30	Failing to comply with a 'Stop' sign.
TS40	Failing to comply with directions of a traffic constable.
TS50	Failing to comply with a traffic sign (excluding 'Stop' signs, traffic lights or double white lines).
TS60	Failing to comply with a school crossing patrol sign.
TS70	Undefined failure to comply with a traffic direction or sign.

Theft or the Unauthorised Taking of Vehicle

UT10	Taking and driving away a vehicle without consent or an attempt thereat.
UT20	Stealing or attempting to steal a vehicle.
UT30	Going equipped for stealing or taking a vehicle.
UT40	Taking or attempting to take a vehicle without consent; driving or attempting to drive a vehicle knowing it to have been taken without consent; allowing oneself to be carried in or on a vehicle knowing it to have been taken without consent.

Special Code

XX99	Signifies a disqualification under the 'totting-up' procedure.

Notes: Aiding and abetting offences are as listed above, but with the 0 changed to 2 (eg UT20 becomes UT22).

Causing or permitting are as listed, but with the 0 changed to 4 (eg PL20 becomes PL24).

Inciting offences are as listed, but with the 0 changed to 6 (eg DD10 becomes DD16).

Speed Limits

A speed limit of 30 mph normally applies to all vehicles on a road where street lamps are positioned at intervals of less than 200 yards. On occasions a higher speed is allowed on such a road, in which case the higher limit is shown by appropriate signs.

Speed limits apply to roads and vehicles, and where there is a difference the lower limit applies. The maximum speed on motorways and dual carriageways is 70 mph and on single carriageways 60 mph. However, these limits apply to cars, car-derived vans and dual-purpose vehicles adapted to carry not more than eight passengers. A different set of speed limits applies to other types of vehicles.

Vehicle	Single Carriageway	Dual Carriageway	Motorway
Cars, including car-derived vans and motorcycles	60	70	70
Cars, towing trailers and caravans	50	60	60
Goods vehicles up to 7.5 tonnes	50	60	70
– towing trailers	50	60	60
– articulated	50	60	60
Large goods vehicles			
– over 7.5 tonnes and articulated	40	50	60
Buses and coaches			
– up to 12 m length	50	60	70
– over 12 m length	50	60	60

Accident Procedure

An 'accident' is generally and legally regarded as one which causes injury to another person or animal, or damage to another vehicle or property.

Any driver who is involved in an accident must stop and give their name, address and vehicle registration number to the other person involved. If there is personal injury you must also produce your insurance certificate to anyone who has reasonable cause to see it. You must give information regarding the ownership of the vehicle. Where it is not possible to exchange these particulars, the accident should be reported to the police as soon as possible and in any case within 24 hours.

These responsibilities apply regardless of who is to blame for the accident so that even if you feel that the accident is relatively trivial and that it was not your fault, you must carry out the procedure described in the chart on page 138.

A police officer may also ask for driver and vehicle details if he believes the driver to have been involved in an accident. The chart gives guidance to the instructor who requires detailed information for instructional purposes. With

Accident Procedure

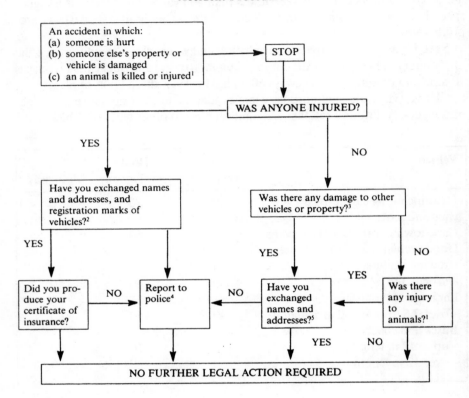

Note:
The chart shows the *minimum* legal requirements.

Notes:

1   Animals: horse, cattle, ass, mule, sheep, pig, goat, dog.
2   With any person who has reasonable grounds to ask for them.
3   Includes roadside 'furniture', eg lamp posts and other fixtures.
4   Report as soon as possible, and at least within 24 hours, and produce certificate of insurance either when reporting or within seven days.
5   With the owner of the vehicle, property or animal.

regard to your responsibility as an instructor, it should be noted that the duty to carry out the foregoing procedures applies to a person accompanying the holder of a provisional licence and not only to the driver of the vehicle.

Legal Obligations of a Supervising Driver

Anyone supervising a learner driver must have held a full GB licence for at least three years and be over 21 years of age. It is the learner's responsibility to check that anyone supervising their practice is covered by these regulations. An offence against the regulations carries a penalty of a £400 fine, discretionary disqualification or two penalty points.

The tuition or practice vehicle must display regulation size 'L' plates which are clearly visible within a reasonable distance from the front and rear of the vehicle. L plates should be removed from the vehicle when it is being driven by a full licence holder, except in the case of driving school cars.

As well as all the legal obligations, any driver supervising a learner has certain moral obligations relating to the safety of passengers and other road users. If a driving instructor commits or aids and abets a traffic offence, the subsequent punishment resulting from a successful prosecution is likely to have disastrous effects. Even relatively minor offences will attract a disproportionate amount of bad publicity which not only causes disgrace and inconvenience, as well as possible loss of livelihood, but also stains the character of the driving school industry as a whole.

In addition to the responsibilities as driver, already covered in this chapter, the instructor has further responsibilities. Where a supervisor sees that the 'L' driver is about to commit an unlawful act, whether it be through ignorance or lack of skill, and takes no verbal or physical action to prevent it, a prosecution for aiding and abetting could ensue. For example, if a learner was about to ignore a red traffic light and the instructor allowed the car to be stopped after passing the solid line, an offence would have been committed by both persons – even though it was the instructor who finally brought the car to a stop.

Tuition vehicle

The driving instructor must pay particular attention to ensure that the tuition vehicle is in a roadworthy condition and that it is taxed and adequately insured for driving instruction and driving test purposes. The vehicle must carry 'L' plates of the prescribed size, showing clearly to the front and rear of the vehicle.

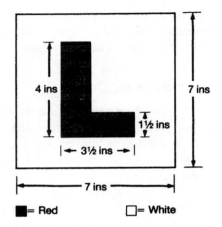

■ = Red	□ = White

Driving licence and eyesight

Before allowing a pupil to drive your vehicle you should make sure that they have a current, valid, signed driving licence and that the eyesight requirements can be met. You must check this even though the pupil may have signed a declaration to this effect on the licence application form. Where glasses are required to meet the minimum standard, they must be worn at all times while driving.

Make sure you are aware of your responsibilities as a driver and an instructor.

Tuition in client's vehicle

On occasions where clients may choose to provide their own car for professional driving lessons, you must give special consideration to all the foregoing points, but in particular to the roadworthiness, MOT certificate and insurance cover of the vehicle.

Before agreeing to give tuition in a non dual-controlled vehicle, you should give serious consideration to the standard, or estimated standard, the client has reached, if you have not yet had an opportunity to make a valid assessment (for example a new client booking by telephone).

Due consideration should also be given to the type of vehicle to see if you can easily reach the handbrake (some cars have the handbrake on the right of the driver or under the dash). Your safety, as well as that of your client and other road users, may be at stake.

ADVANCED DRIVING

The Cardington Special Test

This high-level driving test is open to all Approved Driving Instructors. One of the strictest tests in the country, it is conducted by permanent staff instructors operating out of the Driving Standards Agency's Training Establishment at Cardington near Bedford. To apply, send in your application fee of £65 to The Special Test Booking Section, The Driving Establishment, RAF Cardington, Bedford MK42 0TJ (tel: 01234 742134).

You have to provide your own manual transmission car for the test, which lasts approximately 90 minutes. The test syllabus includes:

- driving on all types of road;
- a left- and right-hand reverse;
- turning in the road;
- reverse parking;
- hill and angled starts.

Commentary driving is not expected and there is no element of theory testing.

You will be assessed on your driving technique and you are expected to demonstrate a systematic and professional approach to all hazards and plan expertly for safe progress at all times. Each individual fault will be fully assessed in the light of the prevailing conditions. The result is normally confirmed by post within 48 hours, and, whether you pass or fail, you will receive a report on those faults observed. If you achieve a grade 'A' you will also receive the Cardington Certificate.

The Institute of Advanced Motorists

The Institute was founded in 1956 for the purposes of raising driving standards and to establish an Advanced Driving Test. The Institute believes that a higher standard of behaviour by all road users, and drivers in particular, could reduce road accidents and their grim social consequences more effectively than any other method. The Advanced Driving Test offers to drivers of cars, trucks, and motorcycles an opportunity to check their own abilities under today's road conditions; membership of the Institute for those who achieve the Institute's standards then demands the responsibility that goes with proven skill.

The standard of the test is based on the police system of car control as taught in Home Office Approved Police Driving Schools. The examiners, all of whom are either serving or retired police officers, have to hold an Advanced Driving Certificate. This qualification has never been challenged by the public as it is probably the highest available in the world. The 120 test routes are designed to provide all types of driving conditions and are about 35 miles long. The test takes 90 minutes, which does not include the briefing and debriefing.

There are many books available on advanced driving, the main ones being *The Highway Code*, *Roadcraft*, the police drivers' text book and *Advanced Motoring*, the IAM's own driving manual, coupled with *Motor Cycle Roadcraft* and *Advanced Motorcycling*.

The advantage of taking an advanced test is that IAM members have a 50–75 per cent lower accident rate. Over 400 commercial concerns put their staff through the test in order to cut costs, as does the British Army. Many insurance companies grant a discount off normal motor insurance premiums of up to 20 per cent. The conviction rate among members appears to be five times lower than the general public. Anyone with a full British driving licence can take the test; it is advisable to receive instruction from an ADI, preferably an IAM member, or contact the local IAM group who will give guidance in preparation for the test.

The Institute is a registered charity and receives full moral support from the Department of Transport, all UK police forces and the Ministry of Defence. The IAM motto is 'Skill with Responsibility'.

The IAM Test

Application forms can be obtained from The Institute of Advanced Motorists, IAM House, 359 Chiswick High Road, London W4 4HS, or telephone 0181 994 4403; Web site: www.iam.org.uk.

Candidates will be expected to make reasonable use of the vehicle's performance within the speed limits and normal parameters of safety with regard to the road traffic and weather conditions. Candidates are expected to reverse into a side road and execute a hill start and will be assessed on their powers of observation.

The test is something which any driver with a reasonable amount of experience and skill should be able to pass without too much difficulty. Candidates do not fail for committing minor faults. Even those who do fail should learn some important lessons from the examiner conducting the test. Successful candidates may:

- display the Institute's badge on their car;
- take advantage of special insurance terms;
- receive *Advanced Driving*, the motoring magazine especially written for those with a keen interest in driving;
- join their local IAM group and participate in the road safety, driving and social events which they organise.

During the test

Examiners look for the following points:

Acceleration This should be smooth and progressive. It should be used at the right time and right place. Acceleration should not be excessive or insufficient.

Braking This should be smooth and progressive. Brakes should be used in conjunction with the mirror and signals. They should not be used late or fiercely. Candidates will be expected to take account of the road conditions.

Clutch control The engine and road speeds must be properly co-ordinated when changing gear. Candidates should not slip or ride the clutch, nor should they coast with the clutch disengaged.

Gear changing Gears should be selected smoothly and fluently. If automatic transmission is fitted, candidates should make full use of it.

Use of gears Candidates must make correct use of the gears. The correct gear should be selected before reaching a hazard.

Steering The wheel should be held correctly with the hands at the quarter-to-three or ten-to-two position. The use of the crossed arm technique, except when manoeuvring in a confined space, is not recommended by the Institute.

Seating position Candidates should be alert and not slumped at the wheel. They should not rest an arm on the door while driving.

Observation Candidates should read the road well ahead and anticipate the actions of other road users. They must be able to judge correctly the speeds and distances of other vehicles.

Concentration Candidates should concentrate on the road and traffic situation and not allow themselves to be easily distracted.

Maintaining progress With regard to the road, traffic and weather conditions, candidates should make use of their vehicle's performance by driving at a reasonable pace, maintaining good progress throughout.

Obstruction Candidates should not obstruct other road users by driving too slowly, by positioning incorrectly on the road or by failing to anticipate and react correctly to the traffic situation ahead.

Positioning Candidates should keep in the correct part of the road, especially when approaching and negotiating hazards.

Lane discipline Candidates should drive in the appropriate lane and be careful not to straddle white lines.

Observation of surfaces Candidates should continually assess the road surface, especially in poor weather, and look out for slippery conditions.

Traffic signals Candidates must observe and respond correctly to signals, signs and road markings and extend proper courtesies at pedestrian crossings.

Speed limits and other legal requirements Speed limits and other legal requirements must be observed at all times.

Overtaking Candidates must overtake safely while maintaining a correct distance from other vehicles and using the mirrors, signals and gears correctly.

Hazard procedure and cornering Candidates must have full control over their vehicle on the approach to a hazard. They must negotiate it in the correct position, driving at an appropriate speed with a suitable gear engaged.

Mirror Candidates must use the mirrors frequently, especially before signalling and making changes to speed or course.

Signals Signals given by direction indicator, or arm if required, should be given in the right place and in good time. The horn and headlight flasher should only be used in accordance with the Highway Code.

Restraint Candidates should display reasonable restraint, without being indecisive.

Consideration Candidates should extend consideration and courtesy to other road users.

Car sympathy Candidates should not over-stress the vehicle, for example by revving the engine needlessly or by fierce braking.

Manoeuvring This should be carried out smoothly and competently.

The RoSPA Advanced Driving Test

RoSPA advanced tests are conducted at locations all over the UK by Police Class 1 drivers and last about 1¼ hours. The cost of the test includes the first year's membership of the RoSPA Advanced Drivers' Association.

RoSPA have a unique system of grading successful candidates into gold, silver and bronze grades, which seems to be a fairer way of assessing performance over a wider range of driving ability. It provides incentives for the less experienced seeking to improve on their standard continuously and, at the same time, gives a meaningful measure of attainment to the more skilful driver. The highest grade is unlikely to be achieved without a thorough knowledge of *Roadcraft*, the police drivers' manual, and the system of car control it advocates.

Applying for the test

Application forms can be obtained from:

The Administrative Officer, RoSPA Advanced Drivers' Association, Edgbaston Park, 353 Bristol Road, Birmingham B5 7ST (tel: 0121 248 2000; Web site: www.rospa.co.uk).

The test

Cars used for the test must be in a roadworthy condition and the candidate's visibility must not be obscured by condensation or for other reasons. Examiners will take a serious view of candidates who, for example on a rainy day, attempt to drive while visibility is restricted by condensation on windows and mirrors. Proper use of the wipers, demisters and window winder is expected. At the start of the test, examiners try to put candidates at ease.

The use of the controls

Before starting off, candidates are required to carry out the cockpit drill followed by a brake test shortly after moving.

Candidates are expected to demonstrate their mechanical appreciation by controlling the vehicle smoothly. Examiners will assess the steering method and position of the hands and arms when turning the wheel. The clutch should be used smoothly. Single de-clutching is acceptable but examiners would prefer to see double de-clutching where appropriate. Slipping and riding the clutch is frowned upon. Examiners will assess the position of the hand on the gear lever when executing selections, the matching of engine revolutions to road speed and the correct timing of gear changes. The intelligent use of intermediate gears will make a difference to the final grade achieved. The use of the brakes is assessed for smoothness, early braking in correct sequence relating to the 'system', skid avoidance through correct technique and progressive reduction in pedal pressure as the vehicle is brought to a smooth stop. The accelerator should be used firmly when needed, precisely and under control at all times. Acceleration sense in overtaking will be assessed along with anticipation and the smooth variation of speeds to meet changing road and traffic conditions without braking.

Candidates are expected to use the mirrors in the correct sequence and have an accurate and continuous knowledge of the traffic situation behind. Over-the-shoulder looks are expected at appropriate times. Candidates are also assessed in their use of the horn.

Driving performance

Moving off and stopping should be smooth and carried out safely. Examiners will assess the correct application of the system of car control, whether candidates brake before or after changing gear and whether they signal too late or to early. Particular emphasis is placed on the way the vehicle is positioned at junctions, on the approach to roundabouts, on the open road and in lanes on the approach to hazards.

Candidates will be assessed on their course when cornering and whether the line taken optimises visibility and safety and that it allows for any tendency of the vehicle to over- or understeer to be compensated for. The use of speed and vehicle controls while cornering will be assessed.

Candidates are assessed on whether necessary signals are omitted or wrongly timed and unnecessary ones are used. The examiner will look for reinforcement of intention by an arm signal where necessary and assess reactions to traffic signs.

Candidates are required to perform a reversing exercise safely and accurately and in normal driving to make reasonable use of their vehicle's performance within legal limits and as safety allows, according to the prevailing road and traffic conditions. Examiners will assess whether candidates are asking themselves the appropriate questions before executing an overtaking manoeuvre.

General ability

Candidates who are slumped at the wheel or resting an elbow on the door will not be considered as advanced drivers. Consideration for others and self-control will be assessed. Temperament whilst driving should be calm, relaxed and decisive.

Candidates are expected not to abuse their vehicles by 'kerbing' etc.

Examiners will assess candidates' powers of observation, hazard recognition and planning. Candidates may, if they choose, elect to give a commentary drive if invited to 'think aloud' for a few minutes by the examiner. Candidates will also be assessed on their ability to judge their own speed and the speeds and distances of other vehicles. This will be linked to candidates' use of braking and acceleration.

The test is concluded with questions on the Highway Code and other monitoring matters such as those contained in most vehicle handbooks.

After the test

The examiner will discuss any points which have arisen during the test and then allocate a grade according to the performance of the candidate. Candidates who are allocated a gold or silver grade are expected to take a refresher test within three years. Bronze grade candidates are expected to re-take the test at intervals of one year. Candidates who are ungraded are permitted to take the test again after three months. All re-tests are free of charge as the fees are included in the annual membership fee.

The Diamond Advanced Motorist's Test

The test is administered by The Driving Instructor's Association and conducted by specially qualified Diamond Advanced Examiners. These examiners are ADIs who have qualified for the Diploma in Driving Instruction, have passed the Cardington Special Driving Test and have also passed the DIA Diamond Instructors' Course.

The test is based on the DSA method of marking, with no more than six minor faults allowed. During the test a wide variety of road and traffic conditions are covered.

One of the advantages of taking this extra qualification is that you should be able to generate more and different types of business opportunities, such as advanced and defensive driving courses.

More details of the test are available from: DIAmond Advanced Motorists Ltd, Safety House, Beddington Farm Road, Croydon CR0 4XZ (tel: 0181 660 3333).

5

The Car

It is not necessary for driving instructors to know every last detail of the construction of a motor car, but the good instructor should have a thorough understanding of the basic principles involved. The reason why this information is required is as follows:

- A better appreciation of the workings of the car will result in a more cost effective use of the tuition car, the possibility of undertaking minor repairs and the better diagnosis of potential major faults.
- The instructor will be in a better position to give effective training – pupils will learn about the controls more quickly if they understand how they work.
- An appreciation of the mechanical principles means that the driver instructor or pupil will develop greater vehicle sympathy and a keener interest in driving generally.

For these reasons it is important to understand what happens when the driver uses the controls. This chapter includes a general view of mechanical principles, vehicle control and operation, vehicle safety checks, factors affecting vehicle stability and a summary of the legal requirements of using a motor car. It also gives an outline syllabus for teaching learners the basics of car mechanics and an understanding of how the car works.

MECHANICAL PRINCIPLES

The motor car is a complex assembly that includes the following main units and systems:

1. The power unit – this includes the engine and the systems essential to its operation – eg cooling, fuel, ignition and lubrication systems.
2. The transmission system (power train) – this includes a gearbox to match the engine speed to the power required for the road conditions and a final drive unit that transmits the power to the front and/or rear wheels.

3. A braking system – to slow or stop the motion of the vehicle in either direction.
4. A steering system – to move the vehicle in the desired direction.
5. A suspension system – to reduce as far as practicable the shock and vibration from the road wheels to the vehicle body/ chassis.
6. A body/chassis – to act as a mounting for all the other units and assemblies.

The Engine

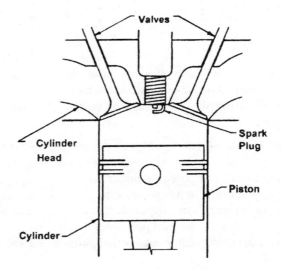

The function of the engine is to convert the heat energy contained in the fuel into mechanical energy for powering the vehicle.

Most motor cars are powered by four- or six-cylinder engines; each cylinder is a hole bored in a cylinder block. Pistons move up and down in sequence inside these cylinders in a sequence called the Otto cycle. The four strokes of this cycle are: induction, compression, power (combustion) and exhaust.

The flow of fuel and air mixture into the cylinders and the flow of the burnt exhaust gases out is controlled by a system of valves incorporated into the cylinder head. The cylinder head bolted to the top of the cylinder block seals off each of the bores, a gasket being fitted between them to make the joint pressure tight. Combustion of the fuel and air mixture takes place in combustion chambers, formed in the cylinder head above each of the cylinders.

Inlet stroke (Fig. 1a) During the inlet stroke, the inlet valve is open and the exhaust valve remains closed. The piston moves downward and the suction or vacuum created by this movement causes air and fuel to be drawn into the combustion chamber.

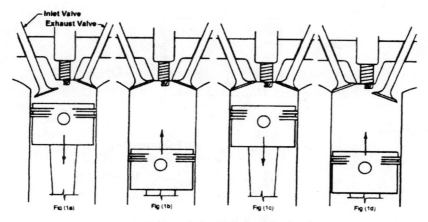

The four-stroke cycle (Otto)

Compression stroke (Fig 1b) During the compression stroke, both inlet and exhaust valves are closed. The piston moves upward to compress the air-fuel mixture into a small volume.

Power stroke (Fig 1c) During the power stroke, both valves remain closed. A spark from the spark plug ignites the air/fuel mixture and the piston is driven downward. This stroke delivers the power to propel the vehicle.

Exhaust stroke (Fig 1d) During the exhaust stroke, the exhaust valve is open and the piston moves upward to push out the burned gases. On completion of the exhaust stroke, the process begins immediately with another inlet stroke.

Power conversion The pistons connected by connecting rods to the crankshaft convert the power produced on the power stroke into a rotary motion. A heavy disc called a flywheel is bolted to the crankshaft to make it revolve more evenly and thus ensure a continuous flow of power to the gearbox and driving wheels. One complete Otto cycle rotates the crankshaft twice.

Valve and ignition timing The arrangement of the valve and ignition timing gears ensures perfect co-ordination with the motion of the pistons; a camshaft controls the opening and closing of the valves. It rotates at precisely half engine speed and in perfect co-ordination with the distributor, which controls the exact timing of the spark to initiate the ignition stroke.

The fuel system (petrol engines)

An engine operates on a mixture of petrol and air drawn from the carburettor. The carburettor basically consists of a tube through which the air passes, drawn in by the downward movement of the pistons, and a float chamber that distributes the fuel pumped from the petrol tank. Air passes into the tube of the carburettor

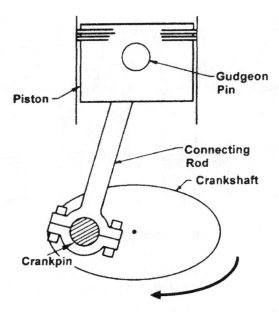

through an air filter, the flow being controlled by a flap known as a 'butterfly valve' and operated by the accelerator pedal.

As the accelerator is depressed, more air is drawn in; this in turns sucks more petrol from the float chamber through small jets which spray petrol into the tube. The combined petrol and air mixture is drawn through a series of pipes, known as the inlet manifold, which are connected to each cylinder. When starting a cold engine, a much richer mixture is required and this means a higher proportion of petrol to air than for normal running. This is achieved by restricting the amount of air entering the carburettor by means of a flap in the air intake known as a choke. Some cars have an automatic choke that is controlled by the engine temperature; others are manually operated.

With a fuel-injection system, the amount of petrol injected and the timing of its supply is controlled electronically. The accelerator operates a throttle butterfly valve that regulates the amount of air that flows through to the cylinder. At the same time a pump pressurises the fuel, which is then directed through the injectors into the cylinders.

Faults

- Dirty air filter: causes rich mixture; increased fuel consumption; loss of power; increased carbon deposits in engine.
- Sediment in petrol tank: causes fuel pipe blockage, dirt in petrol pump and carburettor float chamber that will block the jets, resulting in starvation of fuel at the cylinders.

- Incorrect petrol and air mixture: too rich or too weak. Wrong grade of petrol causing poor engine performance. Driver not returning choke when the engine is warmed up.

The ignition system

The combustible mixture of air and petrol is ignited by a spark that occurs between two electrodes (spark plug) in the combustion chamber, at the end of the compression stroke. It is the function of the ignition system to provide a spark of sufficient heat intensity to ignite the charge mixture at the predetermined position in the engine's cycle under all speed and load conditions.

The ignition system converts the low voltage from the battery into a high-tension voltage by means of an ignition coil. High-tension voltage is transmitted through the HT lead from the coil to the distributor cap. As the engine rotates, the rotor arm inside the distributor acts as an automatic switch that times the spark and distributes it to each cylinder spark plug in turn.

The timing of the spark is advanced or retarded automatically to ensure that it occurs at the correct moment for the load and engine speed. Most modern cars are now equipped with electronic ignition systems that involve less maintenance, longer spark plug life and make starting the car easier.

Faults

- Badly worn, dirty or poorly adjusted contact breaker points and/or spark plugs.
- Cracked, worn or dirty distributor cap.
- Worn rotor arm.
- Poor-fitting, dirty, cracked or perished HT leads, faulty or damaged electronic ignition systems.
- Incorrect ignition timing settings.

Engine lubrication

If two surfaces that rub together are examined under a microscope, it will be seen that each surface has a jagged edge (A). If these edges touch one another during operation, friction and heat are generated. If they are left without lubrication, these components will either wear excessively or weld themselves together, ultimately resulting in component seizure.

If this situation occurred in the internal combustion engine, it would first lead to audible knocking noises, then to a reduction in power output, and finally to the failure of the component concerned.

To overcome these problems, the two surfaces must be separated by a film of oil (B). It is the function of the 'force-fed' lubrication system to maintain a film of oil between all moving engine components under all operating conditions.

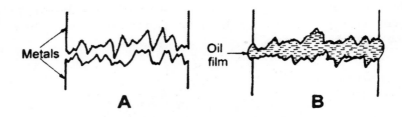

Force-fed lubrication systems are generally of the 'wet-sump' type in which the sump acts as both an oil drain return and a storage container. A pump draws oil from the sump and forces it through a filter up into the engine to lubricate all moving parts. Provision of a dipstick enables the level of oil in the sump to be checked. It is vital that the oil level does not drop too near or under the low mark. Should this happen, the moving parts of the engine are starved of the lubrication and protection they need.

An oil level that is too high can result in 'foaming' of the oil, so that air enters the lubrication system, causing inconsistent oil pressure. Excess oil splash on to the cylinder bores can also give rise to an increase in oil consumption.

It is essential that the engine oil and oil filter are replaced at the manufacturer's recommended service intervals. Failure to carry out this fairly basic service will cause unnecessary engine wear and tear.

An oil pressure gauge or oil pressure warning light indicates a condition of low oil pressure. Should this occur, the engine should be switched off immediately.

Faults

- Excessive oil consumption: oil level too high, wrong grade of oil, worn engine components.
- No oil pressure: low oil level, worn/faulty oil pump, blocked oil ways and/or filter.
- Low oil pressure: low oil level, wrong grade of oil, worn/faulty oil pump, very high oil temperature, worn engine components.
- High oil pressure: wrong grade of oil, faulty oil pump.
- Oil leaks: Worn and/or faulty seals and gaskets; oil level too high.

The cooling system

The principle of the petrol engine, which derives its power from the combustion of fuel and air, necessitates the use of some type of cooling system in order to keep the engine's components at an acceptable working temperature.

A typical water-cooled engine comprises a radiator, a water pump driven by a drive belt from the crankshaft, a series of passages running through the engine and a thermostat. Water is pumped from the radiator, up through the engine

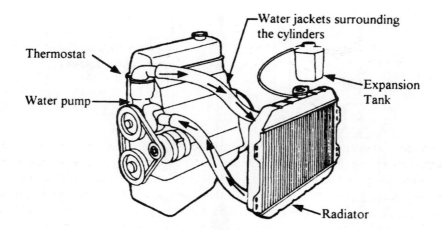

past the thermostat and back into the top of the radiator, where it is cooled by the fan and the natural air flow as the car is being driven. Cooled water from the radiator then flows back into the cylinder block.

Driving school cars in particular do a lot of manoeuvring and slow driving work where there is very little natural movement of air through the radiator to cool the system. Under these circumstances, additional air flow is provided by an electrically operated fan that only functions when a predetermined engine temperature is reached.

Faults

- Engine overheating: water level low, loose or worn drive belt, faulty thermostat, blocked radiator matrix, collapsed radiator hoses, ignition timing incorrect, vehicle overloaded or brakes binding.
- Overcooling: thermostat faulty (jammed open), electric cooling fan continuously operating (faulty thermostat switch).
- Coolant loss: worn out hoses or loose clips, leaking radiator, water pump or core plugs, failed cylinder head gasket, cracked cylinder head or block,

The Transmission System

The transmission of a car consists of a clutch, a gearbox and a final drive unit. Their combined purpose is to transmit the drive from the engine through to the road wheels. Conventionally, cars have an engine and gearbox at the front, with a propeller shaft relaying the drive to the rear wheels via a rear axle unit.

A more common layout is a system in which the engine, clutch and gearbox are in one unit driving the front wheels. This design allows more space for passengers and tends to give improved handling and control. However, it requires more complicated engineering, including the use of drive shafts fitted with constant

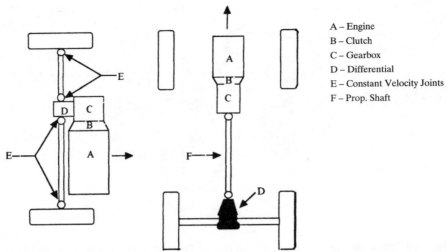

A – Engine
B – Clutch
C – Gearbox
D – Differential
E – Constant Velocity Joints
F – Prop. Shaft

velocity joints (CV). These ensure the smooth transmission of power to the drive/steered wheels throughout all wheel movements.

Clutch

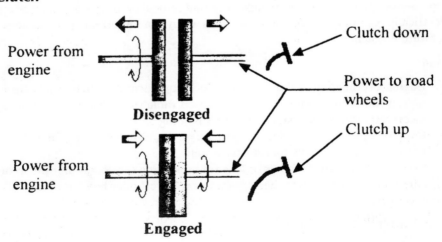

Power from engine

Clutch down

Power to road wheels

Disengaged

Power from engine

Clutch up

Engaged

The clutch enables the engine to be disconnected from the transmission in order to engage or disengage the gears. It provides the means for a smooth engagement of the drive between the engine and the road wheels, and it also enables the car to be controlled at a crawling pace.

The clutch consists of three main parts: a release bearing, a spring-loaded pressure plate and a centre plate. At the back of the engine there is a flat, heavy wheel called the flywheel, which is attached to the crankshaft and revolves at the same speed as the engine.

The clutch centre plate comprises a friction material similar to a brake lining. It is connected to the transmission and held firmly against the flywheel by the pressure plate. When the engine is turning, the clutch is also turning.

When the clutch pedal is depressed, the pressure plate is pulled away from the flywheel, thus freeing the centre friction plate and disengaging the drive. When the pedal is released, the centre friction plate is forced by the pressure plate against the flywheel, and the drive between the engine and transmission is complete.

Partially engaging (slipping) the clutch allows the car to be controlled at a crawling pace. A release bearing is situated behind the pressure plate and provides the means to allow the pedal linkage to operate the clutch.

Faults

- Clutch slip: (no or little power is transmitted when a gear is selected and the clutch pedal is fully released): incorrect clutch linkage adjustment, worn out clutch components, oil contamination of clutch friction faces, riding the clutch (resting foot on clutch in normal driving).
- Clutch judder: worn out rubber engine and gearbox mountings, distorted, damaged or worn clutch components, oil or grease contamination of clutch friction faces.
- Drag or spin (clutch fails to disengage fully when pushed down completely): incorrect clutch linkage adjustment (excess clearance), distorted, damaged or worn clutch components, oil or grease contamination of clutch friction faces.
- Noisy operation: worn or faulty release bearing (noise on disengaging clutch), worn or faulty spigot bearing (noise engaging clutch), worn or damaged clutch components.

Gearbox

The purpose of the gearbox is to enable the car to be driven at varying speeds with the minimum strain on the engine. Lower speeds and harder work will call for lower gears, while for normal cruising a higher gear should be selected.

The modern gearbox has four or five forward gears and a reverse gear. It also has a neutral position that disengages the engine from the road wheels. All forward gears have a synchromesh mechanism that allows changing from any one gear to another to be accomplished quietly and smoothly. Very simply, it synchronises the speeds of the gears to be engaged before actually coupling them together.

Lubrication in the gearbox is as essential as it is in the engine. Most gearboxes have a filler/level plug on the side that allows the oil level to be checked at regular intervals. Failure to maintain the correct level of oil could lead to overheating and unnecessary wear and tear.

Faults

- Noisy or difficult gear selection: faulty or worn synchromesh units, clutch drag.
- Jumping out of gear: worn or faulty synchromesh units, worn out gear selector mechanism.
- Noisy operation: worn bearings, damaged or worn gear teeth.
- Oil loss: worn gearbox oil seals, damaged or broken gearbox gaskets.

Automatic transmission

Most modern automatic transmission systems use a torque converter, together with an epicyclic gearbox. This enables the system to take up the drive smoothly and for gear changes to be made automatically with the power on. A control system determines when a gear change is needed by sensing and comparing the speed of the vehicle with the amount of acceleration. The driver can override the system by changing, for example, to a lower gear by pressing hard on the accelerator (kick down).

Differential units

The differential is comprised of a small unit that is bolted to the crown wheel and pinion assembly that contains a number of small gears. Together they form part of the final drive unit. The differential gears enable the inside wheel to turn at a slower rate than the outer wheel when on a curve.

Sometimes, a 'limited slip' differential is fitted to cars. It is a device that allows normal differential action of the driving wheels when cornering, but prevents loss of traction in the event of either driving wheel losing adhesion. Its action therefore affords the driver better vehicle control under slippery road conditions.

Faults

- Noisy operation: worn out final drive gears, lack of lubrication (check oil level).
- Oil loss: worn oil seals, broken or damaged gaskets, oil level too high.

Exhaust system

An exhaust system is installed for the purpose of collecting burnt gases issued from the engine cylinders and discharging them outside the vehicle. A series of silencers ensure that the gases are exhausted without excessive noise. Exhaust emission consists of a mixture of carbon monoxide (CO), carbon dioxide (CO_2), hydrocarbons (HC) and oxides of nitrogen (NO_x), some of which are harmful to the environment.

To reduce the level of these pollutants, some engine exhaust systems include a catalytic converter.

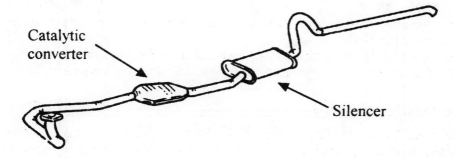

Catalytic converter

Silencer

The catalytic converter functions by providing an additional area for continued burning of HC and CO. HC and CO burn completely (or are converted) to water vapour nitrogen (N) and carbon dioxide (CO_2).

The fuel used in cars equipped with catalytic converters must be lead-free. If lead coats the internal elements of the converter, its effectiveness is greatly reduced.

Precautionary measures

- Use only unleaded petrol.
- Do not use fuel additives.
- If difficult cold starting is experienced, contact dealer as soon as possible.
- If engine misfires, contact dealer as soon as possible.
- Do not use oil additives.
- Allow the engine to return to idle before switching off.
- Keep to the recommended service intervals.
- Never push or tow start the vehicle.
- Avoid running out of fuel.
- Avoid leaving the engine idling for long periods.
- Do not park or drive over inflammable materials.
- Exhaust gas is very hot; keep away from the tailpipe.

Exhaust turbocharging

A turbocharger is a device that uses the exhaust gases to turn an air pump or compressor that forces an increased amount of air into the engine cylinders. If a corresponding amount of fuel is then added, a large increase in engine power will be obtained. Both petrol and diesel engines can use a turbocharger.

Brakes

Most modern cars use a combination of disc brakes on the front wheels and drum brakes on the rear. Disc brakes are more efficient than drum brakes owing to the

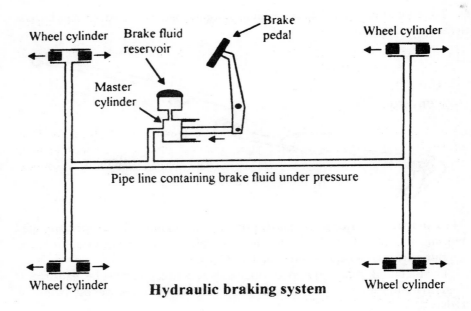

Hydraulic braking system

improved flow of cooling air over the discs. When the foot brake is applied, a hydraulic system multiplies the pedal pressure. Pistons located inside a caliper squeeze the disc between two friction pads, thus providing the braking force required to slow the car down.

Drum brakes work on the same friction principle, but wheel cylinders expand the brake shoes outward against a rotating drum in order to provide the braking force. Drum brakes, being enclosed, are not so easily cooled by an air stream, and generation of excessive heat may result in a condition known as 'brake fade'.

The hydraulic system consists of a master cylinder and a fluid reservoir, connecting pipes, hoses and wheel cylinders. Foot brake pressure is transmitted directly from the master cylinder and applied to the brake shoes and disc pads. This action ensures that the vehicle will pull up smoothly and in a straight line.

All modern brake systems are of the 'divided line' type, where the addition of a second brake line and a special master cylinder (tandem) ensure that in the event of a failure of either line, at least two wheel brakes remain in service.

Faults

- Excess pedal-free travel: drum brakes need manual adjustment. Drum brake automatic adjusters not working. Excess disc hub bearing end float. Distorted discs.
- Brake pulling to one side: other side shoes or pads contaminated. Other side-wheel cylinder piston seized. Other side caliper piston seized.
- Pedal feels spongy: air trapped in system.

- Pedal sinks slowly: external leakage from hydraulic system. Faulty master cylinder seals.
- Brakes binding: drum brakes over-adjusted. Wheel cylinder piston seized. Caliper piston seized.

Handbrake

The parking brake or handbrake is a separate braking system from the foot-brake. It is mounted usually on the floor of the car and is connected by cable to the two rear wheels. Care should be taken when applying the brake to squeeze the pawl, thus saving unnecessary wear and tear on the ratchet.

Faults

- Excess travel: cable or rear brakes need adjustment. Worn handbrake mechanism.
- Rear brakes: binding seized handbrake mechanism.

Anti-lock braking system (ABS)

Increasingly being fitted as standard equipment, these systems provide near optimum braking under most prevailing road conditions. When braking on wet or icy roads, the system virtually eliminates the tendency for wheels to lock up. This means that braking efficiency is used to the maximum, so that very short braking distances can be achieved (it does not make the brakes more efficient). By preventing the wheels from locking, ABS also assists directional control during braking when cornering.

To prevent the wheel from locking, the system provides pressure modulation in the braking circuits. Sensors fitted to each wheel monitor the rotational speeds of the wheels and are able to detect when there is a risk of wheel locking. Solenoid valves are positioned in the brake circuits to each wheel, and these valves are incorporated in a modulator assembly, which is controlled by an electronic control unit (ECU). The ECU controls modulation of the braking effort applied to each wheel, according to the information supplied by the wheel sensors.

Should a fault develop in the system, a self-diagnostic facility is incorporated in the ECU, which can be used in conjunction with special diagnostic equipment that is available to a dealer, to determine the nature of the fault.

The braking system components used with ABS are similar to those used on models with a conventional braking system.

Although ABS provides a major contribution to vehicle safety and driver control, it does not remove the need for responsible driving and awareness of prevailing road conditions.

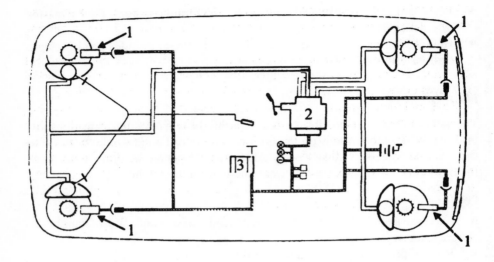

1. Wheel sensors
2. Actuation assembly
3. ABS module

Rack and pinion steering gear

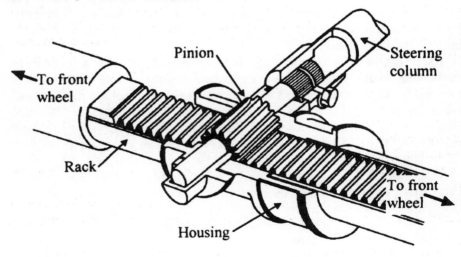

Steering

The steering system is used to control the direction of the vehicle. It is designed to control the front wheels over all types of road conditions, through turns and at different speeds. It comprises a linkage system that is attached to the front wheels, the steering wheel and the steering gear. Manual and power steering units are used.

'Rack and pinion' steering is the most popular system used on front-wheel drive cars. The system is used in conjunction with MacPherson strut suspension that gives more engine compartment room for transverse-mounted engines.

Rack and pinion steering consists of a flat gear (the rack) and a mating gear called the pinion. When the steering wheel and shaft turn, the pinion meshes with the teeth on the rack. This causes the rack to move left or right in the housing. This motion moves the remaining steering linkage to turn the front wheels. This system is very practical for small cars that require lighter steering capacity. It is a direct steering unit that is more positive in motion (less lost motion) than steering box/steering linkage systems.

Suspension

The suspension system of a car is used to support its weight during varying road conditions. The suspension system is made up of several sub-systems. These include the front and rear suspensions assemblies and the shock absorbers. All these systems must work together in order to control three different types of body movement – bounce, roll and pitch. Bounce occurs when a car hits a bump or dip in the road. Roll is produced when cornering, particularly at speed, when centrifugal force causes the car to lean away from the centre of the curve – ie, the car leans to the left when you are trying to steer to the right. In extreme cases, a car will roll over. Pitch is the reaction of the rear wheels following the front wheels over a bump. As the front of the car rises, the rear dips; as the rear wheels strike the bump, the front of the car drops, causing a forward and backward movement, similar to a ship pitching in and out of waves.

The suspension assemblies incorporate springs that are interposed between the wheels and the body so that the body is partially isolated from the axles. When a vehicle rides over rough ground, the wheels rise as they roll over the bump and deflect the springs. The energy created as a result of the movement is momentarily stored in the spring and is then released as the spring returns to its original length (rebound). Various types of spring can be utilised – eg, leaf, coil or helical, torsion bar and gas springs.

The suspension design of most modern cars provides for the inclusion of independent front- and rear-wheel suspension systems. These ensure optimum handling and ride comfort.

Several car manufacturers now offer 'active' ride control systems that allow the driver to switch between 'normal' and 'sport' suspension settings. One such system utilises a hydro-pneumatic springing medium that is controlled electronically via sensors. The 'normal' setting provides maximum comfort and adapts automatically to driving and road conditions. The 'sport' setting provides a stiffer suspension that is more suited to a sporting driving style.

Shock absorbers

Shock absorbers (dampers) are fitted between the car's body and axle in order to prevent excessive rolling and bouncing of the body during motion. They also minimise unwanted up and down movement of the wheel and axle when the car negotiates uneven road surfaces.

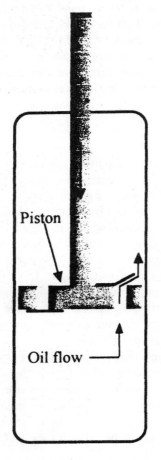

One shock absorber is used on each wheel. Each shock absorber must control one wheel and axle motion. The springs support the body, but the shock absorbers work with the springs to control movements of the car body. The construction of a basic shock absorber consists of an internal piston contained within an oil-filled cylinder. The piston moves with the axle and the resistance to movement produced by forcing the oil through small valves in the piston restricts quick action, preventing a continual bouncing movement.

Faults

● Hard ride: tyres over-inflated. Stiff operation of suspension struts. Excess friction in leaf springs.

● Uneven trim: road spring on front, rear or on one side settled (weak). Broken leaf (if the main leaf is broken, the whole axle unit is partially disconnected from the body). The car should not be driven. Hydrogas suspension loss of fluid pressure, causing collapse of the suspension on either side.

● Noisy operation: worn suspension pivots or mountings. Loose mountings. Defective shock absorbers.

● Poor vehicle handling: worn out or defective shock absorbers. Weak road springs. Worn suspension ball joints. Loose clamping (U) bolts (these clamp the springs to the axle).

Tyres

Basically, there are two types of tyre in use on the modern car – cross ply and radial ply. It is important that a driving instructor understands the difference and value of each.

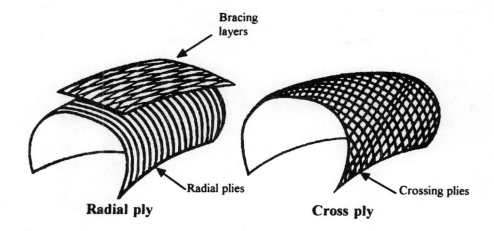

Bracing layers

Radial plies

Crossing plies

Radial ply   **Cross ply**

Modern cross-ply tyres have casings made from plies of rayon, polyester or nylon, laid at opposing angles to each other and at approximately 40 degrees to the circumference of the tyre. They are wrapped around two steel wire hoops or beads which prevent the tyre from stretching and parting from the wheel. The tyre tread, which is moulded to the casing, is manufactured mainly from a blend of synthetic rubbers in order to provide a good road grip, especially in wet weather.

The construction of the radial-ply tyre reduces cornering wear and considerably increases the overall life of the tyre, but this is usually at the expense of a slightly harder ride at lower speeds. It gives greater high-speed cornering grip than a cross-ply of equivalent size.

The cords in the plies run from bead to bead across the crown at right angles, not diagonally as in the cross-ply tyre. This gives great pliability and comfort, but little or no directional stability. Stability comes from the tread-bracing layers, a belt of cords running round the circumference of the tyre beneath the tread. These cords are usually spun from rayon textile or fine steel wire, and are flexible but do not lose their tautness. This firmly restricts any lateral stretching of the tread.

The majority of cars today are fitted with tubeless tyres; these are basically the same as tubed tyres but are made airtight by having a soft rubber lining to the casing, thus dispensing with the need for an inner tube. The main advantage of tubeless tyres is that they are less liable to deflate suddenly when punctured and can be driven without an appreciable loss of air when penetrated by small flints or nails. Statistics show that the risk of tyre failure with a tubed tyre is about three and a half times greater than with a tubeless tyre.

You should ensure that your tyres meet the legal requirements. They should have a tread depth of 1.6 mm throughout the central three-quarters of the breadth of the tyre and around the entire outer circumference.

It is both illegal and dangerous to mix cross-ply and radial-ply tyres on the same axle as they have completely different road-holding characteristics. It is permissible to have cross ply at the front and radial at the back, but it is certainly not recommended.

Faults

- Over-inflation: causes excessive wear along the centre of the tread.

- Under-inflation: causes excessive wear around the outer edges of the tread.

- Serious structural damage: breaks or cuts in the tyre fabric which are deep enough to reach the body cords. Any exposed portion of ply or cord. Any lump or bulge caused by separation of the tyre structure. These faults usually result from heavy contact with the kerb or a foreign body.

- Incorrect wheel alignment: causes wear (feathering) on either the inner or outer edge of the tread.

- Spot wear: unbalanced tyres will cause a steering wheel shimmy, and rapid and uneven tyre wear. Wear in steering and or suspension components may also promote excessive tyre wear.

VEHICLE SAFETY CHECKS

To do the job properly, an instructor should not be worrying about the condition of the driving school car. Both instructor and pupil must have confidence in the knowledge that the car is in a sound condition, both mechanically and bodily. Regular servicing and preventive maintenance are therefore of the utmost importance to an instructor. It is false economy to skimp on car maintenance. Unplanned time off the road causes loss of income as well as the cost of the repair. Cancelling and rebooking lessons causes problems which should not arise if the car is serviced regularly.

Driving test examiners can refuse to conduct a test in a car which their pre-test visual check shows to be in an unroadworthy condition.

Listed below are examples of the regular car checks and services that should be carried out.

Daily Checks

Windows and mirrors should be kept clean and the driver's vision should not be impaired by dangling mascots, badges or self-adhesive 'L' plates. When cleaning, use a solvent to remove any windscreen smears, but avoid damaging the rear window heating-element with any abrasive cleaner. Operation of the lights should be checked each day, with particular attention to the brake lights.

Carry spare bulbs in the car in case of sudden failure. In order to save time in the event of bulb failure, an instructor should consult the manufacturer's manual for instructions on bulb replacement.

There should also be a daily visual check of the car tyres for any cuts or bulges, stones in the tread, etc. Checking the operation of the horn, indicator, screen washers and wipers should be part of an instructor's daily routine.

Weekly Checks

Engine oil level

Make sure that the car is standing on level ground. Remove the dipstick, which is usually situated halfway down one side of the engine, and clean it on a piece of cloth or kitchen paper. Replace it in the dipstick hole, then remove it again and look for the oil mark. The oil level should be between the high (maximum) and the low (minimum) marks. Should the oil be near or below the low mark, up to a litre of fresh oil will be needed to top up to the high mark. Care must be taken not to overfill as this could lead to excessive oil pressure in the engine and cause leaks or damage.

Oil leaks

Oil leaks can be detected quite easily by having a quick look round the engine, gearbox, rear axle and the insides of the wheels. Common places for leaks are drain plugs, oil filters, valve cover gasket or any oil or brake pipe. If the car has a regular overnight parking spot, look for drops of oil on the ground. Any leak inside the wheels could mean a faulty brake cylinder which must receive immediate expert attention.

Cooling system

While the engine is cold, remove the pressure cap from the radiator header/expansion tank. Check the coolant level and top up as necessary with a mixture of water and anti-freeze of the appropriate type and strength. If the water level falls regularly, check for leaks or suspect engine overheating which may require expert attention. Never remove the radiator cap when the engine is hot. High pressure is built up inside the radiator when the engine is running. The steam released when the cap is removed can cause serious scalding.

Brake and clutch fluid levels

Consult the manufacturer's manual for advice on the fluid levels. When topping up brake or clutch reservoirs, always use new fluid. Re-using old brake fluid may damage the brake or clutch systems. Remember that if frequent topping up is required, the fluid must be escaping somewhere. What may be a slight leak one day could be a major loss the next. Never make do with brakes: any suspected fault should receive expert attention without delay.

Windscreen and rear screen washers and fluid levels

It is a legal requirement for screen washers to be in working order and topped up with water. Add a screen washer solvent to the container as water alone is insufficient to clear the combinations of road grit, exhaust fumes, etc that congeal on the windscreen. In winter add a proprietary winter screen wash to prevent the system freezing up. Do not add anti-freeze as this could damage or discolour the paintwork.

Windscreen wipers

Clean the wiper blade rubbers. Dirt and grit stuck on the rubbers could scratch the glass. Renew blades if there is any sign of perishing or brittleness.

Tyre pressures

Check the tyre pressures, including the spare, at least once a week. Don't forget to replace the valve dust-cap. Remove any flints caught in the tread and inspect the side walls for any cuts or bulges. Driving school cars are susceptible to damaged tyre walls as a result of kerbing. Any sign of uneven tread wear should be reported and rectified as soon as possible.

Lights

Check the operation of all lights, including indicator flashers and brake lights.

Battery

Check the electrolite level. Top up if necessary, using only distilled water to about 6 mm above the electrode plates.

Drive belt

Check the tension, look for cuts and fraying. A loose drive belt can affect the operation of the alternator, which may lead to undercharging of the battery. A fan belt is a fairly simple item to replace if it is unserviceable.

Periodically (as per manufacturer's recommendation)

The driving instructor should be able to carry out his or her own daily and weekly vehicle checks. Some instructors may have sufficient mechanical knowledge and experience to tackle the larger services which must be made. It is worth considering further study in this field – for example, evening classes.

Car manufacturers produce handbooks with service recommendations and do-it-yourself advice. There are many good, clear textbooks on this subject, including the *AA Car Duffer's Guide*. The oil companies, like Mobil, Castrol, Shell and BP, produce very good, sound manuals explaining car facts and car care. Vehicle maintenance record sheets are also available and very valuable. The majority of instructors, however, will go to a garage or a professional mechanic. Nevertheless, it is recommended that you should have some knowledge of the work that must be covered by periodic servicing.

Seasonal Checks

At the first sign of winter get the strength of the anti-freeze checked with a hydrometer at a garage. Top up as necessary. If the radiator requires topping up during the winter, use an anti-freeze mixture. In modern cars it is advisable to leave the anti-freeze in all year round as it contains an anti-corrosive additive to prevent rusting in the system. A good quality anti-freeze will keep its strength for about two years, after which the cooling system should be drained, flushed and refilled, using the manufacturer's recommended amount of anti-freeze.

In the springtime the car should be thoroughly hosed underneath to remove all the corrosive salt and sand that has accumulated from the gritted roads.

VEHICLE CONTROLS AND OPERATION

There are three major operating systems in a motor car:

1. *The main controls*: these enable the driver to start and stop the engine and to control the speed, position and direction of the vehicle.
2. *Driving aids*: these assist the driver to see, to be seen by, and to communicate with other road users.
3. *Instrumentation*: this provides the driver with information about the vehicle, how it is functioning and the speed at which it is travelling.

The Main Controls

The steering provides a means of controlling and changing the direction of the vehicle. To operate the steering, keep both hands on the wheel as much as possible and in particular at high speeds, when braking and also cornering. Position the hands at about the 'ten to two' or 'a quarter to three' position. Try to use the 'pull-push' method of steering outlined in *The Driving Manual*, but directional control and accuracy of the steering is the most important objective. The mirror should be used well before changing direction or position in the road. Avoid sudden, jerky movements on the wheel and hold it firmly, but do not grip too tightly. Remember that when cornering, the rear wheels cut into a turn.

The handbrake secures the car when it is parked or stationary for more than a short pause. The handbrake should be used only when the car is stationary, except in an emergency, such as failure of the footbrake system. The ratchet release button should be operated before releasing or applying the handbrake, which is used when parking and also to provide a greater degree of safety and control for some temporary stops. Check that the handbrake is on after entering the vehicle, before starting the engine and particularly before leaving the vehicle.

The gear lever provides a permanent means of disconnecting the engine from the driving wheels (neutral). It also provides a selection of different ratios to allow the optimum and most economical engine speeds to be maintained at all road speeds and load requirements. The gears also provide a means of driving the vehicle backwards. Avoid looking at the gear lever when changing. Use a 'cupped' hand on the gear lever and do not use excessive force when moving the gears.

1st gear: the most powerful, but slowest. Used for moving off, low-speed clutch control and for manoeuvring.

2nd gear: also powerful, but faster than the 1st gear. Useful for rapid acceleration and slow speeds through some hazards.

3rd gear: a faster gear, used for acceleration from over 15 mph. Used for driving through some hazards.

4th gear: the most economical gear, with insufficient power for speeds of
much lower than 25 mph. Used to provide progressive acceleration
from about 25–30 mph and for cruising at constant speeds.

5th gear: used as an aid for cruising at sustained higher speeds.

The clutch temporarily disconnects the engine from the gearbox/driving wheels
to facilitate changing gear and stopping. It provides the means to engage the
power source (engine) smoothly and progressively to the load (the road wheels).

It is operated by the left foot and is used for moving off, low speed control,
changing gear and stopping. Clutch control involves finding and holding the
clutch plates at the first point of contact, the bottom of which is called the 'holding point' and the top the 'driving point'. The full range is called the 'biting
range'. Slipping the clutch is an important part of low-speed control. Excessive
clutch slip over prolonged periods, however, causes undue wear and should be
avoided. Also, try not to rest your weight on the pedal when driving ('riding the
clutch'). Moving off, changing gear and stopping should always be preceded by
mirror checks.

The accelerator (often called the gas) plays a major role in the regulation of vehicle speed. It works by the pedal operating a petrol/air valve which, in turn, regulates the power and speed of the engine. It is operated by the right foot. Any
pedal movement and changes in pressure should be progressive. The response
to pedal movement is more pronounced in the low gears. Changes in speed
should be preceded by use of the mirror.

The footbrake also plays a major role in the regulation of the vehicle's speed. The
footbrake pedal is operated by the right foot. It operates a hydraulic system
which presses high friction material against a rotating wheel disc or drum (similar in principle to a bicycle brake). Any changes in pressure should be progressive. The response to pressure changes on the pedal is immediate. Pressure can
be varied between the barely perceptible up to the point at which the wheels
lock. Braking pressure on bends and corners should be minimised or avoided.
Use of the brake should be preceded by mirror checks. When the brake is
applied, warning lights on the rear of the vehicle are automatically activated.

The Starter Controls

Ignition switch key: a safety and anti-theft device. This activates the engine electrical circuits essential to its operation. It includes an engine cut-out system

when it is switched off. It also activates a number of warning and other electrical circuits. When the key is removed this usually activates a steering lock.

The starter activates the engine via the starter motor. It is usually incorporated into the ignition switch as the final position to which the key is turned. The starter motor should not normally be activated for periods in excess of five to eight seconds. The key should be released as soon as the engine fires. (Some vehicles are fitted with a protection device which will only allow one operation of the starter motor without switching the ignition off.) Before activating the starter circuits, the normal safety checks should be made, ie handbrake on and gear level in neutral.

The choke is used for starting cold engines and during a preliminary 'warm up' period. To operate, pull out fully, operate the starter and switch the engine on. Push the choke back halfway after the first few seconds. Drive off when safe. Return choke fully after the initial 'warm-up' period. There are three main factors which influence the initial warm-up period: the temperature of the engine, the external air temperature and the maintenance of the engine. On a cold winter morning the maximum warm-up period should normally be no more than four or five minutes. On a summery day this may be only a few seconds. (For automatic chokes refer to the manufacturer's handbook.)

Driving Aids

Mirrors: interior and exterior mirrors should be clean and adjusted so as to maximise visibility to the rear and minimise unnatural or unnecessary head movements. Even with the most desirable combination of a large interior and two door-mounted exterior mirrors, there will still be areas to the rear and sides of the car not covered by the mirrors' 'fields of vision'. Before making certain types of manoeuvre these 'blind spots' need to be checked; for example, before moving away from the kerb.

The mirrors should be used at frequent intervals on a continuous and systematic basis to take full advantage of the views afforded by side mirrors. They should be used particularly before any manoeuvre involving a change in speed or direction and specifically well before *moving off, signalling, stopping* and *overtaking*.

Excessively long or staring looks at the mirror should be avoided as these are likely to cause problems with both the steering and forward planning.

Sensible use of the mirrors involves demonstrating an awareness and sympathy for the speed, distance, actions and movement of other road users.

Direction indicators play a major role in a complex system of communication between road users. They are operated by the fingertips, but without losing total hand contact with the steering wheel. They are frequently required for *moving off, stopping, moving to the left or right and turning to the left or right*. Generally they should be used in good time, but some traffic situations require special consideration in the timing of them. They must be correct for the situation and cancelled after use. (Automatic self-cancelling mechanisms are not infallible and it is the driver's overall responsibility to rectify prematurely cancelled signals and to ensure that indicators are switched off after a manoeuvre is completed.)

Windscreen/windows/wipers/washers/demisters/defrosters/rearscreen heater: these play a major role in helping to maintain good all-round visibility for the driver.

The controls vary from car to car (consult the manufacturer's handbook). Avoid using windscreen wipers on dry glass and wiping the insides of windows with bare hands (rings can scratch!). Avoid leaving rear screen heaters on continually when not required. Keep wipers in good condition and the washer bottle topped up with water/solvent. Keep windows clean at all times. Plenty of fresh air inside the car will help to prevent windows misting up. Familiarise yourself with these controls while the vehicle is stationary.

Lights help the driver to see and be seen by other road users. Controls vary considerably from car to car (consult the manufacturer's handbook). Sidelights must be used when parked outside a 30 mph limit or within 10 metres of a road junction at night. Dipped headlights should be used where visibility is reduced by fog, snow or other extreme conditions. High density rear fog lamps should be used in adverse weather conditions when your car might not otherwise be seen by the driver of a following car.

Horn and flashing headlights warn and inform other road users of your presence. Controls vary from car to car (consult manufacturer's handbook). Use of the horn is not permitted between 11.30 pm and 7.00 am in a built-up area or when stationary (except where in danger from another moving vehicle). It should be used sensibly to warn others and not as a rebuke. Try to avoid long 'blasts' of the horn in close proximity to pedestrians but use longer blasts for drivers in motor vehicles. On fast roads, eg motorways, headlamps may be more effective than the horn.

Instrumentation

This group of controls, dials and displays provides the driver with the necessary information on how the vehicle is performing and functioning.

Information displays are becoming increasingly more comprehensive. Most of the information is of great assistance to the driver but some available equipment has yet to be proved useful and may even be found to be counter-productive by causing unnecessary distractions to the driver.

This section is concerned only with essential information and that which can be justified as necessary to the safe and sympathetic use of a motor car.

Speedometer: this is *legally* required to be in working order and should be accurate to an error of no more than 10 per cent. It is an offence to make the mileage recorder read fewer miles than the car has actually travelled. Speedometers are usually marked in graduated scales showing both miles and kilometres per hour. They sometimes incorporate a trip recorder switch which can be set and used to record journey mileages or to calculate petrol consumption. Avoid long staring looks at the speedometer when checking your speed, but where necessary take frequent glances to establish legal status concerning speed limits.

NB: A speed limit means the *maximum* speed permitted for that road, not necessarily the safest!

Fuel gauge: check the fuel level at the start of a journey, remembering some gauges may not be fully reliable. Avoid running on less than a quarter tank of fuel if possible. Ensure that, when topping up the tank, only the correct type of fuel is used. Some vehicles are fitted with dual tanks or reserve systems which include 'changeover' switches.

Vehicles fitted with fuel injection systems normally operate more efficiently and return improved performance.

Unleaded fuel causes less pollution, is generally cheaper than leaded but consumption can be slightly higher.

Petrol engined vehicles can be converted to run on liquid petroleum gas, which requires the fitting of special tanks. When converted, these can run on either petrol or gas.

Where a diesel engine is fitted, do not put petrol into the tank, or allow the fuel to run dry, or it may not re-start without professional assistance.

Where a spare can of fuel is kept for emergencies, it must be suitably marked and have no leaks.

Engine temperature gauge: an internal combustion engine produces mechanical power from controlled explosions (rapid expansion of burning gases) inside the engine cylinders. At precisely the correct time, vaporised petrol gases are ignited by the spark plugs. The force of these expanding gases pushes pistons up and down inside the cylinders. There are usually four of these cylinders, each working in rapid succession and adding continuously to the mechanical power produced by the others.

At a speed of only 30 mph these controlled explosions can be occurring 60 times every second. This generates a tremendous amount of heat which, if allowed to build up inside the engine, would melt the pistons and heat other moving parts until they became one solid mass of scrap metal. These high temperatures require an efficient cooling system if the engine is to operate satisfactorily. Most engines are cooled by water. This is pumped through special channels cut into the engine block to carry the heat away to the radiator where it is then cooled before re-circulation.

The driver requires confirmation that this system is functioning normally. This is provided by the temperature gauge which indicates the normal operating range of temperature. This may sometimes incorporate a separate warning light to provide more visual impact for the driver if the system overheats.

Where an excessive temperature is indicated, the driver should stop and either obtain assistance or rectify the problem before continuing with the journey. The most common causes of overheating are:

- *Broken fan belt:* this normally operates the radiator fan and water pump.
- *Lack of coolant:* water can boil and leak away. Unless the level is checked regularly it may become critical to the cooling system. Also check hoses for leaks and wear.
- *Blocked radiator:* water freezes and will block the radiator with ice during the winter months unless an anti-freeze solution is present in the cooling system. Ice also expands and can crack the engine cylinder block during severe conditions. During the normal course of running, lime scale from hard water sometimes builds up inside the radiator and blocks the water channels.

Oil pressure gauge: without lubrication, an engine can tear itself apart within minutes of driving off. Lubricating oil is forced, under high pressure, along a series of pipes and oilways to all the moving parts. Under extreme pressure, the oil is squeezed between the moving metal-to-metal parts, preventing this damaging contact.

Information about oil pressure is provided by an oil pressure failure light and/or an oil pressure gauge. In the event of a drop in oil pressure, pull up as soon as possible and when safe, to check it. Switch off the engine. Obtain assistance or rectify the problem before continuing with the journey.

Before starting an engine, check that the oil pressure warning system is operational. This can be done by switching on only the ignition circuits and ensuring the oil pressure warning light activates. The light should switch off within two or three seconds of starting the engine. Oil pressure gauges give a more precise indication of oil pressure when the engine is running and sometimes help to pinpoint a problem before it reaches a critical level.

Low oil pressure can be caused by *lack of oil, burst oil pipes, inoperative pump*, or a *very worn engine*.

Check oil levels regularly and look for tell-tale leaks under the car first thing in the morning. Remember too, most cars will use some oil and require topping up between normal servicing.

Brake system malfunction: vehicles are now being fitted with various different kinds of brake warning systems. These can inform the driver of low fluid levels in the system, of uneven pressure in dual-lined braking systems and of worn brake pads. Check these with the vehicle handbook and remember, if the warning systems activate, *stop immediately and obtain assistance*.

Handbrake and choke warning lights: these indicate that the controls are on and in an operating condition. They are intended as a gentle reminder.

Ignition warning light: the ignition warning light is activated when the engine electrical circuits are switched on. Before starting the engine, the system should be checked. This can be done by ensuring the ignition warning light is illuminated when the circuits are switched on and before the starter motor is activated. As soon as the engine starts, the alternator should generate its own electrical supply and the light should switch off.

The alternator is operated by the fan belt. If this fails, the alternator will cease to provide the electrical requirements for the engine and the vehicle will then be running on battery power alone. In this condition the ignition warning light should activate.

A broken fan belt will also cause the engine to overheat (see The Cooling System on page 152). Other causes of the ignition light switching on are *loose wires, burnt out brushes or diodes on the alternator*, and/or *malfunctions in the voltage regulator*.

This does not normally cause any lasting or serious damage to the vehicle but the journey time will be limited by battery power alone. However, there are safety factors which must be taken into account particularly at night and in cold or wet conditions.

Door and seat belt warning/reminders: visual/audible warning systems are sometimes fitted to remind the driver that doors are not properly closed and/or the seat belt is not fastened.

Main beam/sidelights/high intensity rear lights: warning systems are fitted to remind drivers when these aids are operating.

Rear screen heater: a warning system usually reminds the driver that the screen heater is on. Rear screen heaters consume a fairly large amount of electrical power and can cause a heavy drain on the battery during prolonged periods at tickover speeds.

Direction indicators and hazard flashers: these are usually fitted with both visual and audible reminders when the aids are in the operating mode. Hazard flashers should not be used on a moving vehicle.

Automatic Transmission

A vehicle fitted with automatic transmission *should be a safer* car to drive than a manual change, for the following reasons:

1. Both hands are free for the steering of the vehicle 99.9 per cent of the time.
2. Driving an automatic is less tiresome, particularly in heavy and slow-moving traffic.

3. Because of the human error factor in driving, to which we are all suscepti-ble, the automatic car reduces the chances of making an error with a gear or the clutch.

Driving an automatic

One of the problems experienced by people wanting to learn on automatics is that there are not widespread facilities available for tuition, with the result that they are not used to their full potential. Driven correctly, automatic cars provide drivers with as much control over the gears as manual change vehicles. There are certain aspects of driving automatics, however, which the instructor must remember when giving instruction:

1. *The handbrake* is generally required to be used more often and applied more firmly. This is to check the tendency of some automatic vehicles to creep when running at tickover speed.
2. *The footbrake* should be firmly applied before starting some variomatic transmissions fitted to Daf or Volvo cars where the manufacturer recom-mends they are started in gear. This is particularly true when they are 'on choke'. The footbrake should be firmly applied on other makes of automatic transmissions when they are 'on choke' and before drive or reverse gears are selected.
3. *The accelerator* must not be depressed when engaging drive or reverse gears.
4. *Right foot only!* It is advisable to use the right foot only for both the foot-brake and accelerator. There may be some occasions where it is advanta-geous to use the left foot for the brake however – in some lowspeed manoeuvring exercises, particularly if the transmission is not very progres-sive at low speeds.

Disabled drivers

Where a right leg disability is present, the driver may use the left foot for both accelerator and brake (the vehicle will need to be suitably converted).

An automatic gearbox is a tremendous help to disabled clients and older peo-ple – or in fact anyone finding it difficult to drive a manual gear-change car.

The driving test

A person passing the test in an automatic car will only be issued with a driving licence for that type of vehicle group.

Types of automatic transmission

Fully automatic with gear hold position: these have selector positions for forward and reverse with a gear hold for low-speed driving and/or driving downhill.

Variomatic transmission: this type of transmission system is fitted with a hold device which offers a greater degree of engine braking on downhill gradients.

Multi-hold systems: these can retain any particular gear and are fitted to many makes of vehicle from the BL Mini to Rolls-Royce.

Semi-automatic: this generally means the vehicle is fitted with a normal gearbox and clutch but without the clutch pedal. The clutch is engaged or disengaged by the movement of the hand on the gear lever.

Pre-selector systems: on these the gear is pre-selected before it is required. The gear is later engaged by means of a foot pedal in place of the clutch.

Kick down: this is a mechanism fitted to many automatics whereby it is possible to change down quickly to a lower gear ratio, usually for overtaking.

A sharp depression of the accelerator pedal past the full throttle opening will override the normal gear control system.

Using the accelerator: fidgeting on and erratic or excessive use of the accelerator burns fuel wastefully in any car, but in an automatic it will be changing up and down gears according to changes in this pressure. This causes unnecessary wear and tear on the mechanisms involved and should be avoided.

VEHICLE REGULATIONS AND DOCUMENTS

Regulations

There are many laws which lay down the requirements about the way in which cars are manufactured, what equipment they must have and the condition of vehicles when used on the roads.

Most of these rules are contained in the Motor Vehicles (Construction and Use) Regulations. Some of the rules apply only to cars first registered after a specified date; older vehicles may, therefore, not have to include some of the items of equipment mentioned.

Some of the basic rules apply to vehicles of any age. These include the strict rules relating to brakes and steering gear – each part of the braking system and all steering gear must be maintained in good and efficient working order at all times when the vehicle is being used on the road.

The car must be roadworthy. It is sometimes thought the MOT test certificate is a certificate of roadworthiness, but this is not so. The test system looks at the condition of certain main components, but does not necessarily consider the overall roadworthiness of the car.

The regulations contain rules about the dimensions of cars, and about the maximum overhang. The car must have wings or mudguards. The speedometer must work to within an accuracy of plus or minus 10 per cent. Driving mirrors must be fitted, and other compulsory items are: safety glass, windscreen wipers, horn, silencer, seat belts and direction indicators. Lighting regulations are dealt with as a separate section.

Lighting

The regulations require that lights and reflectors must be kept clean and in good working order. They must be maintained so that the vehicle may be driven during the hours of darkness without contravening the regulations.

This chapter includes only a summary of the main requirements, as the original equipment fitted to a modern vehicle will usually comply with the specifications.

Headlamps must be permanently fitted and must have a minimum rating of 30 watts displaying a white or yellow beam. The lamps must be matched and the beam must be capable of being deflected to the nearside so as not to dazzle oncoming traffic.

Sidelamps must be fitted at the front of the vehicle. The two lamps must have a maximum power of seven watts each (or they may be diffused).

Rear lamps must be visible from a reasonable distance to the rear of the car. There must be at least two lamps, each with a minimum power of five watts. Reflectors are also required.

Rear number plate lamp the plate must be illuminated so that the letters and figures are easily legible from a distance of 60 feet.

Direction indicators on cars registered after 1965 must be the amber flashing type. On older cars they may be either flashing or semaphore arm and may be white at the front and red at the rear. Flashing indicators must wink at the rate of 60 to 120 flashes a minute. The indicators on each side of the car must be operated by the same switch and there must be a warning light or audible warning inside the car to show that the indicators are working.

Reversing lamps may be fitted using one or two lamps of not more than 24 watts each. The beam produced must not dazzle anyone 25 feet away at an eye level of 3½ feet from the ground and must only be used when the car is reversing. The lights may be operated automatically when reverse gear is selected or may have a separate switch which includes a warning light.

Fog lamps are to be used as two front fog lamps (or one fog lamp and one headlamp) in darkness and fog, falling snow or conditions of poor visibility. The lights must be placed symmetrically and must be placed more than two feet from the ground unless they are to be used only in fog and falling snow.

Rear fog lamps are obligatory on cars first used on or after 1 April 1980. If one lamp is fitted it must be positioned on the offside of the car, and if two are fitted they must be symmetrical. Rear fog lamps may only be used during adverse weather conditions and when the vehicle is in motion, or during an enforced stoppage.

Stop lamps are compulsory on cars built since 1971. The lamps must be matched and placed symmetrically at the rear of the car. They must operate automatically when the foot brakes are applied and show a steady red light visible from the rear.

During the hours of darkness a vehicle must display:

- 2 headlamps (when the vehicle is driven on unlit roads);
- 2 side lamps;
- 2 rear lamps;
- 2 red rear reflectors;
- 1 or 2 rear fog lamps (for vehicles after 1 April 1980).

Headlamps must be used when the vehicle is being driven on unlit roads (ie a road where there are no street lights or on which the street lamps are more than 200 yards apart). Headlamps must be switched off when the vehicle is stationary (except traffic stops).

During daylight hours headlamps must be used when travelling in conditions of poor visibility such as fog, smoke, heavy rain, spray or snow. If matching fog or spotlights are fitted, these may be used in the place of headlights.

Parking lights at night A car or light goods vehicle may park at night without lights if the following conditions apply:

1. The vehicle is parked on a road with a speed limit not exceeding 30 mph.
2. No part of the vehicle is within 10 metres of a junction.
3. The vehicle is parked with its nearside close to, and parallel with, the kerb, except in a one-way street.

The lighting regulations also permit a vehicle to park without lights in a recognised parking area, and within the confines of an area outlined by lamps or traffic signs. If these conditions are not met, lights must be shown (ie side and rear lights).

Dim-dip lights New vehicles registered from 1 April 1987 must be fitted with a dim-dip device which causes 10 or 15 per cent of the dipped beam intensity to show when the engine is running (or the ignition is switched on) and the sidelights are on.

Hazard warning lights may be used only when the vehicle is stationary for the purpose of warning other road users that the vehicle is temporarily causing an obstruction or to warn following drivers on a motorway that there is a hazard ahead.

Parking

Common law states that a public highway is specifically for the free passage of the general public and vehicles, and there is no legal right to park on the road except in specially designated parking places or with the express permission of a police officer or traffic warden. There is no legal right even to park outside your own home. A stationary vehicle in the road or on the grass verge is technically an obstruction, even where no other road user is inconvenienced.

It is a more serious offence to park a vehicle in a position where it might constitute a danger to others. (See *The Highway Code* for examples of what might be considered dangerous parking.) Parking within the zig-zag lines at a pedestrian crossing is an offence punishable by an endorsement. It is illegal to park on an urban clearway at the stipulated times and on a rural clearway and motorway at any time.

Parking in Controlled Zones A controlled parking zone is indicated by waiting restriction signs situated on all entrances, and is marked with yellow lines along the kerb. Restriction times vary from town to town and care should be taken always to read the signs. Parking meter zones are marked with signs 'Meter Zone' and 'Zone Ends'. It is an offence to park at a meter without paying or to overstay the time paid for, or to feed the meter on return for an extended period.

Use of horn and flashing headlamps

1. Motor vehicles must be fitted with an instrument capable of giving audible warnings of approach. The tone of the horn must be continuous and uniform, with the exception of emergency service vehicles which may use a two-tone horn, siren or bell. Some goods vehicles are permitted to use an instrument to announce goods for sale, but the vehicle must also carry the standard audible warning device.
2. The horn should be regarded as a warning instrument. It should not be used in order to assert a right of way and should not be used aggressively. There are some legal responsibilities regarding the use of the horn. It must not be used when the vehicle is stationary on the road, except to avoid danger due to another vehicle moving, and may not be used in a built-up area between the hours of 11.30 pm and 7.00 am.
3. The flashing of headlamps has the same meaning as the horn. It is an indication of your presence to other road users. The lamps should not be used to tell other people what you intend to do, or to tell them what to do.
4. Flashing headlamps can be useful in certain driving conditions – high speed roads and where there is a high level of noise – but should not be regarded as an indication of another driver's intentions. The signal may not be directed to you but someone else.

Noise and smoke

There are very detailed rules regarding the maximum number of decibels that may be emitted from a car, and it is an offence to drive a car which does not conform to those rules, or to cause a nuisance by making unnecessary noise. It is also an offence to use a motor vehicle which produces smoke, vapour or sparks which may damage or affect other road users and property. Smoke which affects the visibility of other road users is regarded as excessive.

Seat belts

The law requires that seat belts are fitted to all the seats of new motor cars, that they should be maintained in good order and conform to the regulations.

The use of seat belts may be an important factor in the assessment of compensation by a court. Recent cases have shown a reduction in the amount of compensation awarded to non-users of seat belts.

Front seat belts are compulsory on cars and three-wheeled vehicles made after 30 June 1964 and first registered after 31 December 1964 and on light vans made after 31 August 1966 and first registered on or after 31 March 1967. Rear seat belts must also be used.

The use of seat belts by drivers and passengers is compulsory. The maximum penalty for failing to wear a seat belt is £500. Drivers are not responsible in law for the non-use of belts by adult passengers.

There are several exemptions provided in the regulations. For example you do not have to wear one under the following circumstances:

1. When driving and carrying out a manoeuvre which includes reversing.
2. If you hold a valid medical exemption certificate.
3. When you are making a local delivery or collection round using a specially constructed or adapted vehicle.
4. If a seat belt has become defective on a journey, or previously, and arrangements have been made for the belt to be repaired.
5. If an inertia reel belt has temporarily locked because the vehicle is on, or has been on, a steep incline. The belt must be put on as soon as the mechanism has unlocked.
6. If you are an instructor supervising a learner who is carrying out a manoeuvre including reversing.
7. A driving test examiner need not wear a seat belt if he feels that the wearing of a belt would endanger him or someone else.
8. When driving a taxi during normal taxi-ing work, so long as the vehicle displays a plate showing it is licensed as a taxi.
9. While driving a private hire vehicle displaying a plate showing it is licensed as such, or that it is licensed at the Hackney Carriage rate and while used for that purpose.
10. If you are driving or riding a vehicle displaying trade plates and you are looking into or repairing a mechanical fault.

Other exemptions apply to people in special jobs and in certain circumstances, for example the police.

Children under the age of 14 travelling in the rear of cars should be restrained where an approved restraint is available. The essential point is that the seat belt or restraint should be appropriate for the age and weight of the child. The law does not require that all children in the rear of cars should be restrained, only that if an appropriate device is available it should be used. An appropriate child restraint is deemed available if carried in or on the vehicle where there is space for it to be fitted without the aid of tools. Children can be exempt from the regulations on medical grounds.

Seat belt pre-tensioner

The front seat pre-tensioner seat belt works together with the seat belt retractor. It helps to tighten the seat belt when the vehicle is involved in certain types of frontal collisions. The front seats are fitted with a sensor which, in the event of an accident or rapid deceleration, will activate an explosive device to retract the seat belt, providing greater support for the front seat occupants.

Supplementary restraint system (airbag)

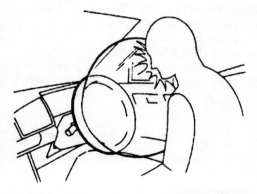

The airbag is designed to supplement the accident protection provided by the seat belt and to reduce the possibility of injury to the head or upper torso in the event of a frontal collision. The seat belt should be worn correctly and the driver should be seated a suitable distance from the steering wheel to enable the system to function effectively. The air bag is located in the centre of the steering wheel and will deploy under a moderate to severe frontal collision; minor frontal, side, rear impact or the vehicle overturning will not activate the airbag. When the airbag system receives a signal from a G-sensor, the airbag inflates as a result of the combustion of a fuel tablet which generates nitrogen gas. The airbag absorbs the impact of the driver's head on the steering wheel and then deflates at a controlled rate. Since the airbag deploys quickly in order to protect the driver, the force of the airbag deploying can increase the risk of injury if the driver is too close to or against the steering wheel during deployment. A self-diagnosis system monitors the entire system. If a fault occurs, the self-diagnosis system switches on an SRS function light (red) on the instrument panel or steering wheel. It is *absolutely forbidden* for unauthorised persons to tamper with, or attempt repairs to, the airbag system.

Mirrors

All new motor cars must be fitted with two rear-view driving mirrors – one inside, the other mounted on the exterior offside. Interior mirrors must have protective edges to minimise the risk of injury in the event of an accident. This regulation also applies to the dual mirrors used by driving instructors.

Windscreen washers and wipers

The law requires that all windows are kept clean so that the driver has an unobscured view of the road. This includes keeping the windscreen free of stickers, novelties and mascots. There is a legal requirement for automatic windscreen wipers capable of efficiently cleaning the screen. The driver must have an adequate view of the road in front of the vehicle and in front of the nearside and offside of the vehicle.

There must also be windscreen washers which work in conjunction with the wipers.

Vehicle defects

Under the Vehicle Defect Rectification Scheme (VDRS) some minor vehicle defects such as lights, wipers, speedometer, silencer may not result in a prosecution if the driver agrees to participate in the following procedure:

1. A VDRS notice is issued.
2. The defect must be rectified within a limited time.
3. The repaired vehicle and the VDRS notice are presented at an MOT garage.
4. The MOT garage issues a certification that the defects have been rectified.
5. The certificate is then sent to a local Central Ticket Office.

Failure to follow the correct procedure will normally result in a prosecution.

Documents

Registration document

A motor vehicle must not be used on the road until it has been registered by the Driver and Vehicle Licensing Authority (DVLA). When a vehicle is first registered, a registration document (form V5 – occasionally called a 'log book') is issued in which the appropriate details are listed. The DVLA will also issue a 'registration mark' for use on the number plates of the vehicle.

The document should normally be kept in a secure place away from the vehicle. The registration document is not in itself an indication of the ownership of the vehicle. It is issued to the 'registered keeper' of the vehicle. Should a registration document be accidentally lost, destroyed or defaced, application for a duplicate can be made to the DVLA, Swansea, for a fee of £2. Any alterations to the registered particulars of the vehicle should be notified immediately.

Vehicle excise licence (tax disc)

Application for vehicle excise licences can be made to the DVLA, Swansea, or to the local vehicle licensing office in whose area the vehicle is normally kept. The following conditions apply:

1. Licences are valid for either 12 months or 6 months. The current rate (April 2001) for a car is £160 per annum, with a rebate of £55 for cars with a small engine capacity.
2. Duty must be paid if you 'keep' your vehicle on a highway, even if the car is never driven.
3. You must renew the licence before it expires. A reminder is usually sent by the DVLA when the current licence is due to expire, and this reminder may be used as an application form so long as all the particulars shown on the registration document are still correct.

When applying for a new licence the following documents are required in addition to the registration document and the appropriate fee:

1. Valid certificate of insurance.
2. Department of Transport test certificate (if the car is more than three years old).

Where the vehicle is kept on a public road, application for renewal of the excise licence must be made before the expiry of the old one. Where a new licence has been applied for before the expiry date of the old one, there is a legal defence against the offence of failing to display a current licence. A vehicle cannot be used or kept on the road within this period unless application was made before the expiry date of the old excise licence.

Renewals may be made at any main Post Office. When the licence disc has been issued, it should be displayed on the windscreen nearside so that all particulars are clearly visible from that side of the road. A licence may be surrendered for any *complete* months unexpired and must be posted to DVLA before the beginning of the month for which the refund is being requested. There is no refund for parts of a month.

MOT test

Most small cars, small goods vehicles and passenger vehicles are subject to an annual test starting three years after the date of the original registration.

Testing is carried out at designated garages which display the sign of three white triangles on a blue background.

The test requirements include brakes, lights, steering, stop lamps, tyres, seat belts (correct fitting, condition and anchorage points), direction indicators, windscreens, windscreen wipers and washers, exhaust systems, audible warning instruments, bodywork and suspension (in relation to braking and steering). A vehicle which passes the test is issued with a test certificate which is valid for one year. The certificate has to be produced along with other documents when applying for a vehicle excise licence.

A vehicle which fails the annual test but which is left at the testing station for rectification of the faults does not incur a further fee for retesting. A fee of half the original is charged when the vehicle is removed and then returned for the necessary repairs to be carried out within 14 days of the original examination.

The certificate lasts one year. The car may be taken for test within a month before expiry. Where a certificate has expired, you may drive to and from a test appointment without a certificate providing that the car does not have a serious fault which would contravene the Construction and Use Regulations.

The certificate must be produced when applying for a vehicle licence, and on the request of a police officer.

MOTOR VEHICLE INSURANCE

Compulsory motor vehicle insurance was introduced in 1930. It was decided that insurance was necessary to make sure that people who were injured in a road accident were not left uncompensated. Property damage should be included within the *minimum* insurance and this cover is required by the Road Traffic Act 1988.

Other types of insurance policies have been in operation for many years, as it is recognised that there is a need for more cover than the minimum requirements of the Road Traffic Act.

Types of Insurance

Compulsory insurance

Users of motor vehicles must be insured with an authorised insurer against third party risks. The cover must include compensation in respect of death, injury to another person and also the cost of any emergency medical treatment. All passengers must be covered and no 'own risks' agreements are allowed between passengers and the user of the vehicle. This type of insurance policy (which is very rare) is sometimes known as a 'road traffic only' policy, and leaves the user with a vast amount of risk. As an alternative to insurance, application may be made to the Secretary of State at the Department of Transport for a warrant to enable a deposit of £500,000 in cash or securities to be made with the Accountant-General.

Third party property damage is a compulsory requirement under the Road Traffic Act 1988.

Third party insurance only

A 'third party' insurance policy usually requires at least the minimum cover described earlier.

This type of policy would normally cover liability for injuries to other people (including passengers in your car), liability in respect of accidents caused by them (for example – causing injury to a passer-by, or damaging his property by opening a car door), liability for damage to other people's property (eg damage to another vehicle may be paid in full or in part by your insurance company). For an additional fee the policy may be extended to include the risks of fire and theft. An additional premium may be required if the car is not kept in a locked garage overnight.

A 'third party fire and theft' policy offers slightly more than the bare minimum but still leaves a lot of risk with the driver/owner/operator.

Comprehensive insurance

In view of the heavy cost of repairs, most owners these days take out a 'comprehensive' insurance policy. However, there is no such thing as fully comprehensive insurance and care should be taken in reading the small print. The term 'comprehensive' as applied to motor insurance means that a variety and a great deal of protection is provided under one policy document, but does not mean that cover is provided against every conceivable contingency of whatever nature.

Most motorists (two out of three) use this type of insurance cover, which will normally include the risks for third party, fire and theft, together with cover for accidental damage to your own car, medical expenses, and loss or damage to personal effects in the car.

The policy will specify the uses to which the car may be put. For instance, a policy restricting use to social, domestic and pleasure purposes will not provide cover for any business use (including use by a driving school). There may also be a restriction to cover driving by specified drivers only, or it may exclude driving by certain persons.

Other restrictions will vary from one insurance company to another, but it is normal practice for the company to specify an 'excess' when the car is being driven by a young or inexperienced driver. The excess is the amount which you would normally have to pay towards the cost of repairing your vehicle in the event of a blameworthy accident. If the accident was the fault of another driver, you may need to recover this amount from that person. In the case of driving school vehicles, the excess may vary and may be up to £250 depending on who was driving the car (or who was in charge of it) at the time of the accident.

Policies are usually invalidated if the vehicle insured is not maintained in a safe and roadworthy condition. Proof that the vehicle is insured in accordance with the Road Traffic Act is given by insurers in the form of a Certificate of Insurance. The certificate is quite distinct from the policy of insurance itself. It is the certificate which has to be produced when renewing the car licence; it must also be produced to a police officer on request.

Driver's Responsibilities

As a driver you must provide details of your insurance to the person who holds you responsible for an accident which results in damage to their property. The law also requires you to give insurance details following an injury accident.

For your own convenience you should be prepared to give your insurance details following an accident, or to a police officer, who can ask to see evidence of your insurance at any time.

Therefore it is in your interest, as well as those of accident victims, to keep your insurance details to hand when driving. You are advised, however, not to leave them in the car in case they are stolen.

Even with the new insurance requirements, drivers and other road users can find themselves without a source of compensation. This can happen where the accident is nobody's fault, or where you yourself are in some measure to blame. It is for you, as a driver, to consider whether you take out additional insurance cover against such risks as injury to yourself or damage to your own car in these circumstances.

EC Requirements

All UK motor insurance policies must include cover against any third party liabilities which are compulsorily insurable in any other EC member state. The full cover provided under a comprehensive policy can be extended for travel in Europe, if required. A 'green card' is no longer legally necessary but it may be prudent to obtain the card from the insurance company in order to have much wider cover. Possession of the green card can also help to eliminate some of the problems of procedure and language.

We would like to express our thanks to David Bayliss of Kidderminster for his help in updating this chapter. David is experienced in the teaching of mechanics and was inspired to take his ADI examination after reading this book.

6

Driving Theory

Although driving is predominantly a practical skill which can only be fully developed through practice and experience, it nevertheless involves a complex mixture of awareness, skill, knowledge and attitudes. In order to help the new driver, you should be able to identify these and other aspects of driver behaviour.

It is extremely unlikely that 'the perfect driver' exists. However, perfection is something which we should all try to achieve in our own driving. As instructors, we should take a natural pride in our driving and be able to analyse our own performance, as well as being able to criticise constructively the pupil's driving. In striving for perfection we need to recognise some of the main ingredients and characteristics of 'the perfect driver', including elements of skill, knowledge and attitude.

PROFILE OF 'THE PERFECT DRIVER'

Skill

Much has been written over the years on the subject of 'vehicle sympathy'. To the perfect driver, this means being in total control of the vehicle at all times and completely in tune with it – with all movements and actions being smooth, positive and precise. The vehicle will always be in the correct position on the road, travelling at a safe speed for the road and traffic conditions and with an appropriate gear engaged to suit the speed and power requirements. Observation and anticipation – both of which require total concentration – are essential at all times. Perfection in driving requires not only the ability to think for oneself, but often to read effectively the road and traffic conditions so as to help other road users avoid trouble. Too often, a driver's ability is judged purely on the basis of manipulative and control skills. Perfection in these skills alone will not compensate for lack of knowledge or defective attitude.

Knowledge

Obviously, the perfect driver will know and understand all the laws, rules and regulations relating to road procedure. Without this knowledge, even the most skilful driver will not become a complete driver. An understanding of the qualities of a good driver is an additional requirement.

Knowledge is thought to generate favourable attitudes. In driving instruction, as in general education, there is an implied suggestion that the acquisition of knowledge is a factor in generating attitudes which in turn determine driver behaviour.

Attitude

Knowledge of the subject and skill in handling the car are not sufficient qualities in themselves. The knowledge and skill acquired need to be applied in a safe and sensible manner, taking into account errors which other drivers might make and being prepared to make allowances accordingly.

Attitudes have a profound effect on the quality of driving, and although they are relatively easy to define in general terms, they are more difficult to assess in the individual person. The perfect driver is considerate, courteous and tolerant, and never drives in a spirit of competition or takes retaliatory action. In an instructor, these qualities are even more important, as the attitude displayed during the lesson or on a demonstration drive will be transmitted to the new driver.

Attitude is assumed to influence the behaviour of drivers and reckless or unsafe actions are often attributed to negative attitudes. When making a judgement on a traffic situation or another driver, opinions are often not objective. Judgement in any situation may be influenced by attitudes assumed in advance towards a similar event. Attitude tends to make drivers see things not as they actually are, but as they imagine them to be. One of your most important jobs as an instructor will be to develop favourable attitudes in your pupils and change any negative ones they may have.

Motivation describes the personal needs and drives of the individual, ranging from the need to survive to a feeling of well-being and achieving a fulfilment of desires. Motivation can be used in a positive sense to improve driver behaviour. However, it may sometimes cause illogical and potentially unsafe driving. For example, a driver may take risks which are uncharacteristic if late for work or for an important appointment; to get the better of another driver; to demonstrate a superiority of skill; or to gain the admiration of friends.

Emotion is the general term used to describe feelings such as love, hate or fear. Intense emotions like anger, frustration and grief tend to focus the attention of the mind on itself. This lowers the attention on the driving task and limits the perceptive abilities of the mind. Anger may result from an argument; frustration may result from being held up behind a slow moving vehicle; anxiety may be the result of worries about work or other personal problems.

Inexperienced drivers lacking in confidence may suffer from their own, ill-founded fears that they cannot cope. Driving is, in itself, a stressful activity. Deficient knowledge or skill can result in frustration and may generate destructive emotions.

Personality is described as 'distinctive personal qualities'. However, the individual's perception of oneself is different from the personality as it is perceived by others. Personality tends to be inconsistent: faced with different circumstances, drivers may display different sides of their personality. There is some evidence to suggest that extrovert drivers are more likely to be involved in accidents than drivers with a more introverted personality. This may be partly explained by the driver's inability to concentrate on the driving task for longer periods of time.

Perception is the brain's interpretation of information provided by the eyes, ears and other senses. The perception of a particular traffic hazard involves the primary information-processing functions of the brain. This process involves the need to compare existing knowledge and previous experience with the current situation. Hazard recognition requires an active and rapid assessment of the potential risks involved in a particular situation. In order to do this, the driver must anticipate events before they occur. This relies heavily on stored memories of previous learning or similar experiences. Other relevant factors include the driver's personality and levels of arousal, motivation and attitude. Perception is the driver's visual and mental awareness. It provides information on speed, position and timing.

It has been shown that drivers have limited perceptual capacities and that they are frequently faced with an overload of information from the road and traffic environment. A decision has then to be made to attend to some of the available information, and to reject or ignore other aspects of it. New drivers should be encouraged to recognise this discrepancy between the demands of the task and their own personal capabilities.

A more detailed explanation and an analysis of driver behaviour, including the classifications of educational objectives, are given in Chapter 7, Driver Training.

ON THE ROAD

Most driver training is carried out in a car on the road and most driving theory is learnt at home, using *The Highway Code* and *Driving Manual* as learning aids. Because of commercial pressures, there tends to be an over-emphasis in the car on the superficial acquisition of simple skills and routine procedures in preparation for the Driving Test. Since the introduction of the theory test there has been a shift in emphasis towards theory learning based on 'question and answer' books. However, new drivers cannot learn how to handle the car effectively by studying driving theory alone. Equally, they are unlikely to obtain all the knowledge which is needed to develop positive attitudes and awareness skills from in-car practice alone.

Structured training, combining theory and practice, can reduce the cost of learning and may also achieve a higher level of skill and understanding. In-car and in-class training should be integrated in a way which will complement and reinforce one another. Classroom lessons and home study programmes provide instructors with the opportunity to present a wider variety of experiences for new drivers. Producing study units for individual Highway Code rules or sections of *The Driving Manual* relating specifically to what the pupil is learning in the car should result in a better understanding.

Road Sense

Driving is a continuous process of attending to, perceiving and responding to constantly changing needs involving the vehicle, the road layout and traffic conditions. Drivers must continually check, assess and re-assess the hazards and the responses they are making to them. These responses involve the mirror/signal/manoeuvre and position/speed/look routines.

Within the individual elements of these routines drivers should:

- look, assess and decide what action can safely be taken relating to information received from the all-round situation;
- look, assess and decide whether a signal is having the required effect on the actions of following drivers;
- look, assess and decide what effect any changes in position and speed are likely to have or are having on other road users, and decide what further looks may be required.

New drivers should be taught to assess their part in the changing road and traffic environment. For example, they should not only respond to developing situations, but should also see themselves as an active part of those situations, often contributing to them.

Assessing the risks, and deciding on the appropriate response to a hazard, involves a continuous process of assessing and re-assessing the constantly changing traffic situation. This involves:

- assessing the degree of risk;
- deciding on the priorities;
- focusing attention on the most important aspect;
- deciding on a specific course of action;
- responding and re-assessing.

Anticipation is the driver's ability to predict the actions of other road users and is closely linked to visual search skills.

Drivers should know:

- what to expect and the kind of things to look for;
- why, where and when they must look;
- how to see effectively as opposed to just 'looking'.

Risk assessment is influenced by a driver's knowledge and previous experience and may be learnt on a trial-and-error basis or from controlled exercises. Because of lack of experience, a new driver may recognise that there is a bend in the road, but may not think there could be an obstruction hidden from view.

Most collision accidents result from deficiencies in the driver's information processing skills and not from deficient car control. A large proportion of collisions would be avoided if drivers were more aware of the risks involved and knew what to look for and what to expect.

Visual awareness

New drivers tend to look for long periods at only one aspect of the traffic scene and this often results in steering errors and a lack of information on other aspects of the road and traffic situation. An active visual road scan will not only provide more information at an earlier stage, but will also give more time to respond.

The eye movements of experienced drivers are very rapid, moving quickly from one point of interest to another, checking and re-checking areas of risk. Drivers should practise an effective visual search system which involves:

- looking well ahead to steer – this allows you to steer a safe and smooth line;
- keeping the eyes moving – this helps you to build up a more complete picture and improves awareness;
- getting the big picture – looking all around assists with the judgement of speed and position;
- allowing others to see you – position your car where you can see and be seen;
- looking for alternatives – work out an alternative action which may be required if events change.

Hazard recognition

The natural inclination of most drivers is to keep going, unless it is obviously unsafe. New drivers usually need encouragement to actively search the road ahead and assess the safety of proceeding. They should be taught to recognise the consequences of their own actions or inaction. There is a tendency among new drivers to attend to the driving task in a completely passive way. Because they are not actively establishing the safety of proceeding, they tend not to respond early enough to potentially unsafe situations. One of the main aims of the instructor should be to encourage new drivers to obtain as much relevant information about the road and traffic environment as they can. For example:

- To steer accurately and adjust to safe speeds before reaching a hazard, they should be persuaded to look well ahead for bends, gradients, road signs, junctions and obstructions such as parked cars, roadworks and traffic holdups.
- To maintain tyre and road surface friction, encourage them to drive smoothly, approaching hazards at a suitable speed, taking into account weather conditions, condition of the road surface and any camber on bends.
- To anticipate, and act on the actions of other road users, they must be encouraged to scan the road for anything with a potential for moving into or across their path.
- To be able to stop well within the distance they can see to be clear, drivers should identify any blind areas in their field of vision and adjust their speed accordingly.
- To avoid collisions with road users at the sides and rear, drivers should make full use of mirrors and peripheral vision. They should understand the principles of communicating with other road users and of lane discipline.

Making decisions

Lack of experience often results in new drivers making decisions before they have sufficient information on which to base them. Decisions frequently polarise between 'stop' and 'go' where neither is correct. Inadequate information and hurried assessments are often major causes of incorrect decisions. New drivers should be encouraged to make decisions which provide extra time and alternative choices. For example, there may be three possible choices when approaching a parked vehicle with a stream of slow-moving traffic approaching from the opposite direction:

1. It is safe to proceed.
2. It is unsafe at the present time to proceed.
3. More information is needed to assess the situation before a decision can be made.

Any decision – whether to proceed, hold back, give way, or stop – must be continually reassessed. Assessments should be worked out in advance and all options kept open. For example, when approaching a green traffic light, anticipate the possibility of the lights changing and be ready with the decision to stop. At some point on the approach, however, you will be too close to pull up safely. Once this point has been reached, the only decision is to continue. You need to continually re-assess what to do if the lights change – decisions may be made in advance, leaving the response to be triggered by the events.

Response and Control Skills

Communication

Methods of communication between road users are complex and much broader than just traditionally recognised signals such as direction indicators, stop lights, arm signals, flashing headlights and hazard warning flashers.

An effective communication system also involves:

- the lateral position of the vehicle on the road;
- the speed of the vehicle;
- implied signals of intent;
- eye contact with other road users;
- courtesy signals and acknowledgements.

Signalling by position

It is said by some experts that the driver who maintains a correct course and position on the road does not need to signal. Although such statements are not completely valid, they do contain some element of truth. Anticipating an intended act from the vehicle's position or steering line is an important means of communication which should not be ignored.

Correct positioning helps to confirm a signal given by the direction indicators. Where the position does not confirm a direction signal, other drivers may become confused. For example, a vehicle ahead may be signalling left, but if the position is that usually taken for a right turn, others may understandably become confused because they are receiving conflicting information.

Signalling by speed

Speed, and changes in it, are also used by other road users as evidence of intended actions. For example, where a vehicle is signalling to turn left, positioned to turn left and is seen to be appropriately slowing down for the turn, there is a combination of evidence to suggest a left turn will be made. Other drivers and road users are not relying upon one single factor.

Another example of where speed signals the driver's intention to other road users is when a car approaches a junction too quickly to allow it to give way, or perhaps when a car accelerates when it should more appropriately slow down.

By slowing down well before a pedestrian crossing, a driver can clearly signal his intentions to the pedestrians waiting to cross.

Defensive signals

These are the signals a driver might use to warn other road users of his presence. They consist of flashing the headlights or sounding the horn.

Another warning signal is the hazard flasher, which should be used in an emergency situation only.

Implied signals, eye contact and courtesy signals

Not only must drivers learn to recognise and interpret speed and movement, they must also be alert to the conditions of implied or potential movement such as the pedestrians standing at the edge of the pavement near a zebra crossing.

A vehicle waiting at the give way line in a minor road has the potential to move into the path of a vehicle travelling on the main road and should be treated with concern.

Eye contact is another valid form of communication. For example, when slowing down on the approach to, or waiting at, a pedestrian crossing it helps to reassure pedestrians they have been seen. When waiting to pull into a line of slow-moving traffic it often persuades others to wait long enough for you to move out into the traffic stream.

Speed adjustment

The senses used in the judgement of speed are: sight, hearing, balance and touch.

The interpretation of speed can be very misleading at times, particularly in a modern car with sound-insulated interiors. In the absence of vibration and noise on a smooth road with no nearby side features such as buildings, fencing or hedges, speed can seem deceptively slow.

Speed seems to be assessed from a combination of factors which appears to involve an established speed 'norm' learnt through previous experience.

The speed is judged from:

- the rate at which visual images disappear to the sides;
- road, wind and engine noise;
- the sense of balance when changing speeds and direction;
- the general 'feel' of the vehicle on the road;
- comparisons with established 'speed norms';

(These speed norms can be very misleading, for example when approaching the intersection at the end of the slip road after travelling for a long distance at high speeds on a motorway.)

Speed adjustments are required to maintain sufficient safety margins with respect to being able to stop in accordance with traffic conditions, visibility and regulations. These adjustments must take into account the critical perceptual/attention overload limitations of the driver in dealing with the traffic workload.

As speed is increased, the focus point for drivers is further ahead with a corresponding reduction in their field of vision or periphery vision. Where drivers need to attend to foreground detail, speed must be reduced. Periphery vision also assists drivers to judge their speed and position. Failure to reduce speed will result in important risk factors being ignored and reduced awareness of lateral positions and safety margins.

Awareness of position and direction is a perceptive skill developed by practice *and* experience.

Awareness is achieved mainly through an active visual scanning process observing the road and traffic environment in its entirety. The driver steers and positions along a safe course by observing the road geometry, features, signs and markings while visually searching for the movement or potential movement of other road users in order to compensate for them.

Maintaining a correct and safe position not only involves steering, but the driver's awareness and ability to control the speed.

Position

Positioning involves adjusting speeds to maintain an adequate safety cushion between the vehicle ahead and in order that the driver can pull up under control in a precise position along the road as well as laterally when faced with an obstruction.

Positioning with safety and consideration involves:

- the driving position in the road;
- driving in the centre of a lane;
- not changing lanes or lateral position unnecessarily, quickly or unexpectedly;
- allowing sufficient safety cushion between own vehicle and the one ahead;
- allowing sufficient safety margins when passing parked vehicles or other obstructions;
- allowing sufficient safety margins to allow for unexpected movement of other road users;
- selecting safe parking positions;
- manoeuvring into a suitable position at road junctions prior to, or in order to, take effective observations safely before emerging into a new road. (Too far back may mean the driver cannot see, too far forward may be dangerous.);
- positioning correctly when turning in order to cause the minimum of disruption to the flow of other traffic.

Other important aspects of positioning, concerned with maintaining good sightlines and visibility of the road ahead, are:

1. Keeping too close to the left kerb prior to passing stationary or overtaking moving vehicles severely restricts visibility of the road ahead.
2. Holdback position – when giving way to oncoming traffic before passing a parked vehicle, the driver should be prepared to wait well back from, and

well out into, the road to maintain the sightline beyond the obstruction. (Not too far out, however, as to impede the flow of oncoming traffic.)

Other considerations involve:

3. When waiting in a traffic queue, not blocking the access to side roads.
4. When waiting in a traffic queue, not pulling up so close to the vehicle ahead as to be unable to pull out should the need arise.

There is a tendency for many drivers to make commitments before they have sufficient information to reason properly through the problem. It is emphasised that driving is not a series of decisions to stop or go, and there is a particular need in traffic situations to slow down and see without making any definite commitment to stop or proceed while keeping both options open. This is an information-gathering exercise which serves two purposes:

1. It allows the traffic situation (hazard) to develop or clear.
2. It allows the driver more time to reason through the information and choose the best possible moment to make the final commitment to either wait or proceed.

Precautionary measures

In some situations where there is doubt and where a positive response to slow down is necessary to provide more time and information, many novice drivers will react passively and do nothing until a hazard becomes obvious, by which time it is often too late to take any kind of safe action at all. In most of these situations the driver should 'slow down and see'. Failing to take precautionary measures in doubtful situations can only result in extreme measures becoming critical.

These precautionary measures should be taken not only when the driver can see a potential threat, but anywhere when vision is restricted or where there may be an unseen hazard.

Holdback procedure

There are varying degrees of holdback procedure. These range from momentary easing of the accelerator to taking the more active measures necessary to maintain safe options. This is normally achieved through more positive braking control with a view to waiting or holding back from a traffic hazard.

Holdback procedure involves *actively* reducing speed and slowing down with a view to looking, deciding or waiting. Maintaining safe options in moments of uncertainty should almost always be met with some degree of *active* precautionary measure to create a 'safety cushion' relating to speeds, distances and safety margins.

Progress

Whereas the holdback procedure involves slowing down with a view to looking, waiting or deciding what further action is required, powered progress involves the conclusion to proceed as a conscious decision after seeking and considering all the available information. This includes creeping forwards, using first gear/clutch control, in order to look round any obstruction before making a final commitment to proceed.

The appropriate gear should be selected just prior to making the decision to make 'powered progress'. It is emphasised that the gear is only selected with a view to proceeding and not as a result of slowing down. While the gears may be used after reducing speed, it is important that the learner driver associates them with making progress and not slowing down.

Speed Control and Steering The main car control skills involved in driving can be summarised as the ability to decide on:

1. *Making powered progress* This involves moving off under control on all gradients, sometimes using sustained clutch control to hold or achieve low-speed control. This is normally followed by making controlled rates of progress with the accelerator and gears to take account of changing gradients.
2. *Holdback procedure* This involves slowing down by use of deceleration or controlled rates of braking taking into account the varying gradients, possibly leading to stopping and finally securing the vehicle in a stationary condition.

These two procedures alternate according to the road and traffic environment, from one of making powered progress to one of holding back progress. This simplified version of car control is essential to the new driver who will otherwise see driving as an extremely complex and inconsistent series of isolated skills.

New drivers require a thorough knowledge of the skills involved in speed control. In addition they need to understand about the safe use of speed in relation to:

- the acceleration, braking and cornering limitations of the vehicle;
- the qualities of adhesion between the tyres and road surface.

They should also be aware of the overall stopping distances in both good and poor driving conditions and should be able to relate to these in practice.

Encourage your pupils to learn about speed limits. Teach them the necessity of being constantly aware of the speed limit that applies to the road they are travelling on. Confirm that they should always drive at a speed at which they can pull up safely, under control and within the distance they can see to be clear.

You should ensure your pupils are aware of the need to make proper progress in relation to the speed limits and the traffic flow. They should be made aware of the inconvenience and dangers they may cause by driving too slowly and being over-cautious.

All drivers should be aware of the importance of checking what is happening all around (including mirror checks) before any changes in speed are made.

System of Car Control

The natural phenomena and forces that affect the stability of vehicles in motion are scientific facts of which any system of car control must take proper account. The early development of an efficient system helps to provide new drivers with a firm foundation on which to link other skills. It also gives them more time to look for and recognise 'high risk' situations, and to correctly assess their responses to the road and traffic conditions.

Any system taught to new drivers should have a built-in set of safety margins which help compensate for human error, deficient skills, minor lapses in concentration and mistakes made by other road users. An efficient system will ensure drivers have time to control their vehicles in a proper and sympathetic manner.

Many driving instructors incorporate the following tried and tested principles as an integrated part of the system of car control they teach.

1. Vehicle speed should never exceed that which permits the driver to bring the vehicle to a properly controlled stop well within the distance that can be seen to be clear. Drivers should look for and respond to:
   (a) actual obstructions to the intended course;
   (b) the potential of other road users to move out of blind areas behind obstructions, into or across the intended course;
   (c) restrictions to the driver's sightlines caused by road features such as bends, hillcrests and hollows (dead ground);
   (d) potential obstructions which may be hidden by restricted sightlines.
2. Vehicle control and speed should take account of the natural phenomena and forces that affect the stability of a vehicle in motion. Drivers should be made aware of:
   (a) the physical roadholding and handling limitations of their vehicles;
   (b) the tyre and road surface adhesion and increased stopping distances resulting from wet and icy conditions;
   (c) the effects of camber and gravity on hills;
   (d) aerodynamic forces acting on the vehicle.
3. To minimise the effects of the natural phenomena and forces that affect the stability of a vehicle in motion, drivers should:
   (a) apply and remove acceleration, braking and cornering forces smoothly;
   (b) avoid excessive acceleration and/or braking forces when negotiating a curved path;
   (c) avoid changing gear when negotiating severe changes in direction;

(d) avoid unnecessary gear changing. Be selective when changing down, for example: keep both hands on the wheel whilst braking; after slowing down to less than 10 mph and as the braking pressure is being gradually reduced and/or released, change direct from fourth gear to second. Gears enable drivers to maintain efficient engine speeds through a wide range of road speeds and different power requirements. Although in some circumstances gears can be legitimately used as a braking source, the practice is no longer generally considered good driving practice;

(e) keep both hands on the steering wheel when braking and cornering;

(f) keep both hands on the steering wheel when accelerating;

(g) use gentle controlled power when negotiating a curved path. When stationary for more than the time it takes to comfortably apply and then release the handbrake, it should be applied, even on a level road. For example a one- to two-second pause will normally involve the use of the handbrake. Having said this, it should also be stated that experienced drivers rarely come to complete stops for this length of time. By planning their approach to situations likely to require stops, they creep at very slow speeds on the final two or three yards before the stop is required. This often gives the situation time to clear, enabling them to move off again before stopping completely. In such circumstances using the handbrake is inappropriate.

4. Drivers who are sympathetic to the needs of their vehicles not only prolong its working life but make more efficient use of fuel. Drivers should:

(a) avoid unnecessary or fidgety movements on the accelerator;

(b) use the accelerator and/or footbrake early/smoothly;

(c) avoid excessive clutch slip, drag and unnecessary coasting;

(d) avoid excessive tyre wear by cornering at lower speeds;

(e) avoid using gears unnecessarily to reduce speed;

(f) switch off engine while stationary for prolonged periods;

(g) avoid switching the car's interior heating system on before the engine is hot;

(h) avoid additional drag caused by roof signs;

(i) avoid unnecessary loads in the boot;

(j) keep engines properly tuned;

(k) check tyres regularly for uneven wear and pressure;

(l) have brakes and vehicle serviced regularly;

(m) keep a regular eye on the bodywork for corrosion.

Gear-assisted braking

Changing down to reduce speed is unsympathetic to the vehicle, wastes fuel and is not normally acceptable as good driving practice. However, a lower gear can be engaged to offset the effects of gravity on downhill gradients. The brakes should be used first, however, to bring the speed under control before selecting an appropriate lower gear. This provides increased engine braking and reduces the risk of brake failure from overheating due to their continuous use down long hills.

Selective gear changing

To slow down, keep two hands on the wheel and use the footbrake to reduce speed. After slowing down, change down, if necessary, before reaching the hazard, eg:

- Approaching a simple left turn in, say, fourth or fifth gear, use the brake to slow down to less than 10 mph and change direct to second as you are easing the pressure from the brake or after it is fully released.
- Approaching the end of a road in third or fourth gear where your view is restricted, use the brake to slow down until you have almost stopped. Push the clutch down and gradually ease the braking pressure to let the vehicle roll. Just before it stops, change into first gear, ready for moving away.

The power change

This technique permits lower gears to be selected smoothly when travelling at higher than normal speeds. It matches the engine speed to the lower gear and lets them be engaged quickly without the loss of road speed or power. It is beneficial when extra power is needed for overtaking or climbing a hill.

To change, hand on the gear lever and cover the clutch; clutch down quickly, depress the accelerator, release it immediately and select the lower gear; raise the clutch and accelerate as appropriate.

Double de-clutch

This specialised gear-changing technique is generally only necessary in some heavy goods vehicles. Although it is still recommended in some advanced driving manuals, it is inappropriate in a modern vehicle with synchromesh gears. It also increases unnecessary wear on the transmission system.

To change up: hand on gear lever and cover the clutch; clutch down, off the accelerator and move the gear lever to neutral; clutch up quickly and then down again; engage the higher gear; finally raise the clutch and accelerate.

To change down: hand on gear lever and cover the clutch; clutch down, off the accelerator and move the gear lever to neutral; clutch up and depress the accelerator quickly, releasing it immediately; clutch down quickly and engage the lower gear; finally raise the clutch; continue braking/accelerating.

Factors Influencing Stopping Distances

The overall stopping distance is made up of two separate components – thinking distance and braking distance.

Thinking distance is based on the assumption that an average reaction time in normal driving situations (as opposed to an artificial 'emergency stop') is approximately $^2/_3$ of a second – that is, the time between reacting to the emergency and beginning to apply the brakes. This means that, at 70 mph you will travel about 70 feet (or 21 metres) *before* the brakes start to work.

The conversion of speed from miles per hour to feet per second shows that, at a speed of 60 mph with a reaction time of $^2/_3$ second, the 'thinking distance' will be approximately 60 feet. This distance will be proportional over the complete speed range. However, the exact distance may vary from one driver to another and from one situation to another, depending on the driver's health, fitness, reaction and state of mind.

Braking distances are affected by a combination of factors:

- the size and weight of the vehicle;
- the effectiveness of its braking system;
- the type of tyres, their pressure and depth of tread;
- the condition of the road surface.

On a dry road, a car with good brakes and tyres can stop within the distances shown on the chart below. However, stopping distances will be much greater when travelling downhill and are increased considerably on wet or slippery roads.

Shortest Stopping Distances in metres and (feet)

Speed mph	Speed mps (fps)	Thinking distance m (ft)	Braking distance m (ft)	Overall stopping distance m (ft)
20	9 (30)	6 (20)	6 (20)	12 (40)
30	14 (45)	9 (30)	14 (45)	23 (75)
40	18 (60)	12 (40)	24 (80)	36 (120)
50	23 (75)	15 (50)	38 (125)	53 (175)
60	27 (90)	18 (60)	55 (180)	73 (240)
70	32 (105)	21 (70)	75 (245)	96 (315)

It can be seen from the chart that thinking distance increases proportionally with the speed. Braking distance increases much more rapidly – when the speed is doubled, the braking distance is quadrupled! In other words, if you increase your speed from, say, 20 mph to 40 mph in a built-up area, it is going to take four times the distance to bring the car to a standstill.

The cause and correction of skidding

Although the vehicle and road surface condition may contribute to a skid, the main cause is without doubt the driver. There are three different types of skid and they are all caused by:

● excessive speed for the road conditions and/or traffic situation; or
● excessive acceleration, braking and/or cornering forces applied to the tyres; or
● combinations of both.

The rear-wheel skid occurs when the rear wheels lose their grip. It is usually the result of excessive speeds and cornering forces. These may be in association with acceleration or more usually excessive braking force. It is easily and instantly recognised because the rear of the car slides away from the centre of the corner. Uncorrected, the vehicle may turn completely round. It is essential to eliminate the cause, eg release the accelerator and/or footbrake and compensate with the steering. Because the vehicle is pointing in the wrong direction, the driver's natural reaction is normally to steer back on course. There is a danger however, particularly with the quick response of radial tyres, for drivers to over-react and steer back too far.

The front-wheel skid occurs when the front wheels lose their grip, leaving the driver with no directional control. It is usually the result of turning sharply into a corner or bend at excessive speed and/or under hard acceleration or braking. It is recognised when the vehicle fails to go where it is steered. Eliminate the cause and regain steering control by momentarily straightening the wheels and/or reducing pressure on the accelerator or brake.

The four-wheel skid occurs when all four wheels lose their grip. It is usually due to excessive speed for the road conditions or traffic situation, resulting in uncontrolled overbraking. On a wet or slippery surface drivers may even feel they are increasing speed. They are left with no control over direction and the result may be a combination of turning broadside and no response to steering corrections. Steering control can be partially restored by momentarily releasing the brake to allow wheel rotation to recover and then quickly re-applying the brake in a rapid on-off action.

The prevention of skids is better than the cure! It is important to recognise the danger signs early and act on them. For example, slowing down early upon sighting a group of children playing near the road will mean that less braking pressure is needed if one of them dashes out. Concentration, planning and the early anticipation of the possible actions of others is essential. In snow and ice, slow down early with light braking pressure. Gentle braking is less likely to cause skidding than changing into a lower gear. Use gradual acceleration and keep in the highest gear possible without distressing the engine. When going uphill in snow, try to maintain a steady momentum by staying well back from the vehicle ahead.

Drive at safe speeds for the road surface conditions. Accelerate, brake and corner gently. Drive more slowly on wet, icy and slippery surfaces. Watch out for loose gravel, fallen leaves and damp patches under trees. Make sure your tyres are correctly inflated and that they have a minimum of 2 mm of tread all around. Never mix crossply and radial tyres on the same axle.

Keep off soft verges! Read the surface conditions and slow down well before reaching any bumpy parts of the road. Also slow down if the edges are rough and broken. Avoid heavy braking on loose gravel and muddy surfaces and on damp patches under trees. The combination of oil, rubber dust and water can make the surface very slippery after a light summer shower following a long dry spell. In freezing temperatures, remember that black ice forms on exposed bridges first.

Emergency braking

Drivers should be realistic about the distance it takes to stop, particularly in wet conditions. Pivot promptly to the brake and apply it progressively and firmly. Keep both hands on the wheel and try to keep the vehicle on a straight course. Maximum braking force is applied to the vehicle just before the wheels lock; it is most important to avoid braking so hard that the wheels lock, as this will considerably lengthen the stopping distance. Pushing the clutch down too soon will increase the risk of locking the wheels and lengthen the stopping distance. If the wheels do lock, the brake should be released and quickly re-applied.

If too much pressure is applied and the wheels lock up, particularly in wet, slippery conditions, the brake should be momentarily released and then quickly re-applied. This will allow the tyres to regain their grip. This method of rapid on-off braking can be likened to the very rapid on-off action of anti-lock braking systems. It gives the driver greater braking efficiency and increased directional control in emergency situations where the natural reaction is to lock the wheels. This braking technique, sometimes known as 'cadence braking', relies in part on the fact that as the brakes are applied some weight is transferred to the front wheels. The brakes are then released, ensuring that the wheels do not lock.

Reading about the theory of driving will only give you the knowledge of what should be done. In practice, to drive well you will need to:

- exercise self-discipline;
- concentrate all the time and read the road well ahead;
- drive at speeds at which you can stop comfortably within the distance you can see is clear;
- anticipate actual and potential hazards;
- be courteous, patient and considerate;
- apply the controls gradually and smoothly.

As an instructor, your driving should be an example to your pupils. Your aim should be to teach them to drive confidently and to a similar style.

Remember: PRACTISE WHAT YOU PREACH! – try to maintain a good, professional standard with your driving at all times.

Driver Training

In this chapter we deal with the main elements involved in the process of teaching people to drive – how to structure the training, encourage safe attitudes, and develop appropriate teaching and learning programmes. The chapter covers:

- methods of learning;
- teaching and learning;
- the learner's needs;
- skill training;
- structuring the learning;
- syllabus for driver training;
- instructions and terminology;
- adapting your instruction;
- assessing progress;
- 'L' driver errors.

METHODS OF LEARNING

The basic requirements for any effective learning to take place are attention, activity and involvement.

Attention is not a completely conscious activity. Long periods of undivided concentration are difficult to maintain without a break or change in the type of activity concerned.

Activity and involvement (in the task) are vital if the pupil is going to learn efficiently and effectively. Activity should not only be thought of as physical. For example, although learning to drive a car involves a large degree of physical activity, mental involvement is also necessary to initiate the physical responses.

The saying which is often used in general education – **'What I hear, I forget; what I see, I remember; what I do, I understand!'** – is particularly relevant in driver training.

Keeping the novice actively involved in the learning experience will normally result in more being remembered. However, physical activity alone is not sufficient; learners should also be encouraged to think about what they are doing and why!

Learning by Repetition (rote)

Learning by rote, or repetition, is the traditional approach and consists of nothing more than memorising lists, numbers, facts and formulae etc, without requiring any understanding. For example, you probably remember learning your multiplication tables by reciting them over and over again.

Most of us have the ability to memorise information 'parrot fashion'. However, the information can only normally be recalled in the order in which it was learnt. Can you say, without thinking about it, which letter of the alphabet comes before the letter 'R'? You will probably have to break into the alphabet a few letters before the 'R' to answer the question.

Rote is the lowest form of learning and is really only a foundation on which to add more information to give a greater meaning. Some driving skills, such as changing gear, are learnt by rote or repetition – that is, carrying out the physical actions over and over again until they are perfected. These are often referred to in teaching as psychomotor skills – because they involve mainly physical actions.

Learning to Understand (Gestalt)

Learning by the Gestalt method is based on understanding. Understanding can be defined as being able to attach meaning to information.

Learning to drive involves combining physical actions with a knowledge of the rules and regulations and is therefore learnt through the Gestalt method and classed as an intellectual or cognitive skill.

The need for rote and Gestalt

Both methods of learning are important for retaining new information. You may need to teach some basic facts or skills in a rote (memorising) manner in order to help the learner to acquire the basic competence to handle the car. When these basic skills are mastered, you then need to encourage your pupils to extend their knowledge and understanding by analysing the effect their actions have on the vehicle.

What started out as a memorised list of actions begins to take on some meaning. However, it does not imply that this initial 'meaning' will automatically result in an understanding of how to apply the same information to a new situation. You will therefore have to teach the learner how to adapt the skills for moving off, which were initially learnt by rote, in a wide variety of situations; for example, moving off uphill, downhill and from behind parked vehicles.

As an instructor, you will discover that a mixture of the two methods of learning will be required in most situations. It is poor teaching to overemphasise the traditional rote learning method without encouraging learners to understand how and why actions need to be taken. It would be equally as bad to overemphasise progressive learning by allowing them to make and act on their own interpretations of situations before they have an adequate knowledge of the essential rules and skills.

Developing Safe Attitudes

As a teacher, it will be your responsibility to ensure that the new drivers you are putting on to our roads have the correct attitude towards their vehicle, themselves and other road users. To achieve this, you will need to develop an understanding of the effect their actions have. This type of teaching and learning is called 'affective' because you will be developing safe attitudes through an understanding of the effect their actions, or lack of them, have on others.

Defensive driving is becoming a necessity on our roads and it is important, if you are to achieve this to any great degree, that your learners understand the need to keep themselves safe at all times.

Learning to drive the car safely and considerately is classed as an attitudinal skill because the phrase 'safely and considerately' describes the attitude of the learner. This makes the difference between merely learning to handle the car (a psychomotor skill) and following the rules of the road (an intellectual skill).

Attitude and behaviour

The attitude of drivers will normally influence their behaviour. Attitudes are formed through personal experiences from birth onwards. Reckless or unsafe driver behaviour is frequently attributed to negative attitudes. These are often inherent in the person who has always 'done his own thing' without a thought for the consequences on other people.

Those with a positive attitude, who have learnt to be more thoughtful towards others, will normally respond favourably as their understanding of correct behaviour and of the consequences of bad driving develops. For example, the person who drives at 30 mph through a busy shopping area, where there are parked vehicles on both sides of the road and a high volume of pedestrian activity, has a negative attitude.

Such actions may be caused by the driver simply not understanding the risks involved or simply not caring about them. Knowing and understanding the risks, however, may still not have the effect of slowing the driver down if a negative attitude is present. The driver with a positive attitude will normally listen to your reasoning, analyse the effects of the reckless behaviour and work on correcting it.

Road user error

The design of our roads, and sometimes local knowledge, allows for a certain degree of road-user error. This may reinforce wrong actions because drivers with a negative attitude get away with deficient behaviour. It may encourage the development of a feeling of immunity and eventually result in changing the individual's attitude towards the degree of risk they become willing to take.

Let us take an example. A driver who lives on a quiet estate may emerge from a junction without taking effective observations because there is usually no other traffic about at that time of the day. No other road user is present and therefore nothing happens, which gives the driver a false sense of security. The same situation may recur a number of times, thus reinforcing the 'safe' feeling. Eventually, other road users will be present and an accident will happen.

It will be your responsibility to try to change negative attitudes. This can be done by explaining the risks involved in any situation; persuading the driver to act safely in order to protect himself and others; and by setting a personal example.

You may find that some of your pupils will resent your efforts to change their views, remaining subjective and even offering excuses for not complying; those with a positive attitude will normally listen to your reasoning and become more objective and flexible when they understand the consequences of their actions.

You should recognise that all human beings have their limitations. Try to remember that a driver who is normally patient and tolerant may sometimes, for a variety of personal reasons, such as emotional problems, become hostile. Explain how conflict with others can be avoided if a little time is taken to relax and regain composure.

At the end of their course of training, new drivers should be able to:

- recognise features in the road and traffic environment where accidents are most likely to occur;
- identify the causes of accidents and assess their personal risk of becoming involved in them;
- recognise their own driving capabilities and limitations;
- apply defensive driving techniques to minimise the risk of becoming involved in accidents.

Transfer of Learning

It is unusual these days for anyone to present themselves for driving lessons without having some of the basic knowledge or skills required.

For example, all of your pupils will have been pedestrians and have learnt how to cross busy roads successfully. A lot of them will have ridden a bicycle and some will have had some experience on motorbikes. They have therefore developed skills in the judgement of speed, distance and timing of traffic. As these are some of the most essential skills involved in driving, you should be able to take advantage of this knowledge and transfer it to driving.

There are numerous other associations through which you will be able to help your learners relate or transfer existing skills and knowledge to driving.

Interference in learning

Previous learning can, however, sometimes work the other way round and interfere with learning a new skill. For example, where people have been passengers over a number of years, they will have probably developed a 'partial sense of speed'. They will have subconsciously learnt an impression of the speed norm of experienced drivers and this can cause problems if they try to copy the experienced person.

By driving at what they have learnt to accept as the normal speed, this 'previous learning' can severely interfere with progress, because these basic control skills need to be carried out initially at slower than normal speeds.

The following are examples of interference of learning:

- Always change up through the gears as soon as you have moved off.
- Always change down progressively through the gears when you are slowing down or stopping.
- Always signal for passing parked cars.

If pupils have been previously indoctrinated with certain views, it is likely to cause conflict with the new information you are giving. You must recognise that your pupils are not learning in a vacuum and will therefore be subject to all kinds of conflicting pressures from others.

Where this type of interference occurs, you must be tolerant and show an understanding of your pupils' problems during any difficult periods of 'unlearning'. You must also try to avoid saying that the information they have been given is totally wrong.

Motivation

Motivation describes the personal needs and desires of an individual. The fact that someone is prepared to pay for a course of lessons will normally show that they are motivated by a desire to learn.

The student will normally be alert and keen at the beginning of the course with a willingness to follow instructions in eager anticipation of the next session. The initial enthusiasm, however, may not always be enough to maintain full interest and attention for the entire course, particularly if difficult patches are experienced where very slow progress is achieved.

An important part of your work as a teacher will be to try to maintain their motivation. Help your pupils over any difficult periods by maintaining your enthusiasm and showing that you are interested in their progress. Motivation and interest can be stimulated through success. Even small successes are important to a pupil who is finding the learning hard work. By creating the right conditions, you can do much to ensure success. This can be done by properly grading the tuition in short, progressive steps. You should then try to maintain this interest by giving suitable encouragement and approval for effort.

Traditional methods of driving instruction mean students are often learning in total isolation from others and this can frequently cause problems for both the instructor and student. While 'individual' tuition is advantageous, it does limit contact and comparisons with other students. Deprived of the group learning situation, students are unable to measure their progress against that of others. More importantly, if they have no means of assessing their own progress and improvement, they may often feel they are making no progress at all. This may be a result of the instructor not giving feedback on where improvements have taken place.

If students feel they are making slow progress, encouragement alone from the teacher may not be sufficient to allay their fears of inability. In this situation, emphasise where some progress has been made and do not be excessively critical in other areas. An unsympathetic teacher may cause students to feel so discouraged, isolated and incompetent, that they become completely demoralised and may even give up the idea of learning to drive.

If you set up some easily attainable, intermediate targets, you will help to reinforce the student's feeling of achievement. Intermediate goals also help to organise the learning situation and do much to prevent pupils from being 'thrown in at the deep end before they can swim'.

One of the first goals to achieve in learning to drive is clutch control. It is important to remember that many of the driving skills are conditioned responses. That is, they not only require the right approach in order for them to be learnt properly, but they also need continual repetition to master them. This goal should be attained before students are asked to deal with difficult uphill junctions.

The confidence of some learners is destroyed because they are taken into difficult situations which require good clutch control before they have mastered this skill. Imagine how you would feel if you were sitting at a red traffic-light on your first driving lesson and you stalled the engine a couple of times!

Clutch control should initially be developed by full talk-through instruction to ensure that confidence is built up. However, in the final analysis, it is only by practice and success that the skill will become 'second nature' as the pupil learns to control the clutch correctly in all situations.

It is important that your pupils develop at their own pace and these intermediate goals should ensure that they progress with confidence. This, in turn, will keep the motivation at a good level.

TEACHING AND LEARNING

You should know from experience that learning is an inconsistent process over which there is little reliable control. Teachers have no mystical power by which to pour knowledge into the minds of their learners, so whatever students learn (whether it be a psychomotor or an intellectual skill) they must learn for themselves.

You will merely be providing the circumstances from which learning may occur. These 'learning conditions' may be in the form of a practical driving lesson; a lecture or discussion; or some other teaching or instructional method.

Your role as a teacher will be essentially one of establishing the quality, and of planning and organising the conditions, of this learning situation.

The teacher manages the learning experience by:

- preparing the material;
- organising the material;
- presenting the experience to the student;
- observing the student's reactions;
- assessing progress.

No matter how carefully prepared and presented the lesson may be, success can only be judged by how much knowledge or skill the learner gains from it.

Teaching Driving

The complete experience in learning to drive involves the car; the classroom, or some other location; and the personality and teaching methods of the instructor. It will also be dependent on the attitude, knowledge and skill of the student.

Whatever natural abilities and aptitude students have, if they are to gain the full benefit of learning the new subject, they will only do so through paying attention and becoming actively involved in the learning experience. Motivation is vital to students' willingness to learn. You must motivate your students and create an environment and situations from which they can learn.

You should think of yourself as a manager of the learning experience, with responsibilities extending far beyond the act of teaching. You should always be aware that what you are teaching – or are neglecting to teach – could at some time in the future be a matter of life or death to your students.

Apart from the quality and content of your lessons, your responsibilities will range from the organisation of the course to the final assessments you will need to make before your students take their driving tests.

The key to the successful management of learning will be your ability to present, adapt and adjust the same basic knowledge and skills for the wide range of learning abilities of the different pupils you will be teaching. You should not only be master of your craft and skills, but you should also have an infinitely variable range of instructional techniques at your command. You will have to call on these skills as and when the situation, or your pupils' needs, demand it.

Teaching driving is a challenging task which requires thorough training. Make sure you are prepared for it properly.

THE LEARNER'S NEEDS

The most successful instructors are those who have a concern for their students and are most sensitive to their learning requirements.

Learner drivers' needs are as varied and complex as the differences between the students themselves. Avoid grouping people into preconceived categories such as young and old, or quick and slow to learn. Making pre-judgements before you get to know pupils may prevent you from treating them as individuals and stop you from seeing them with 'open' and 'more sensitive' eyes.

One of your first priorities will be to create a good working relationship with your students. A good test of this will be the rapport which develops between you; and, perhaps more significantly, the level of communication. For example, if a good relationship develops:

- pupils should feel they can readily admit their mistakes without the risk of being made to feel silly;
- they should be able to discuss freely with you their fears and anxieties;
- you should be able to laugh together about silly mistakes.

Learning should be founded on mutual co-operation in order to develop students' ability and confidence. You can encourage this by structuring the learning so that they are only asked to carry out tasks which can be achieved with some degree of success.

Points to Remember About Learning

- Begin with what the learner already knows or can do and build on this.
- Structure the learning in short progressive steps.
- Be consistent with your instructions and terminology.
- Ensure your terminology is understood.
- Keep your explanations short and simple.
- Emphasise the key points.
- Ensure your instructions are positive, ie tell learners what to do rather than what not to.
- Explain the purpose of any demonstration before carrying it out.
- Carry out demonstrations at the correct level according to the ability of the learner.
- Keep initial explanations and demonstration commentaries simple – too many variables will confuse.
- Give the learner plenty of practice – people learn by doing things for themselves.
- Ensure the learner is in no doubt about what is expected.
- Try to ensure that initial practice is successful.
- Initial failure will sap confidence and inhibit progress.
- Success will stimulate interest and involvement.

- Praise and encouragement will help stimulate progress.
- Excessive criticism may destroy motivation.
- Give the learner continuous feedback of progress.
- Correct errors positively before they become habitual.
- Positive correction should be made to improve learners' performance.
- Confirmation of minor successes is important to those who may be finding the going difficult.
- Lack of sympathy for learners who feel they are making little or no progress may completely demoralise them.
- Reassure them that periods of slow learning are quite natural and common.
- Avoid comparing learners with other students.
- Easier, intermediate goals may help to promote progress.
- Allow your students to learn at their own pace.
- Avoid excessive repetition, it can be boring – a change in activity may help sustain interest.
- Older students may benefit from longer periods of practice.
- Fear of failure is a prime cause of anxiety.
- Reassure your learners and give them emotional encouragement.
- Ensure, as far as possible, that the learner can cope with the conditions, particularly where the route and volume of traffic are concerned.
- Be prepared to vary your methods of instruction.
- Avoid attempting to expand on variables before students have grasped the key points of a new topic.

SKILL TRAINING

The term 'skill' describes an activity in which the performance should be economical and effective in order to achieve a consistent and satisfactory result. Although it is relatively easy to recognise the skilled performance of an expert driver, it is considerably more difficult to define why it is so. It is even harder to explain and analyse the many skills involved in the complete task.

Driving instructors are obviously highly skilled drivers. Many drivers are unaware of the numerous individual tasks they are putting into practice because, with experience, these have mostly become subconscious actions.

As an instructor you need to be able to analyse each of the skills in detail before being able to teach the complex tasks involved in the process of learning to drive.

As a driver you have to:

- obtain relevant information from the environment;
- process it; and then respond by:
- making decisions; and
- executing the appropriate car control skills.

The driving task involves:

- attending to;
- perceiving; and
- responding safely to driving-related stimuli.

The activities involved relate to three different areas:

- **the psychomotor** (or physical skills);
- **the cognitive** (or knowledge-related skills); and
- **the affective** (or attitude).

When driving, you allocate attention by using your senses to gather information about the performance of your vehicle and also the conditions of the road and traffic environment. You must process the information by comparing it with existing knowledge, memories and previous experiences. You then assess its relevance and either ignore it and do nothing, or decide on a particular response or course of action to be taken to maintain a safe environment.

As an instructor you will have to recognise all of the different aspects of the task and teach your pupils how to drive safely in order to survive.

Analysing the Learning Task

To assist your pupils in the acquisition of new skills you need to be able to identify key learning points and to isolate any areas of weakness. To do this you will need to identify the elements of knowledge, attitude and skill involved in a particular learning task.

Essential elements

Knowledge: describes what you know. It is assumed that knowledge influences attitude and assists in the acquisition of skills.

Driving involves considerable knowledge of the Highway Code, traffic law and the principles of road safety procedures. Certain aspects can be learnt more effectively in a classroom or at home rather than in the hustle and bustle of today's road and traffic conditions.

Knowledge, however, is only a basis for 'real' learning. Although it may influence attitudes, in practice, knowledge alone is not always sufficient to ensure we have the will or skill needed to behave in the correct manner.

For example, although most drivers know they shouldn't drink and drive, this doesn't always prevent them from doing it. Legislation and the consequences of being caught, however, place incentives on drivers not to break the law.

Other incentives include the consequences of accident involvement. This knowledge may also help influence our attitude towards alcohol and driving. On this basis, the more we know, the better equipped we are to make our decisions.

Attitude: describes what we really think, and this usually influences our behaviour.

Attitudes are formed over a lifetime of experience and learning. They will not normally be changed overnight! Unsympathetic attitudes towards others, and towards the established principles of road safety, are a contributory factor in causing many road accidents.

You must teach your pupils to develop safe attitudes towards others. You can do this by constantly persuading and providing them with good examples.

In addition to knowledge, an attitude has motivational and emotional elements which influence behaviour. These elements can be so powerful that we may sometimes lose control of our actions. Uncontrolled aggression and love are two extreme examples of this.

A skill: describes what we can do! There are two main types of skill:

Manipulative skills: physical actions such as turning the steering wheel, pressing the footbrake or operating the clutch pedal.

Perceptive skills: these are skills associated with awareness, thinking, reasoning and making decisions. These are the most predominant skills used in the overall driving task. They rely heavily on visual sense and include the judgement of:

- reductions in speed caused by differing amounts of braking pressure;
- detecting changes in direction when steering;
- awareness – the general state of the mind involving comparison with previous experience and hazard recognition;
- assessing and predicting risk and making decisions.

Driving skills: these include:

- attention – staying alert and concentrating;
- visual search – a systematic scanning of the road and traffic scene;
- responding to situations and taking the appropriate action to control the car;
- using the car's controls smoothly and efficiently.

Use the following test to help you break down any task into its various elements. At the beginning of a lesson, or part of a lesson, ask yourself these questions:

What precisely do I want my pupil to do? What does the pupil need to know in order to do it?

For example: find the 'holding point' and keep the feet perfectly still! To do this efficiently and consistently, your pupil should know that only a small proportion of the total clutch pedal travel has any noticeable effect upon the behaviour of the vehicle. The first 'two or three' inches from the floor have no effect at all.

What senses will your pupil need to use?

For example: many new drivers are taught to lean over and check the passenger door is properly closed. Is this really necessary when experienced drivers would use their ears to assess whether it was shut, or look in the nearside door mirror for the bodyline of the car being flush?

What should your pupil be thinking about when a particular action is required, either when you are there or they are eventually on their own?

For example: drivers need to recognise the possibility of, and the dangers associated with, cars emerging from side roads. They must be prepared to act in the interests of their own survival.

After studying this kind of question, you should be able to decide what and how to set about teaching your pupils. Decide what you want them to be able to do at the end of the lesson. Be realistic about what they can achieve in the time available. Don't attempt too much.

Organise your lessons into short progressive steps and let pupils work through them at their own pace. Aptitudes and abilities vary, so adapt the pace of your instruction to the ability of the individual. Build on what the pupil already knows and can do, then move on one step at a time.

Before attempting a new skill, the pupil will require some basic knowledge upon which to build. Each physical action has a 'get set' position from which the actual skill commences. This involves preliminary movements and positioning of the hands and/or feet in anticipation of carrying out the skill or sub-skill.

This 'get set' position is important for ensuring the efficient and smooth execution of the overall task. For example:

- siting the hand over the gear lever in anticipation of a change; whilst:
- positioning the foot over the clutch pedal;
- extending the fingers ready to use a signal;
- raising the appropriate hand ready for the first pull movement on the steering wheel.

Teaching a Skill

Before you can teach a new skill you have to establish the present standard and abilities of your pupil. You can then decide on the level at which the skill should be introduced, demonstrated and practised. Be prepared to adjust this level, up or down, depending on the pupil's responses and performance.

At the beginning of each session, explain to your pupils what they are going to do and why. They should understand how the skill is to be performed and what is expected of them. Relate the subject matter to what they already know and can do, so that they feel the task in hand is attainable.

It may be necessary to break some skills down into their component sub-skills to ensure success is achieved.

The generally accepted pattern of skill training is:

explanation → demonstration → practice

The explanation

Introduce the topic for instruction. This introduction should include an indication of:

- what the topic involves;
- why this particular aspect is important;
- when and where it is carried out;
- how it is to be carried out.

Keep your explanations short and to the point. They should be appropriate to your pupil's ability. For example, it would be pointless to go into lengthy explanations on how to exercise clutch control at busy uphill junctions if the pupil cannot move away under control on a level road. Establish and consolidate the main principles of the subject before introducing the finer points and variables. Once basic rules and procedures are established, it will be easier for the pupil to understand and retain additional information given at a later date.

There are three main constituent parts to most explanations. These include details and information concerning:

Control – of the vehicle's speed.
Observation – of hazards and general attitudes towards them.
Positioning – of the vehicle by using the steering.

Control: explanations should include the general control of the vehicle for dealing with hazards. Control is mainly a manipulative skill, for example:

- co-ordination of the car's controls when moving off;
- low-speed clutch control for manoeuvring;
- smooth, gradual use of the steering wheel;
- smooth and progressive use of the accelerator and gears;
- smooth and progressive use of the brakes for slowing down and stopping;
- securing the car when stationary.

Observation: you should explain about the visual search required to deal safely with any hazard or when manoeuvring. The use of any necessary signals should be included and any special danger cues the pupil should be looking for.

It is your responsibility to encourage safe attitudes and you should include information on the perceptive skills and safety margins. Explain about the decision-making process required to respond correctly.

Positioning: your explanations should include:

- the rules relating to positioning and when to adjust to suit the situation;
- steering – the physical use of the steering wheel;
- maintaining general accuracy throughout the required course;
- lane discipline where appropriate.

Points to Remember: a general guide for lessons is to:

- tell your pupils what they will be doing during the current session;
- explain how to do it;
- allow plenty of time for practising;

Do it with a KISS: KEEP IT SHORT AND SIMPLE

- keep your explanations as brief as you can for the subject;
- get straight to the point;
- use simple terminology;
- use visual aids where these will help your pupil understand what you mean;
- use official materials such as *The Highway Code* and *The Driving Manual* to validate points under instruction;
- emphasise the key points – leaving out unnecessary detail.

It can prove to be totally unproductive to introduce complex procedures until basic car control skills have been adequately developed.

The demonstration

The demonstration has a number of applications. It can be used to:

- show pupils how an expert would carry out a manoeuvre or procedure;
- emphasise or reinforce individual components of any skill;
- show the key elements of a manoeuvre prior to giving a fuller explanation;
- dispel the pupils' apprehension.

To obtain maximum effect from a demonstration it must be preceded by a briefing. Outline the key points and emphasise these while giving your demonstration by talking yourself through the procedures.

Conclude your demonstration with a summary of the key points. This may then lead to a more in-depth explanation. Consolidate the explanation and demonstration immediately by giving your pupil plenty of practice under controlled conditions.

Quite often new drivers are genuinely 'blind' to mistakes. A demonstration may help them to 'see' exactly what you mean. This particularly applies where safety margins, holdback positions and also the use of speed when approaching hazards are concerned. Because of inexperience, pupils can fail to recognise the dangers involved. If you demonstrate safer clearances and speeds, it may result in a better understanding of the problems.

You could tell your pupil to slow down more before a corner and get no result whatsoever. This could mean your pupil's concept of the word 'slow' is different from your own. Under these circumstances, a demonstration can be invaluable.

It should, however, be used as part of your explanation and not as a substitute for it.

Points to Remember about the Demonstration:

- It should be at the correct level for the pupil's ability.
- It should follow an explanation of the subject.
- It should be a perfect example of the skill or procedure carried out at near normal speed. (Slightly less than normal may be advantageous at times, but it should not be so slow as to become unreal.)
- Commentary should be restricted to the main points using key words (too many variables may confuse).
- It must be consolidated with plenty of practice in controlled conditions.

PUPILS' PRACTICE

Your pupils can only learn practical skills by carrying them out! The practice should, however, be structured and follow a pattern of:

- controlled practice;
- prompted practice; and
- distributed practice.

Controlled Practice and Talk Through As far as possible try to ensure your pupils 'get it right first time'. Talk them through each action and stage of the operation, skill or exercise until they develop the ability and confidence to do it for themselves.

This 'talk-through' technique enables initial practice of new skills or procedures to take place realistically and in relative safety. It also helps to prevent vehicle abuse and inconvenience to other road users.

The need for the full 'talk through' is greatest in the early stages when terminology is least familiar and pupils are more likely to misunderstand the instructions given.

Make sure pupils are familiar with the terminology and can carry out your instructions before they move away. Instructions should be clear and you should give them so that pupils have plenty of time to interpret and execute them comfortably.

In order to build up confidence, it is essential that initial practice of a new skill should be successful. The 'talk through' ensures, as far as possible, that nothing goes wrong at this early stage.

While this method of instruction is usually successful for introducing pupils to the basic skills, it is not entirely without its problems. Due to the limitations of speech, the timing of some skills is slightly artificial. We can only speak, or give instructions, in a specific order – one at a time. Some skills require perfectly co-ordinated movements at the same time and it is therefore impossible to give instructions exactly as they should be carried out.

Another problem lies in pupils' speed of interpreting and then carrying out the instruction. There will be a delay of varying lengths for different pupils. The pupil may also temporarily become confused over an instruction which will cause more delay.

There are no real alternatives to this method of instruction during the initial stages of training. The driving simulator is perhaps a safe alternative, but it falls a long way short of being ideal. This is because no sensation of movement, direction or change of speed is felt.

New skills should normally begin to develop after two or three talk-through exercises. When you can see progress taking place, encourage your pupils to take some personal responsibility for their actions.

There are a number of ways in which development of this responsibility can be encouraged:

● Ask pupils to talk themselves through the sequence. This gives them the responsibility but it may also give you forewarning of any errors. You can then verbally rectify these before they are actually committed.

● Break the sequence into three parts (ie preparation, observation, action) and get pupils to talk themselves through each.

If pupils become confused with the unfamiliar terminology it is not important as long as they understand what is required. Don't be too particular about making the pupil use your precise phrasing. This may result in them feeling inadequate and inhibit their performance of the skill.

If pupils 'dry up' when repeating the sequence, give a cue or prompt; then, if they can, let them continue. Practise until the whole sequence can be completed unaided.

Insist that previously learnt routines are carried out properly. Errors must be corrected before they become habitual. Excessive criticism and pettiness, however, must be avoided as it can destroy confidence.

Encourage improvement by pointing out progress. Identify weaknesses and help the pupil overcome them. Devise simple exercises to help with any problems. Experiment and be prepared to vary your methods of instruction if problems persist.

Your students should feel that they can approach you without feeling foolish or incompetent. If the problems still persist, try something new for a while and let them go back to the subject. Reassure those who find things difficult. Let them know that periods of slow progress are quite common.

At the end of practice sessions, decide if the objectives have been achieved. After observing the pupil's performance, ask questions to ensure that the subject has been clearly understood before you proceed to the next.

Practice sessions should finish with a review of what has been achieved and a look forward to what will be covered in the next. Before practising new skills in the next lesson, revise and reinforce those learnt in the previous one.

Prompted Practice Some pupils may become very good at following instructions, but when left to carry out a skill unaided they are unable to do so. Others who find it more difficult to follow individual instructions are often far more advanced when allowed to work on their own initiative.

While controlled practice is an essential part of basic training in new skills, it should gradually be phased out when you feel pupils can cope for themselves. Some pupils will require lots of encouragement to act and think for themselves.

Prompting, where required, is perhaps the natural progression from the controlled practice or talk-through. The amount of prompting required will largely depend on the ability and willingness of pupils to make decisions for themselves.

The type of decision required is also significant. For example, if the conditions become too busy for pupils' ability, there will be a tendency for them to refrain from making any decisions at all. Where these situations arise, you must be prepared to prompt as required.

The ultimate objective is to get pupils to carry out all of the skills under normal traffic conditions without any prompting at all.

Revision is important and it requires continuous consideration, particularly in the early stages of establishing a new skill. A true and wholly accurate assessment cannot be made of the driving skill where it is still necessary to prompt.

The use of detailed instructions should decrease as ability increases. For example: a pupil hesitates and shows minor signs of distress at the beginning of a lesson after being asked to move off. You know from your previous experience that this pupil can carry out the procedure without any assistance. All you may need to do is give a simple cue such as, 'Select first gear'. Normally this will trigger the actions required as the sequence is remembered.

Remember that a simple cue like this is often sufficient to bring back a whole sequence of complicated actions without further instruction. Try not to help too much by giving all the necessary information. If capable, the pupil needs to be given the opportunity of achieving some success independently.

Lots of practice will be required to build consistency, stamina and to reduce the time taken to complete any sequence. When the skill becomes consistent and is carried out in a reasonable length of time, other important aspects can be introduced with more emphasis being placed on the visual search and timing.

Skills must be applied and practised progressively in more difficult traffic-situations. For example: moving off from junctions and traffic lights; moving off and maintaining low-speed control in conjunction with steering.

Prompting should not be necessary in any form if you consider your pupil is at DSA driving test standard.

Transferred Responsibility There comes a time when you must hand over to your pupils the responsibility for making their own decisions and acting on them.

As control skills develop and confidence grows, you should place more emphasis on the development of perceptive and hazard recognition skills. Point out what pupils should be looking for and where to expect it. Explain the dangers involved and why particular responses are called for.

Encourage pupils to think and to make their own decisions. Get them to *look* for information and encourage them to use their knowledge of the rules and previous experience in order to *assess*. Build the confidence they need in order to *decide* and act for themselves.

The question-and-answer technique becomes very useful in this stage of training. By asking questions relevant to the traffic situation, you can find out what pupils are thinking. How they respond will tell you of any misunderstandings which may be occurring and you can make the necessary corrections.

Distributed Practice No matter what skills are being learned, there is no substitute for practice. It should be organised sensibly. 'Cramming' everything into a few marathon sessions is not an efficient way of learning. 'A little and often' is a more efficient strategy.

Carefully distributed practice, divided evenly over four or five weeks, is more efficient than working for the same amount of hours during an intensive one-week course.

For example, one hour of training a day is considerably more efficient than:

- one hour of training twice a day;
- two hours' training once a day;
- two hours' training twice a day.

The General Learning Curve

While you can see the manipulative aspects of the driving task improving by simply watching your pupils execute them, prompts and verbal guidance during the early stages of learning will still be necessary.

When the skill is sufficiently developed, hints and reassurance should be all that is required. Pupils' progress will vary depending on the type of skill being learnt.

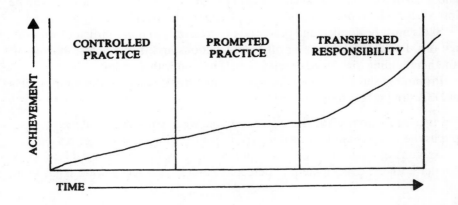

When learning some skills, pupils reach a stage which is called 'the plateau of learning'. Once this level has been attained, further progress will seem to come to a halt. However, this is not necessarily the limit of performance. After a short while most pupils will overcome the problem and then progress to their own personal limits.

STRUCTURING THE LEARNING

There are nine main principles involved in structuring a course of driving instruction. As there is a great deal of common sense involved in teaching any practical skill, most good instructors follow the principles intuitively. The general principles are:

Principle 1   Set out the aims and objectives of your course of lessons. Each part of the course should be clearly specified in terms of observable behaviour.

Principle 2   The subject matter to be learnt, and routes used, should be appropriate to achieving the specified aims and objectives.

Principle 3   The course content, and individual lessons, should be organised in short progressive steps which follow a logical sequence.

Principle 4   The content of lessons, and the routes selected, should be graded in difficulty so that your pupils make as few mistakes as possible.

Principle 5   Your pupils should be introduced to new materials and skills at a level of difficulty which relates to their ability, previous experience and current attainments.

Principle 6   Your pupils should be allowed to proceed through the course at their own pace.

Principle 7   They should be 'actively' involved in the learning process.

Principle 8   You should give your pupils continuous feedback of progress.

Principle 9   Pupils should master each skill and section of the course before you go on to the next stage.

Principle 1: The aims and objectives of a course of lessons, and each part of it, should be clearly specified in advance in terms of observable behaviour.

Objectives are written statements which describe what your pupils are expected to know, think or be able to do at the end of a lesson, or course of lessons. They should be stated in terms of observable behaviour. Your pupils should know what new skills they are expected to be able to carry out, or what knowledge should be gained by the end of each section of learning.

Driving instructors have little control over the 'superficial' procedures and other aspects of driving they teach because these are mainly dictated by driving test criteria. However, it is obviously useful for instructors to decide beforehand what changes they want to bring about in the learner's behaviour. This particularly concerns the important aspects of driving which are not effectively assessed on the driving test. These are knowledge, attitudes and some vital aspects of hazard recognition skills.

Objectives in the affective domain are concerned with stating what your pupils should think and how they should behave. Those in the cognitive domain are concerned with intellectual skills and state what the learner should know.

Objectives in the psychomotor domain are concerned with stating what the learner should physically be able to do.

It is essential that your pupils are taught at least to comprehend and apply their knowledge, otherwise it will remain more or less useless. It is generally accepted that knowledge helps to generate favourable attitudes. Conversely, inadequate or incorrect knowledge might result in the development of negative attitudes, resulting in unsafe driver behaviour.

The objectives of the driving test are stated in *The Driving Test*. You may wish to extend these or write your own set of intermediate or structured 'short-term' objectives.

The following are examples of structured or short-term objectives relating to the psychomotor (physical) domain. These are specifically concerned with the use of the gear lever on a first lesson.

On completing this stage of the lesson, your pupil should be able to:

Step 1　With the car stationary, carry out instructions to move the gear lever to specified positions while looking at it.

Step 2　With the car stationary, carry out instructions to move the gear lever to specified positions without looking at it.

Step 3　With the car moving, carry out instructions to select specified gears while steering and without looking at the gear lever.

Step 4　Carry out specified gear changes on command while steering and without looking at the gear lever.

Principle 2: The subject matter to be learnt, and routes used, should be appropriate to achieving the specified aims and objectives.

The content of the lesson, support materials and routes used, should ensure that the aims and objectives can be achieved. Research into the causes of road accidents shows that deficiencies in perceptive abilities, personality and other psychological characteristics are more significant than deficiencies in car control skills.

Instructors should classify the matter to be learnt in order of importance. For example:

Essential material is what the learner *must* cover in order to achieve the course objectives.

Desirable material is what the learner *should* cover but which is not essential in order to achieve the objectives.

Useful material is what the learner *could* cover but which is not completely relevant to the objectives.

For instance, how to carry out an oil change is probably more suited to a course on car maintenance than it is to a course on learning to drive.

The facts, skills and techniques selected for learning should not only be relevant to the course objectives, they must also be accurate and reliable. There is a vast source of learning material available to the 'L' driver in books and films.

Some of this material is useful to the novice, but sometimes discrepancies occur. For example the DSA states 'Slow down and keep to the left approaching a left-hand bend'. The police and Institute of Advanced Motorists state 'To improve visibility round a left-hand bend, you should approach in a more central road position'.

Check the source of your information. The DSA is the highest authority on driving in Britain and their advice is sought and respected worldwide. What you teach your pupils must be compatible with road safety principles. You should bear in mind that they will be assessed on the driving test to the criteria laid down by the DSA.

Principle 3: The course content, and individual lessons, should be organised in short progressive steps which follow a logical sequence.

Intermediate targets will help to stimulate interest and progress. They can help to reinforce learning by providing positive evidence of progress through each section and also organise the learning situation.

The driving task should be analysed and organised into short progressive units of instruction. Considered as a whole, driving is a complex task. It is made up of many sub-skills such as moving off, steering, stopping etc. The sub-skills are each made up of several sub-divisions.

A course of driving lessons should be structured to proceed from:

the known to the unknown
the simple to the complex
the basic rules to the variations
concrete observations to abstract reasoning.

Once your pupil has grasped the basic rules and concepts, it becomes easier for them to develop new skills and understand the variables.

Principle 4: The content of lessons, and routes selected, should be graded in difficulty so that your pupils make as few mistakes as possible.

Make sure students experience success during the early stages of the course. Avoid setting standards which are too high. Be prepared to accept some technical inaccuracies and deficiencies until pupils have developed more confidence in their ability.

Initial failure may deter pupils and inhibit progress. Build confidence and understanding upon a firm foundation of practical skills. Progress from what the student knows and can do to the unknown and the new. Simple skills should be taught before complex procedures are introduced. For example, it is unreasonable to expect pupils to deal with right turns at busy traffic-light-controlled junctions before they can control the vehicle properly.

Principle 5: Your pupils should be introduced to new materials and skills at a level of difficulty which relates to their ability, previous experience and current attainments.

There are considerable variations in the rate at which students learn. This should cause few problems when giving individual tuition because the course can be tailored to suit the needs of each student. Your pupils should be allowed to work through each unit of learning at their own pace. New skills and techniques can then be introduced at a level commensurate with ability, knowledge and previous achievement.

One of your first tasks, when meeting new students, is to find out what previous experience they may have had and how much they know and can do. In order to plan the level of training, it is necessary to establish the pupil's current knowledge and ability. Consult your pupils, find out what they know and encourage them to take some responsibility for the decisions you will be making together.

As skills develop, and mastery of the controls is attained, keep your pupils informed of what they are doing and why. They should never be left confused or in doubt. However, some of the basic skills must be taught as simple conditioned reflex procedures. Initially, it is more important for pupils to respond correctly to an emergency than to understand why the particular response was required.

Principle 6: Your pupils should be allowed to proceed through the course at their own pace.

Learning is more efficient when pupils are allowed to proceed at their own pace, as quickly or slowly as they are able. This enables the learning to be more effective.

Principle 7: Pupils should be 'actively' involved in the learning process.

Keep your pupils physically and/or mentally involved in the learning experience. Whatever is learnt can only be achieved by pupils thinking and doing things for themselves. Activity will help to hold your pupils' attention.

Where students may be sitting passively in a classroom, supposedly listening to a necessary, but boring, lecture, it is easy to see how they may become 'switched off'. This may happen where the students do not think the content of the lecture is particularly relevant to their personal needs.

You may think driving a car at 40 mph along a quiet road, with relatively little happening, is a far cry from a boring lecture! In some ways that is correct. But it requires little physical activity other than steering. The problem in this situation is that there is very little to occupy the mind as it may not be actively involved in the driving at all. These situations will provide ideal opportunities for you to develop your pupil's visual search and observational skills and relate them to the reasoning of the experienced driver.

Observing the physical activity of the student is relatively straightforward. Observation of what the pupil is thinking, however, is a far more difficult problem. An active mind is essential to learning and an extremely important part of driving.

In the early stages of learning a task, keep the student's mind active – ask questions about the relevant road features or any intended actions. Avoid distracting your pupils when they are busy, however.

There will be many instances where, once the learning experience has been set up, you will be able to 'take a back seat' and play a passive role and simply observe the quality of the pupil's work.

Principle 8: Give your pupils continuous feedback of progress.

Learning should be reinforced with feedback of progress, helpful comments, constructive criticism and encouragement.

Active involvement facilitates learning. However, this does not ensure that the learning is of the right kind, nor that the pupil is making progress towards the final performance as stated in the objectives.

Make sure that your pupils do not just perfect faults. Reinforce learning and improve performance, by giving continuous information on progress. This feedback should occur as soon as possible after an event, or between each step in an exercise or manoeuvre. This will help prevent further faults appearing.

Comments such as 'good' or 'very good' may be useful as an indication of progress where there is insufficient time to give more detailed information. These comments do not, however, tell the pupil anything about the actual performance. Comments such as 'Our position was a little wide on the approach to the turn' or 'The gear change was left a little late' or 'The approach speed needs to be a little slower' are all more helpful because they give information on the actual performance.

Positive comments which state the action required to rectify the error are even more beneficial. For example, 'Position about three feet from the kerb when turning left', 'Change down to second a little earlier next time' or 'Slow down more before reaching the corner'.

Short comments and corrections made on the move, such as those outlined above, will be of great value in improving your pupil's performance. However, avoid giving detailed verbal corrections when on the move. Where these are required, they should be given as soon as practicable after the incident when a suitable parking position is found.

Principle 9: Pupils should master each skill and section of the course before you go on to the next stage.

There is sometimes confusion over what is meant by 'complete mastery' and some instructors argue that this cannot be attained until a very advanced stage is reached. You should not expect 'total mastery of the full task demands' during the intermediate stages. You can reduce the demands placed on your pupils by setting properly structured objectives and choosing your routes carefully.

If a course is properly structured, complete mastery can, and should, be attained in each sub-skill, technique or procedure before introducing new and progressively more complicated variables.

Consistency is an essential feature of good driving. To achieve this, each skill or task should be 'over-learnt'. Full mastery of each unit or stage of learning should be achieved before proceeding to the next. Progress based on mastery of each phase of learning will do much to develop a sense of achievement and confidence.

Staging the course into a number of progressive learning units also helps to increase pupils' motivation to learn by sustaining a continuous sense of urgency.

Syllabus for Driver Training

The Driving Standards Agency officially recommended syllabus covers the complete range of driving and is not restricted simply to 'learning to pass the 'L' test'. The syllabus therefore provides a basis for structuring courses for:

- pre-driver training;
- learner driver training;
- post-test training under the 'Pass Plus' scheme;
- advanced/defensive/fleet training.

The main elements of the syllabus include:

- legal requirements;
- car controls, equipment and components;
- road user behaviour;
- vehicle characteristics;
- road and weather conditions;
- traffic signs, rules and regulations;
- car control and road procedure;
- motorway driving;
- riding mopeds and motorcycles;
- towing larger trailers or caravans.

Full details of the objectives within the syllabus are included in *The Driving Test*.

When structuring your own course you should use this syllabus in conjunction with *The Driving Manual, The Driving Test, The Highway Code,* and any other material which will help develop and reinforce safe procedures and attitudes.

The syllabus lists the skills in which your pupils must achieve basic competence in order to pass the driving test. They must also have:

- a thorough knowledge of the Highway Code and the motoring laws;
- a thorough understanding of the driver's responsibilities.

You must teach your pupils to have real concern, not just for their own safety, but for the safety of all road users, including pedestrians. It is your responsibility to influence safe attitudes.

You should be able to teach your pupils most of the subjects listed during their practical on-road lessons. However, some may be difficult for you to cover because of the road and traffic conditions in your area.

You may not, for example, be able to give practical experience at dealing with level crossings, floods or dual-carriageways, because these situations do not exist locally. However, it remains your responsibility to give your pupils sufficient knowledge on all of the subjects listed within the syllabus.

You can do this by various means. You may have classroom facilities available to you where you can teach your pupils in groups; you can spend time in the car going over the rules and procedures; or you can give your pupils homework by referring them to the various reading materials and ask relevant questions on subsequent lessons.

A Structured Programme for Learner Drivers

Learn to Drive in 10 Easy Stages, published by Kogan Page, is a systematic programme designed to support professional instruction. Each stage identifies key points and explains what should be learnt in the car.

The book contains a special chart linked to DSA requirements. You can use this to identify any areas of weakness and organise appropriate revision exercises. The page references direct pupils to the relevant text and Highway Code rules needing most revision. It encourages pupils to read the rules and complete the appropriate checkpoint before practical on-road lessons. By doing this, your pupils will learn to apply the rules in a sensible manner as they will be concentrating on those which relate to what they are currently practising in the car.

Linked to the book is a special appointment card used by instructors around the UK. This will give your pupils instant feedback of their progress throughout the course and also serve as a progress check for you.

The principles outlined in the previous section are followed and the book is based on the four phases of skill development described later in this chapter.

Stage 1.   Before driving – planning lessons, driving schools, instructors and private practice.

Stage 2.   Vehicle Familiarisation (Part 1) – explanation of use of controls.

Stage 3.   Vehicle Familiarisation (Part 2) – practice in a moving car.

Stage 4.   Systematic driving practice.

Stage 5.   Gaining confidence.

Stage 6.   Development of manoeuvring and reversing skills.

Stage 7.   Applying commonsense.

Stage 8.   Developing defensive attitudes to avoid conflict and accidents.

Stage 9.   Driving at higher speeds. Dealing with emergencies.

Stage 10.   The Driving Test.

The four phases of skill development

New drivers progress through four phases of learning before they reach a competent standard. These are: Dissociated Passive – Dissociated Active – Injudicious – Safe.

Phase 1 Dissociated Passive This phase of learning is very superficial. Pupils are only passively attending to the driving task while you, the instructor, will play the dominant role in talking them through routines and procedures. (For future reference this is referred to as 'controlled practice'.) Novice drivers are: visually inactive; slow to respond and often experience 'near misses'; slow and hesitant with a tendency to make sudden 'unusual manoeuvres'.

'Controlled Practice' (Lessons 1, 2, 3 and 4 in *Learn to Drive*.) During this phase give your pupils full instruction through each routine or skill. Restrict the initial stages of training to developing their car control skills. Although routines may be superficial at this stage, you can still try to develop good habits such as the MSM sequence.

    The aim of the first lesson is to familiarise pupils with the car's controls. It will also give them an opportunity to get a feel for the controls by practising some simple exercises while stationary. When you have explained the terminology you will be using, make sure your pupils understand, and are able to carry out, basic instructions before moving away. For example, handbrake ready; cover the clutch; clutch down; set the gas; find the holding point; and cover the brake.

    Talk your pupils through the routines and let them practise and develop their car control and steering skills on the nursery routes. You should tell your pupils exactly what to do and when to do it. This helps them get things right first time and will build confidence.

    Keeping to the quiet routes, use step-by-step exercises to encourage your pupils to do more for themselves. Let them practise each step of each exercise separately until they have mastered it reasonably well.

Phase 2 Dissociated Active At this stage your pupils will become more 'active' in the manipulative skills but will still be visually inactive with slow perceptive responses. You will often need to prompt them into action. (For future reference this phase is referred to as 'prompted practice'.) Near misses, sudden unusual manoeuvres, late over-reactions tend to be the norm and pupils seem to actively take risks.

'Prompted Practice' (Lessons 5 and 6 in *Learn to Drive*.) Your pupils will require considerable prompting at the beginning of this phase. Progression through the phase should be structured within their capabilities. First teach them to deal with static hazards. The circumstances of routes and movement of pedestrians and traffic, however, will sometimes create unforeseen situations with which they are unable to cope. Under these circumstances, reassure your pupils and talk them through the situation.

To develop pupils' skills, use quiet estates with wide roads, rounded corners and as few parked cars as possible. Practise simple MSM routines turning left and right into side roads. Once they have mastered these, practise the system approaching and emerging from roads. At first, only practise on junctions which provide clear views into the main road.

Once pupils can cope with the quiet estates, give them the opportunity to practise on sharper corners and major roads with more traffic. Avoid very busy junctions and those on uphill gradients.

When pupils have mastered the system of car control at basic junctions, and their confidence increases, practise on busier roads, uphill junctions, and those with restricted sightlines.

Introduce the manoeuvring and parking exercise when your pupils' control skills are adequately developed to ensure initial success.

As your pupils improve towards the end of this phase, encourage them to assess situations, take on more responsibility for themselves and begin to make decisions for themselves.

Phase 3 Injudicious Your pupils will now be beginning to become 'visually aware', developing perceptive response and actively attending to driving the car. They should become more responsible for their own actions. (For future reference this phase is referred to as 'transferred responsibility'.) At this stage pupils will make false assumptions, still be prepared to take risks, make occasional misjudgements, suffer near misses and still make some unusual manoeuvres.

'Transferred Responsibility' (Lesson 7 in *Learn to Drive*.) Once your pupils have mastered the car control skills and the basic rules and routine procedures, give them some experience on busier roads and in traffic.

Try to keep them calm and build their confidence in these conditions by giving them plenty of practice. Provide them with plenty of experience on a wide variety of roads and junctions. Practise in laned traffic; on one-way streets; turning onto and off dual carriageways; roundabouts; and turning right at busy traffic-light-controlled crossroads.

Excessive criticism of your pupils will destroy their confidence. A little praise will encourage them to do better next time. Tell them when they execute procedures well, commend them for making good decisions and flatter them for their concentration and effort.

Avoid heavy, fast-moving traffic and multi-lane roads containing combinations of parked vehicles, pedestrians and complex junctions until the final stages of training when they will be able to cope with these situations.

Phase 4 Safe Road accidents claim almost 4,000 lives, maim over 250,000 people and cost over £2,000,000,000 every year. Nine lives are lost and 685 people are seriously injured every day. The cost is around £230,000 per hour.

Newly qualified drivers are those most at risk. Proper training could reduce accidents by as much as 50 per cent.

It is your responsibility to teach your pupils to recognise and accept that other road users make mistakes. They can be taught to avoid accidents by compensating for the mistakes of others.

By the time your pupils reach this phase of learning they should be more visually active and aware. They should be developing a quick perceptive response to recognised risks and be able to react in an unhurried and skilful manner. There should no longer be any near misses or unusual reactions.

'*Safe*' (Lessons 8, 9 and 10 in *Learn to Drive*.) Assessments and mock tests should be constructive. They should help to provide your pupils with evidence of progress as well as any weaknesses.

Before presenting pupils for the test, ensure, as far as you possibly can, that they are able to cope with busy road and traffic conditions. It is insufficient for them merely to satisfy the minimum standard required by the examiner.

Route planning

Route planning is an essential element of lesson preparation. It requires a thorough knowledge of local geography and traffic conditions. When planning routes you must take into consideration any specific driving skill or procedure which is to be practised.

An unsympathetic route can have disastrous consequences when novices are unnecessarily exposed to conditions with which they are unable to cope. In extreme cases, and with particularly nervous pupils, it may even make them give up the idea of learning to drive at all.

Ideally, a fairly wide selection of planned routes containing various types of traffic hazards and conditions will be required. These need not be considered as rigidly fixed routes from which there must be no deviation.

Flexibility is an important consideration when planning a route because it allows for changes to be made midway through a lesson. This may become necessary to allow more time to be spent on an area of driving which may be proving unexpectedly troublesome, and yet still allow the lesson to be completed on time for your next appointment.

Excessive repetition over the same routes will often prove counter-productive. It frequently leads to a reduction in the pupil's interest. This in turn may result in boredom and slow progress. Some repetition, however, can be helpful at times when it is carried out deliberately for a specific purpose relevant to the lesson. For example, practising control skills on the approach to uphill junctions would need to be restricted to a localised area where the same junctions may have to be used several times. This will give pupils more opportunity to practise the skills.

Training routes and areas fall loosely into three groups:

- Nursery routes
- Intermediate
- Advanced.

There is no definite dividing line between these groups and there may frequently be considerable overlap between them. On occasions there is justification for incorporating all kinds of route on one lesson; for instance, when making an initial assessment of a new client with previous driving experience.

Starting with the nursery routes, introduce new traffic situations at a controlled rate which is sensitive to the needs of your pupils and sympathetic to their ability.

In reality, the nature of traffic conditions can be very erratic. Even the most carefully planned route may suddenly prove unsuitable, and the pupil will be faced with new situations they cannot yet cope with. Route preparation will, however, help keep these incidents down to a fairly isolated and acceptable level.

Training routes are often a compromise between the ideal and the reality of local geography and traffic conditions. In general, instructors working near the centre of a large city may experience difficulty in finding suitable nursery routes. However, their counterparts, operating in isolated rural areas, may experience problems in finding suitably varied conditions for the advanced routes. Extending the length of some lessons may be a satisfactory answer in both instances by allowing more travelling time to better suited areas.

Nursery routes

Various kinds of roads are required, but, in general, these routes should avoid areas containing many turns or junctions. As far as possible avoid busy roads and initially, in the very early stages, areas where there are parked vehicles.

These routes should not include pedestrian crossings, traffic lights or roundabouts and should progressively incorporate:

- fairly straight, wide roads, long enough to allow uninterrupted progression through all the gears and preferably free from parked vehicles;
- quiet, fairly wide roads on up/down/level gradients; suitable for practising the manipulative skills. Roads should be selected to allow minimum interference with the flow of other traffic;

- roads containing right/left hand bends, allowing for use of the gears on the approach;
- simple left turns from main into side roads;
- simple left turns into main roads;
- right turns from main into side roads and right turns into main roads;
- some routes containing parked vehicles will become necessary towards the end of the initial stages.

Intermediate routes

These routes should, wherever possible, be planned to avoid dual carriageways, multi-laned roads and one-way streets. Junctions which do not conform to basic rules should also be excluded. Right turns on to very busy main roads, and any other particularly difficult situations, should not normally be incorporated into these routes where they can be avoided.

- There will be overlap between some of these routes and the more advanced nursery routes.
- Include all types of basic rule crossroads and junctions with give way and stop controls.
- A route with plenty of uphill, give way junctions should be included for practising first gear hold and control.
- You should now begin to include traffic lights and roundabouts which conform to basic rules.
- Roads selected for the initial practice of the 'turn in the road' and reversing exercises should be reasonably traffic-free and obstructions on the footpaths should be avoided. Driving test routes should also be avoided.

Because of the length of the tuition periods, local geography and road design have to be taken into consideration. If complicated situations cannot be avoided then you may either have to drive pupils to more suitable areas, or give them full instruction and talk-through.

Advanced routes

These routes will incorporate most of the intermediate routes. They should be progressively extended to include as many variations to the basic rules as possible. Where possible, include dual carriageways, multi-laned roads, one-way streets, level crossings, busy shopping streets, and rural roads providing an opportunity to practise overtaking.

Advanced routes all provide an opportunity for you to conduct 'mock' tests in situations similar to those used for the driving test. It is stressed, however, that you should avoid actual test routes.

You should, where possible, incorporate:

- pedestrian crossings – zebra, pelican and school;

- level crossings;
- dual carriageways;
- multi-laned roads to practise lane selection and discipline;
- one-way streets;
- motorway-type dual carriageways;
- rural roads.

Points to Remember When planning and selecting routes, primary consideration should be given to the following:

- the standard and ability of the pupil;
- the specific skills you wish to practise;
- which particular hazards you wish to include or avoid;
- how much time is available;
- what danger or inconvenience might be caused to other road users;
- if any excessive nuisance is likely to be caused to local residents;
- avoiding excessive repetition of routes because of boredom;
- avoiding using test routes and not using corners or roads used by driving examiners for manoeuvre exercises during the normal testing hours (8.40 am to 5 pm);
- awareness that other traffic can be a severe distraction to pupils while they are learning basic skills.

Giving route directions

The quality of your pupil's performance can be totally destroyed if you give late or unclear directions. You must give your pupils sufficient time to interpret and respond to any request. You must also remember that inexperienced pupils may take a long time to react to your instructions.

Your instructions must be clear and precise, stating the direction required and identifying the location where the action is to take place. You should first of all alert your pupil to the forthcoming change of course.

Most instructions concerning the route contain three basic ingredients, which are:

- Alert – draw your pupil's attention to the imminent request.
- Direct – the instruction to turn or pull up.
- Identify – confirm where the instruction is to be carried out.

Examples:

Alert – I would like you to
Direct – turn left
Identify – at the junction ahead.

Alert – I would like you to

Direct – take the second road on the right
Identify – this one being the first.

Alert – I would like you to
Direct – take the road leading off to the right
Identify – at the roundabout. That is, the third exit.

Alert – I want you to
Direct – take the next road on the left, please
Identify – that's the one where the pillar box is.

Confirmation can be given where required by adding further information such as 'It's just out of sight around the bend' or 'It's just before the telephone box, bus stop' etc.

Instructions and Terminology

General instructions

You should try to keep your instructions standard. In this manner pupils will be familiar with the type of terminology the driving examiners use.

The following are general instructions for normal driving and special manoeuvre exercises:

General Route Brief I want you to follow the road ahead unless otherwise directed by road signs or markings. When I want you to turn, I will ask you in good time.
Drive on when you are ready, please.

Stopping – Parking – Angled Start – Moving Off. I want you to pull up and park on the left at the next convenient place, please.
I want you to pull up just behind the stationary vehicle, but leaving yourself sufficient room to move out again.
Drive on when you are ready.

Emergency Stop Shortly, I will ask you to stop the vehicle as in an emergency. The signal will be 'Stop'. When I give this signal, stop immediately and under full control, as though a child has run off the pavement.
Drive on when you are ready, please.
After the exercise, let the pupil know exactly what is happening next by saying:
Thank you! I won't/will be asking you to do that exercise again.
Drive on when you are ready, please.

Left/Right Hand Reverse Exercise Left – The road on the left is the one I want you to reverse into. Drive past it and stop, reverse in and continue back for some distance into the side road. Keep reasonably close to the kerb.

Right – The road on the right is the one I want you to reverse into. Drive on the left until you have passed it, then move across to the right and stop. Reverse in and continue back for some distance down the side road, keeping reasonably close to the right hand kerb.

Turn in the road I want you to turn the car round by means of forward and reverse gears. Try not to touch the kerb whilst turning.

Parallel Parking Pull up on the left in a convenient place, please. This is the parallel parking exercise. Will you drive forward and stop alongside the vehicle ahead. Then reverse in and park reasonably close to, and parallel with, the kerb. Try to complete the exercise within about two car lengths from the vehicle.

Lane Selection Wherever possible you should encourage your pupils to make lane selection decisions for themselves. During early practice in new situations, however, and at more complex junctions, assistance may still be required. For example:

- Approach in and maintain the left hand lane through the roundabout.
- Select and maintain the centre/right lane.

Route Confirmation When confirming a straight ahead direction, use the term, 'Follow the road ahead,' at a junction or roundabout.

Avoid 'Go straight on' or 'Carry straight on'. These terms may be taken literally and the pupils may ignore traffic signs, markings or give way rules.

Directional errors

Giving clear directions in good time may not always guarantee the correct response. People often get confused between left and right, particularly when they are under stress. This can be embarrassing for them, so, providing no danger or inconvenience is caused to other road users, it may be advisable to let them continue in the chosen direction. Make sure, however, that they do proceed in the direction for which they are indicating. Try not to overemphasise the problem as it will only make your pupil feel even more foolish.

Obviously you should try to cure this problem as soon as possible. One way of helping a pupil who is right-handed is by saying 'I write with my right and what's left is my left.' Almost all people wear their watch on their left wrist, similarly wedding and engagement rings are worn on the left, so this could also be used as a point of reference.

Although candidates are not tested on their ability to distinguish between left and right, excessive errors of this nature could prove very difficult for the examiner.

Encouraging independence

When giving directions to pupils who are nearing test standard, it is important that these are as neutral as the circumstances allow. While your directions should always be clear and precise, guard against giving the pupil too many reminders of what they should be observing for themselves.

Telling an advanced pupil to 'Turn left at the traffic lights' provides the information 'traffic lights' which the pupil should be left to work out independently. Such information, however, may be justified in special circumstances on a particularly complex route.

In certain areas it may be virtually impossible to ascertain which lane will subsequently be required without previous knowledge of the area. Under such circumstances you may have to tell your pupil which lane to select and give a reason for doing so.

Points to remember

- Late instructions are likely to cause:
  - rash, hurried decisions;
  - poor control;
  - poor observations;
  - erratic steering;
  - lack of confidence;
  - difficult/dangerous situations arising;
  - over-use of the dual controls.
- Avoid using the word 'Stop', except in an emergency. It could result in the pupil stopping in a dangerous position. If you want the pupil to hold back, or avoid moving away unsafely, the word 'Wait' can be used quite effectively.
- Avoid beginning an instruction with the words: 'Turn' or 'Pull up'. You could get an immediate and incorrect response.
- Try to avoid using the word 'right' for anything other than a directional change. For example, 'Right, turn left at the crossroads please'. This could cause obvious confusion. Avoid saying 'That's right!' when in fact you mean 'That's correct!'

The use of instructions and terminology

Any instructions you give while the vehicle is in motion should be firm, concise and clearly understood. Your terminology should be consistent, particularly in the early stages of tuition. For example, if, after mostly referring to the 'holding point', you change your wording to 'biting point', there is a possibility of confusion.

Similarly, if, after giving frequent instructions to 'signal' right or left, you change your terminology to 'indicate', it could lead to momentary hesitation. This could lead to serious consequences if there are other road users about.

If you wish to instigate correct and immediate response, your pupils must be able to recognise and interpret your terminology.

The need for most instructional jargon is at its highest during the early stages of tuition. However, this is when pupils are least familiar with it. A new pupil should, however, in a short time, become accustomed to your style of terminology.

Pupils who come to you with previous experience may be used to a completely different style of instructional language. In order to make life easier for them, it may help if you can adapt to the difference rather than expect them to learn new vocabulary.

This is not always easy, or successful, but it should help you appreciate the difficulties caused by unfamiliar phraseology.

TERMINOLOGY

Koplings – Bremse – Girkasse

Unless you are Norwegian, the above words will be strange and unfamiliar names for three of the car's controls.

When talking to an absolute novice about the clutch, brake, or gearbox, you might as well be speaking in a foreign language. When introducing these controls and explaining the function and use of each, pupils must be given sufficient time to assimilate the new and strange words.

Wherever possible, your terminology should be in simple and consistent language which will be easily recognised and clearly understood.

Some Standard Instructions

The following instructions can be used to instigate set responses from your pupils. Make sure you give adequate explanation and practice at using the terms before expecting pupils to remember them. In most cases the basic responses can be practised while the car is stationary.

Vary the tone of your voice according to the personality of the learner and the nature or speed of the response required. For example a short, firm 'Brake harder' is far more likely to achieve a positive effect than the same instruction given in a very quiet and slow manner.

Get to know your pupils and adjust your voice to suit the urgency of the situation as well as taking into consideration how they are likely to respond.

Make sure your pupils can understand and carry out the following instructions before attempting to move off:

The Instruction	What it means
Handbrake ready.	Hand on the handbrake, ready to release it.
Set the gas.	Increase the engine speed to a faster tickover.
Find the holding point.	Clutch up until the engine is slowed down at the point of clutch take up. This is often called the 'biting point'.
Cover the clutch.	Foot over the clutch pedal.
Cover the brake.	Foot over the brake pedal.

Instructions Used for Moving Off and Increasing Speed
   Make an initial check all around.
   Clutch down; hand on gear lever, palm towards me, and select 1st gear.
   Set the gas.
   Find the holding point and keep your feet still.
   Check the interior and door mirrors.
   Look over your right shoulder to check the blind spot.
   Signal if helpful to warn or inform others.
   Handbrake off; hand back to the wheel.
   Increase the gas slightly; and slowly raise the clutch.
   Cancel signal (if used).

Instructions Used to Change Through the Gears
   Hold the wheel firmly with your right hand and cover the clutch.
   Hand on gear lever, palm towards me.
   Push the clutch down and come off the gas.
   Move the gear lever into 2nd.
   Clutch up smoothly; increase the gas gently.
   Hand back to the wheel; rest your left foot.

For changing into 3rd and 4th use the same instruction. If the palming method of gear selection is used, you should say 'palm to you'.

Instructions Used to Change Down the Gears
   Keep both hands on the wheel; off the gas and cover the brake.
   Brake gently; off the brake but keep it covered.
   Hold the wheel firmly with your right hand and cover the clutch.
   Hand on gear lever, palm towards (whichever direction is appropriate for the
      gear).
   Push the clutch down.
   Move the gear lever into –.
   Clutch up smoothly.

Further instructions will then depend on whether you wish the pupil to keep slowing down or to speed up again. For slowing down more, it would be:

   Keep the brake covered; clutch down etc.

For building up the speed again, it would be:

   Increase the gas so that we can change up again.

After any gear change, make sure the left foot is clear of the clutch and the hand returned to the wheel.

Instructions Used in Normal Driving
   Hold the wheel firmly.
   Look well ahead; look where you want to steer.

Prepare to turn the wheel left/right.
Check the mirrors.
Signal left/right.
Increase the gas/off the gas.
Brake gently/brake harder/ease off the brake.
Clutch down.
Handbrake on/select neutral.

Instructions and Prompts used to Alert Drivers to Risks and Hazards
Look for pedestrians/cyclists/animals/vehicles moving into/across your path.
Look for and act on things which restrict your view, such as parked cars.
Look for and act on signs/signals/road markings.
Look for and act on bends/junctions/obstructions.
Look, and keep looking both ways.

Instructions to Reduce Speed
Hold back for _____

Once explained and demonstrated, the 'hold back' procedure provides a usefully abbreviated expression. It can be used to replace abstract instructions relating to braking pressure. It also involves the pupil in learning how to judge speed and timing. It does, however, require considerable practice.

The procedure involves slowing down early enough in order to give the situation more time to clear. Thus it reduces the likelihood of having to bring the car to a complete stop.

Once understood, this procedure will give your pupils more freedom and help them develop a sense of responsibility for their own actions.

The holdback position describes that in which drivers would normally:

- wait behind parked vehicles or other obstructions for oncoming traffic;
- follow behind cyclists when waiting for oncoming traffic to clear.

The following are positive commands which should leave pupils in no doubt as to the action you require of them:

Slow down for _____.
Give way to _____.

Both of these instructions leave pupils with more freedom and responsibility for their own actions to avoid a stop.

The command 'Stop!' should only be used in an emergency. It is the verbal equivalent of using the dual controls. The tone of your command will affect how your pupil responds. Used in a careless manner, this command could result in an emergency stop, particularly if the learner is under stress.

Instructions and Prompts Used to Stimulate Thought New drivers, because of their inexperience, often fail to recognise or anticipate danger in many common 'high risk' situations. Short comments or questions, directed at drawing their attention to the danger, can help to improve anticipation and responses.

Provided that the prompts are used in plenty of time for pupils to respond, this technique helps to make them think about and consider the consequences of their own inaction. For example:

I would approach much slower than this.
I would give way to the oncoming driver.
Are you ready to move away when it's clear?
What's happening behind?
Is it safe to go yet?
Can you see?
How far can you see?
Is it clear?
Do you need to signal?
Do you know how much clearance you should give to a parked car?
Can you tell me what the normal driving position is?
What's the speed limit on this road?

Approaching a row of parked vehicles at an excessive speed, ask:

What will you do if a child runs out?
What will you do if a car moves out?
What will you do if a car door opens?
What will you do if the cyclist pulls out?
What will you do if the oncoming car keeps coming?

Approaching a pedestrian crossing at excessive speed, ask:

What will you do if that pedestrian steps onto the crossing?
Do you know what's behind us?

Driving too close to the vehicle ahead, ask:

What will you do if the car in front has to stop quickly?
Do you know how close the car behind is?
What is the stopping distance at x mph?

Approaching a bend or corner at excessive speed, ask:

What will you do if there is a car parked just around the bend?
What will you do if there is a pedestrian crossing the side road?

Corrections Made on the Move Under normal circumstances, detailed explanations should be avoided while the vehicle is in motion. This applies particularly if your pupil is concentrating on something else, such as emerging from a junction or when waiting at red traffic lights.

However, most incidents involving minor errors may not be recognised by the learner at the time they are committed. Ten minutes later, most of those that were recognised will also have been forgotten.

Some brief feedback, therefore, should be given on errors committed at the time, or as soon as possible afterwards. This will draw attention to them, making incidents easier to recall when later referred to and corrected in detail.

You can use short comments as cues to help pupils deal with difficult situations, or as minor rebukes for errors which may have been committed.

Where corrections are made, they should be of a positive nature and ideally state the action required to cure the error. For example, it is better to say 'Hold the clutch still' rather than 'Don't let the clutch up', or 'Drive about two or three feet from the kerb' rather than 'Don't drive in the gutter'.

Serious errors, or repeated minor ones, which appear to involve misunderstandings, should be corrected as soon as reasonably possible after they have occurred, when a suitable parking place has been found.

Using the Dual Controls

Because of their inexperience, new drivers lack anticipation and fail to recognise or respond to potentially dangerous traffic situations. You should never completely trust pupils to follow instructions or do the correct thing. Make sure they are aware of their legal responsibilities. Remember too that you could be prosecuted for aiding and abetting offences committed by them.

You must sometimes be firm and take whatever action necessary to protect your pupil, the car and other people. Look, think and plan well ahead. Get to know individual pupils and watch them. You will soon learn to predict how they are likely to respond in given situations.

You must anticipate changes in the traffic situation and give instructions early enough for pupils to react. If anticipated early enough, most awkward situations can be avoided by giving verbal commands or, if it becomes necessary, taking action with the dual controls. Uncorrected errors will lead to the development of potentially dangerous and frightening situations.

There are four main reasons why you should intervene:

- to prevent risk of injury or damage to persons or property;
- to prevent an offence against the law;
- to prevent excessive stress to the learner in certain unplanned circumstances;
- to prevent mechanical damage to the vehicle.

A verbal command is often sufficient if given in time. However, if your pupil does not react to this, you will need to act. For example, you may sound the horn; turn the wheel; switch the engine off; select a missed gear; release a partially engaged handbrake; or prevent an unsympathetic gear change by covering the lever.

If it becomes necessary, use the dual controls. However, these should not be used as a matter of routine. If they are used, you should tell the pupil afterwards and the reason should be given.

Continual steering corrections and excessive use of the duals does little to build pupils' faith in their instructor. It could also lead to resentment, particularly if the pupil does not understand why the controls were used. Even where use of dual controls is totally justified, some pupils will be upset by such action.

There are various methods which you can apply in order to maintain a safe learning environment:

Verbal intervention

The verbal command is the most common form of intervention. This will usually be successful if you are concentrating on the task, planning well ahead and giving instructions early enough for your pupil to respond.

These commands range from a mild memory prompt to a more positive command for a specific and immediate action.

The prompt is usually associated more with the earlier lessons but may be extended to more positive instructions such as:

- Use the mirror before changing direction.
- Brake harder, or, ease the brake off.
- Clutch down, or, hold the clutch still.
- Increase the gas, or, off the gas.

The more positive commands, needed to relieve potentially dangerous traffic situations, are usually those you will need to give when you want your pupil to slow down earlier when approaching hazards.

'Hold back', or, 'Give way' are positive commands requiring a specific reaction from the pupil but these also leave the pupil with some freedom of judgement.

'Stop' is the final and absolute command. It should generally only be used in a situation which is fast getting out of control and/or where other instructions have not been followed or are unlikely to achieve the desired response.

Physical intervention

Physical intervention should normally be restricted to those situations where it has become essential: where verbal intervention has not worked or where there is insufficient time to give it.

The main methods of physical intervention are the use of the dual footbrake and steering corrections made from the passenger seat.

In any traffic situation you should consider the method of intervention best suited to correcting the current problem. There are occasions when both steering and braking corrections may be required. For example, it may be essential to hold the steering wheel while using the dual footbrake. This is to resist the tendency the pupil may have of swinging the wheel.

In order to generate more time for you to intervene and turn the wheel from the passenger seat, it may be necessary for you to reduce and control the speed of the car with the dual brake, particularly if the pupil has 'frozen' on the accelerator.

Using the dual footbrake:

- Keep your foot readily accessible for the brake with the minimum amount of movement.
- If you see a potential need for using the brake – get your foot ready over the pedal.
- Avoid fidgeting with the brake – this is likely to unnerve the pupil.
- If your pupil becomes frozen on the accelerator, it is generally inadvisable to use the dual clutch as well as the brake. This could result in a 'blown' engine.
- If pupils see a sudden movement towards the pedal, or where they feel a pressure change on theirs, they may react instinctively by braking harder. This double pressure can be dangerous to following traffic or may possibly lock the wheels. Be aware of this possible reaction.
- Before using your brake, check your dual mirror.
- After using the dual controls, explain to the pupil why it was necessary.
- Reducing the speed with the dual brake sometimes allows pupils more time to turn the wheel in circumstances which might otherwise have been difficult.

The steering wheel – points to remember:

- Turning the wheel from the passenger seat is generally more difficult than using the dual footbrake.
- In certain circumstances it may be the only safe or practical method of intervention.
- The need for this kind of intervention can be kept to an acceptable minimum by ensuring the route and conditions are commensurate with your pupil's ability.
- Other than for minor course corrections, if you intend turning the wheel left, go for an initially high position. This will give more leverage. For turning it right – go for a lower position which is more suitable for pushing the wheel.
- When turning the wheel, try to avoid physical contact with the pupil, though circumstances may make contact with the hands or arms inevitable.
- Where 'frozen' to the wheel, even a very frail person can become immensely strong and may resist any attempt you make to turn it.
- Minor corrections to steering course and positioning are frequently more practical and safer alternatives to using the dual footbrake. For example, where the pupil is steering loosely towards the kerb or too close to oncoming traffic, parked vehicles, cyclists or pedestrians.

- There is sometimes resentment by pupils of physical intervention with the steering wheel, particularly if they fail to recognise the reason.

The dual clutch and accelerator

- Assisting pupils by using the dual clutch is usually unnecessary. It should be avoided in all but the most exceptional and isolated of instances where it must be used to avoid danger or damage.
- Dual accelerators are uncommon in the UK. If they are fitted, they must be removed while the vehicle is being used for a driving test.

The horn

- This should be used sensibly. It is better to remove a danger at source by giving a warning, than to later find more drastic intervention has become necessary.

Other forms of intervention

- You can engage a missed gear at a critical time or place.
- You can prevent damage to a racing engine by switching it off – as long as you can reach the key.
- Operating the indicator in critical circumstances may prevent a dangerous occurrence where the pupil is unable to attend to it.
- Correcting a mistake in the use of the handbrake, eg releasing it properly if your pupil has only partly done so; or applying it properly if this has not been done.
- Preventing an unsympathetic gear change by covering the lever until the speed has been increased/reduced.

Even where it may be fairly obvious, you should confirm why you have taken any physical intervention.

Where much verbal or physical intervention is still required by a pupil nearing a driving test appointment, it is extremely doubtful that, independent of such help, they will be able to cope unaided on test.

Dual Eye Mirrors The extra rear view mirror will help you to keep in constant touch with the all-round traffic situation. The dual eye mirror, strategically placed and focused on the pupil's eyes, will enable you to check that the pupil is checking mirrors sufficiently.

The importance of your dual mirrors should be obvious. They should be placed fairly high on the windscreen so as not to impede the pupil's view in any way. However they should be low enough to provide an adequate view to the rear. They should be correctly adjusted and perfectly directed for you to check just as you would adjust the mirrors if you were driving. They should give maximum vision with minimum movement.

Some instructors use nearside door mirrors for their own convenience. This can be counter-productive and defeats the commonsense purpose of encouraging pupils to make all-round observations.

If your car does not have a nearside mirror, there are some circumstances when you must encourage pupils to turn their head to check blind spots prior to executing certain manoeuvres. However, looking round unnecessarily in this manner, when driving forwards at speed, is an unnecessary risk factor and could result in steering problems.

You can verify the safety of some manoeuvres for yourself by checking to the nearside.

Avoiding Common Driving School Accidents

Safety is no accident! It is your responsibility to maintain a safe learning environment for your pupils by:

- planning routes commensurate with their ability;
- looking and planning ahead and concentrating on the traffic situation all around;
- being alert to and anticipating their actions;
- giving directions and instructions clearly and in good time so that they have plenty of time to respond.

Popular belief is that learner drivers are far more likely to have accidents than experienced motorists. However, the novice who is learning in a dual-controlled car under professional supervision is far less likely to have these problems.

If a driving school car is involved in an accident it is most likely to be a 'rear end shunt'. There are two main reasons for this:

1. Most novices have a reluctance to slow down, give way or stop, because of their inexperience at hazard recognition. This initial reluctance to deal with a traffic hazard may subsequently develop into an emergency. Where the situation is allowed to reach this critical level, there are two possible unwanted reactions from the learner:
   (a) Do nothing, remain frozen on the controls and proceed on a collision course;
   (b) Over-reaction – this can often result in harsh unregulated braking, which will usually bring the car to an uncontrolled and abrupt stop yards before it is necessary.

Whether it is the instructor or pupil who stops the car under these circumstances, the result is likely to be the same if the driver behind is not concentrating or is following too closely.

2. The 'false start', or 'stall', when moving into a roundabout or pulling out of an 'open' junction. Often, as the learner starts to pull out, the driver behind

is looking to the right whilst moving into the space he thinks has been vacated. Unfortunately, and unknown to him since he was not paying attention by looking in both directions, the learner has stalled while moving into the space (or the instructor may have stopped the car because of approaching traffic). This emphasises the need for proper route selection according to the student's abilities.

How to avoid rear end collisions

1. Keep your distance, slow down earlier and allow the car to run gently to a halt.
2. Act promptly to prevent a pupil from trying to move off at the wrong time. To allow a pupil to move off in this manner, necessitating a stop within a few feet, is potentially dangerous because it also encourages the following driver to move.

Other accident-prone situations

Pay special attention when approaching traffic lights. Because of a lack of understanding of the real meaning of the lights, some pupils are apt to stop abruptly if the lights change. This can sometimes happen when they have already crossed the stop line.

The right turn at traffic lights is a particularly dangerous manoeuvre and careful attention should be paid to observations when emerging from blind junctions or where visibility is restricted by parked vehicles or other obstructions. Look for yourself and be sure it is safe to proceed before allowing the pupil to do so.

You must remember that inexperienced learners are not usually as quick off the mark as experienced drivers. This can make emerging into busy roads and large roundabouts potentially dangerous manoeuvres. Again, choose your routes to match your pupil's ability.

Be ready to compensate for any sudden movement of the car on low-speed manoeuvre exercises. A slight error on the part of your pupil could have disastrous consequences.

When emerging from junctions, pay particular attention to the blind areas behind your pupil's head. At the same time, position yourself so that the pupil's sightlines are not restricted by you.

Always make sure for yourself that your pupil is emerging safely.

Assessments and Standards

To be able to judge how effective your teaching is, you will need to be able to assess your pupils' performance as they progress through the different stages of learning to drive.

To test the different aspects involved in learning, ie knowledge, attitude, personality and skills, you will need to know about the different methods of assessment. These are:

- interviews/oral (question and answer);
- written tests/examinations;
- objective tests;
- aptitude tests;
- practical tests.

As an instructor you will mainly be concerned with assessing the practical skills involved in the driving task. You can also test your pupils' knowledge of the Highway Code and other relevant motoring matters either orally, or by setting written papers at intervals throughout the course.

To assess the effectiveness of your training you will need to:

- ascertain the level of pupils' ability at the beginning of their course;
- state what they should know and be able to do as they progress through each stage, by specifying objectives for each topic;
- test their ability at the end of the course.

Initial assessments

To make an initial assessment of current knowledge and skill, you will need to use a mixture of interview technique and aptitude testing. From information gained, you will then be able to establish a base from which to commence your tuition.

ADAPTING YOUR INSTRUCTION

As a driving instructor you need to be able to adapt the style of your teaching methods to suit the ability of the person you are teaching. Your instruction and approach with someone who has never driven before should be totally different from that you should use for a driver with years of experience.

You should find it much easier to develop efficient and correct skills, together with safe attitudes in the new learner, than you will in changing the style of the experienced driver who has recently been ordered to take an extended test.

Dealing with Learner Drivers

It can be helpful to find out a little about pupils prior to their first driving lesson, particularly if there are any disabilities which may mean that you will have to adapt your teaching methods.

Be punctual and look professional, both personally and in the presentation of your car. Show the pupil that you are interested. The first lesson should be used for getting to know them, establishing how you will address them, and to find out what they already know and can do.

It is important that you use this first meeting to build up the pupil's confidence in you and to get them used to your style and terminology. Reassure them that learning to drive can be enjoyable and motivate them by confirming that driving is an asset and that if you work together it will be easier.

If your pupil has had no previous experience then you should drive to a quiet location and explain how to get into the car safely and about its main controls and how they work. Depending on ability and the length of the lesson, the pupil should have had some experience in moving off, stopping and changing gears by the end of the session. This will go a long way to satisfy their expectations.

For those who have had some experience, use this session to confirm the standard they have reached. Do not rely entirely on what you are told – some learners are not as good as they think, others understate their ability. It is vital that you make your own assessment by asking a few relevant questions and then taking them somewhere appropriate so you can validate what you have been told. Point out to them, and make allowances for, the differences in your car and the one they have been driving. Be prepared to adapt your terminology if they do not understand you.

Only when you have carried out this process can you establish the level of instruction to be used and the point in your syllabus at which to begin.

Dealing with Experienced Drivers

When you are assessing or training experienced drivers you may have to display a great deal of tact and diplomacy. Do not make the mistake of treating them as learners – treat them as equals.

For example, if habits, such as the crossing of hands on the steering wheel, have been practised for 20 years, you should not expect to completely eradicate them. As long as the driver has the car under control, and is in the correct place on the road, try not to over-emphasise the fault. You may find the driver feels you are 'nit-picking'. This could easily result in resentment to the point where no learning or improvement takes place in more important areas such as forward planning, hazards awareness and anticipation.

Where weaknesses in style of driving and knowledge are apparent, you can only advise and give valid reasons for adapting and changing. You should find that reasoning is a more positive way of changing attitudes than retribution.

Licence and Eyesight Check

If you have not already done so, check that the pupil's driving licence has been signed. If it is not available for any reason, it is your responsibility to ensure that they have one before they drive your car. Ask to see it at the beginning of the next lesson. If you are in any doubt, it may be advisable to postpone the lesson.

You should also check for yourself that the pupil can read a number plate at 20.5 metres with glasses if normally worn. If the number plate cannot be read, or there are problems with some letters or numbers, try several plates. If difficulties persist and you are not satisfied, postpone the lesson and advise the pupil to get their eyes tested professionally.

As with your learners, you should also check the driving licence and eyesight of your experienced clients – do not take anything for granted.

Getting to know your new learner

You can use the time spent driving a new pupil to a suitable training area to establish previous experience and other details. Avoid long periods of silence as these could increase tension, particularly if the pupil is already feeling a little apprehensive. An informal chat will help relax pupils. This short period can also serve the following purposes:

- To help break the ice by relieving initial tension.
- New learners are often frightened of appearing inadequate – this informal chat will help keep their mind occupied.
- Light conversation should help provide you with a basis of information which in turn may enable you to assist your pupil achieve the final goal.

Do not press too hard if pupils are reluctant to talk about themselves. Other opportunities will arise later. You may find some pupils particularly talkative – this could be to cover up anxiety on their part. In any case, keep the conversation professional, polite and sympathetic.

Try to keep your questions relevant. You could include:

- Are you still at school or college?
- What kind of work do you do?
- What interests or hobbies do you have?
- Why do you want to learn to drive?
- Are you learning for pleasure or do you need to drive for your job?
- Do you have any previous experience in driving a car, riding a bicycle or motorcycle?
- Do you have any particular worries about learning to drive?

Give your pupil an outline of the course

Outline the progressive stages of learning to drive. Explain that everyone is different and reassure pupils that the course will be structured to their own capabilities.

Selecting a suitable route

When choosing a route for initial assessments, the following should be taken into consideration:

- As far as local geography allows, the route should be suitable for the absolute novice.
- It should be flexible enough to allow for progression on to intermediate routes where pupils' ability to cope is satisfactory.
- For pupils with previous experience, the route should begin in a quiet area affording the opportunity of familiarising them with your car. It should then become progressively more difficult. Make sure, however, that it is possible to escape from the more difficult area if the pupil is unable to cope.

ASSESSING PROGRESS

Question-and-answer Technique

It is your responsibility to produce thinking drivers. Road and traffic conditions are such that it is no longer appropriate to teach new drivers merely to scrape through the 'L' test robot-fashion.

Learn how to use the question-and-answer technique to encourage your pupils to look and plan well ahead and respond early to developing situations. By asking relevant questions, you will discover whether they are learning the appropriate Highway Code rules as they progress through their course.

At the beginning of each lesson find out what a pupil already knows and can do. This will ensure that the lesson can begin with the known and progress to the new subject matter. It is important to ensure that your instructions are clearly understood. Give new information at a level to suit the pupil's ability.

Questions should be short, to the point and phrased in a manner to encourage the required response. Begin questions with: how, why, what if, when, where, or which.

Sometimes questions should only have one correct answer. If this is the case, make sure the question is phrased so as not to mislead. The following questions could be ambiguous:

'Do you know the main causes of skidding?' A correct response could be either 'Yes' or 'No'.

'What do you know about correcting skids?' Could result in the pupil saying 'Nothing'.

Neither of these responses would be what you were looking for. The above questions would have been more direct if phrased as follows:

'What is the main cause of skidding?' and

'How would you correct a skid where the rear of the car is sliding to the left?'

Allow pupils time to think when using more open-ended questions, such as 'What kind of things should you be looking out for about four seconds ahead?' Don't worry about the silence – they need time to interpret your questions, search for the answer and then find the words with which to express themselves.

If the pupil is having obvious difficulty in finding an answer, phrase the question differently or give some clues about what you are looking for. For example you might add 'Think about the movement of other road users' or 'What about the restrictions to your sightlines?'

Listen to what the pupil is trying to say and make the most out of incorrect answers! Give a little praise for partially correct or thoughtful answers and then provide the correct information.

Avoid questions which go far beyond what the pupil is likely to know. You could easily cause embarrassment if a pupil is never able to give you a correct answer.

The timing of questions can be as important as the wording. While the car is on the move, avoid asking questions which need a lot of thought. This can be a distraction and cause the pupil to lose concentration on the driving task. If you wish to find out what your pupil is thinking about in relation to the current driving situation, keep questions simple. For example, if you see a dog wandering about near the pavement edge you could ask 'What can you expect the dog to do?'

Each stage of development should be concluded with a few questions to ensure the student has grasped the main points. A recap at the end of each lesson is probably most effectively done by using the question-and-answer technique. It can also be useful as revision on subsequent lessons.

Answering questions with questions

Students should be encouraged to ask you questions which are relevant to the points under instruction. If irrelevant questions are asked, give a simple answer and tell your pupil that you will cover the subject in detail at a more appropriate time. Avoid leaving questions totally unanswered.

Socrates, the Greek philosopher, is famous for his inductive technique of answering questions with questions to reach new definitions. This 'Socratic method' is probably one of the most effective ways of teaching. It allows pupils to acquire knowledge through their own personal involvement and effort.

For example, if a pupil asks you 'What shall I do about the bus signalling to move away from the bus stop?' you could respond with 'What will you do if it starts moving?'

Highway Code and driving-related questions

New drivers generally require some kind of motivation to learn the Highway Code rules. Continually emphasising the importance of the Code and its relevance to practical lessons is not always enough. Asking questions which relate directly to the subject currently under instruction can do much to change attitudes towards learning the rules.

Words of encouragement and a few simple oral questions relating to what is being learned in the car generally help to arouse a degree of interest. Organise between-lesson projects and provide self-test exercises consisting of multiple choice objective questions. Supply an answer code to enable students to check their scores.

There are various types of test questions which can be devised to reinforce learning and/or assess your pupils' knowledge of the Highway Code and driving-related matters.

Objective questions

These are designed so pupils have to select a response from several answers. For example:

1. Triangular signs usually give:

   (a) orders;
   (b) warning;
   (c) information.

2. Tyres must have a minimum legal tread depth of:

   (a) 1mm
   (b) 2mm
   (c) 1.6mm

Short answer questions

These are questions which require a specific answer. They can be used to reinforce specific learning points. For example:

1. Give reasons for each of the following:
   (a) Drivers must allow adequate clearance for parked cars.
   (b) Drivers should reduce speeds in busy shopping areas.
   (c) Drivers should take extra care on country roads without footpaths.

Examples of questions more commonly used in driving instruction and testing are given below:

2. What is the stopping distance when driving at 30 mph in good conditions?
3. Give six examples of places unsuitable for parking.
4. What are the characteristics of a safe parking position?

Designing questions

Questions should be written simply, so as not to mislead. For example 'What must you not do before turning right?' is a negative question.

After considering this question, you should find two basic flaws which could prove counter-productive if put to a novice driver:

1. Because the question asks what not to do, the learner will probably go up a number of 'blind alleys' prior to reaching the correct answer. There are literally dozens of correct and sensible answers to this negative question. While occasionally there may be justification, it is normally far better to ask questions in a manner which requires positive and constructive responses.
2. Changing the question to 'What must you do when turning right?' narrows down the field of correct answers. While this has improved the question, the word 'what' implies it requires a specific answer. However, there is not one specific answer to this question as the full procedure for turning right involves several actions. If you require a short, exact response then more information should be included in the question.

Examples

1. What must you do before signalling to turn right?
2. When turning right into a side road, what must you particularly look out for just before turning?
3. What position should you be in for turning right on a wide road?

If a more general answer is required, the question could be phrased as follows:
Outline the basic procedure for turning right into a side road.
While this kind of question may frequently be necessary, one of the problems is that it also tests a pupil's ability to communicate. The procedure may be understood but the pupil may have difficulty in explaining the details. Patience and understanding should be shown and, where necessary, give further help by asking different questions of a more specific nature.

Practical Assessments

To assess progress, take pupils into traffic conditions which are appropriate to previous experience and observe their behaviour.

This type of assessment will be mostly visual. It consists of watching pupils' actions within the car. Observe their use of the controls, ancillary equipment, instrumentation and mirrors. The assessment should also include watching pupils' behaviour towards the external traffic situations.

You should guard against:

● watching the pupil too intently. This may result in you missing important changes in the traffic situation to which your pupil should be responding;
● watching the road and traffic too intently. You may miss faults of a physical nature inside the car. These could include an incorrect signal being applied; riding the clutch; poor mirror use; attempting to select a gear with the clutch engaged.

You must divide your attention over a wide range of your pupil's activities in fairly rapid succession. The need to read the road and traffic conditions at all times should be, in the interest of safety, fairly obvious.

However, there are some areas of performance where prolonged observation of the pupil is required in order to make a more thorough assessment. These are:

- observation of the pupil's mirror checks;
- assessing the pupil's pattern of observations on the approach to, and emerging from, different types of road junctions.

In order to limit the time required to check the pupil's use of mirrors, and also to leave you with more time to keep in touch with the all-round traffic situation, an additional mirror can be discreetly focused onto the pupil's eyes.

This extra mirror does away with the need to look directly at pupils at the appropriate times to ascertain whether they are using their mirrors. Looking at them could give a cue to make a mirror check when it may otherwise have been omitted. This lack of 'prompting' allows you to make an entirely objective assessment.

Similarly, your observations of the road and traffic situation, before pupils emerge from junctions and before and during any of the manoeuvre exercises, must be carried out very discreetly unless they are intended to be prompts.

Driving examiners are trained to be very discreet where these observations are concerned. The pupil is unlikely to get the kind of prompt during the driving test, which an unknowing instructor could be giving.

Examinations and intermediate assessments of a student's knowledge and ability are an integral part of a teacher's work. A considerable amount of your time will be involved directly in, or as a result of, these.

You will be involved in two different forms of practical assessments. The first form of practical appraisal is called continuous. This is sensitive to pupils' needs and is particularly concerned with improving their driving performance.

The second form of appraisal is a practical test similar to that used by the DSA. This is called a 'mock test'. This objective type of assessment is useful for keeping accurate records of progress made by the intermediate and advanced learners. Because of the 'pass or fail' nature of this kind of assessment, it is unsuitable for basic training sessions.

Mock tests

An objective assessment is one which measures the learner's actual performance against a pre-fixed standard. This pre-fixed standard is the 'perfect driver'. This is a satisfactory yardstick by which any level of driving can be measured.

The perfect driver can be defined as one who is in complete harmony with the vehicle and traffic conditions. He is always in the correct position on the road, travelling at a safe speed for the conditions and visibility, and with the ideal gear engaged to suit the varying speed and power requirements. He is totally aware of his surroundings and shows consideration for the rights of other road users.

Technically, anything which detracts from this perfection is an error. However, perfection to this degree is extremely rare, even in an experienced driver. Therefore, it would be unrealistic to expect the inexperienced 'L' driver to achieve this standard consistently.

It is therefore necessary to devise some means of grading faults. Such a system of grading should attach significantly more importance to serious and dangerous faults than to those of a minor nature.

Grading of Errors You should try not to class driving errors as either 'black' or 'white'. There are many shades of grey, and, when assessing the seriousness of a fault, you should take into consideration the following points:

- An error can involve varying degrees of importance.
- Some errors are of a more serious nature and can result in more severe consequences than others.

Continuous Assessment

This type of assessment is more sensitive to the needs of the learner driver progressing through a course of lessons, than is the more decisive objective assessment previously discussed.

During the early stages of learning, it would be unreasonable to compare the performance of the novice with the 'perfect driver'. Although this type of assessment should still be objective, it should take into account previous experience, practice and general progress, as well as the ability of the learner.

Your assessments should take into consideration the reasons why faults may be occurring. You should seek ways in which to correct them, encourage greater understanding of the causes and thereby improve the overall knowledge and performance of your pupils.

When an 'L' driver makes a mistake there is usually a valid reason for it, for example there may be a basic misunderstanding of what is required. If you are to prevent the same, or similar, errors recurring, you must look to the cause so as to cure it at source rather than superficially treat the symptoms.

There are literally hundreds of different errors waiting to be committed by the 'L' driver. Their causes are relatively few. If you concentrate on curing the cause of an error, improvement should result in other areas where similar mistakes may be occurring.

The 'halo effect'

It is not possible to remove the human element from driver assessments. If you develop a particular regard for a pupil with whom you get on well, it is possible to subconsciously ignore minor errors. You may even gloss over those of a more serious nature.

You may even find an easier route for the pupil by avoiding some of the more difficult traffic situations. Acceptance that this phenomenon, known as the 'halo effect', exists, is in most cases sufficient to guard against it. Try to remain objective, otherwise your pupil may suffer in the long term.

The opposite can also occur with the unpopular client. In this case you may subconsciously treat relatively minor errors as more serious ones and perhaps fail to notice improvements in performance and give credit where it is due.

Assessment records

At any one time you could have about 30 or 40 pupils. All will be at different stages of learning. Even those at similar stages will not have covered identical aspects of driving in exactly the same order.

Your students will be of a wide range of abilities and aptitude and will all have their own personal likes and dislikes.

For teaching purposes alone, this information is of vital importance in helping you create suitable and effective learning experiences for each pupil.

Without some form of record it will be impossible for you to carry all of this detailed information around in your head from week to week.

Apart from obvious information such as name and address, records could usefully contain some of the following details:

- driving licence details – driver number, categories, expiry date;
- eyesight – contact lenses? spectacles?
- theory test – application, date, result;
- practical test – application, date, centre;
- test fees, lesson fees;
- basic tuition record – topics covered;
- assessment and progress report – skills and procedures;
- route record – intermediate and advanced routes – avoid repetition.

Patterns of Errors A properly kept progress record will show where any distinct patterns of errors are developing. These may otherwise not be so obvious to you. If allowed to go unchecked, these errors could eventually mean the difference between a pass or fail on the driving test.

Oral and Written Assessment Reports You may be required to produce reports where relatives or employers are paying for lessons or assessments. These need not necessarily include detailed information of faults but should give a clear and honest outline of the pupil's performance. In certain cases an employer may require a complete assessment before employment is granted.

The following general headings may assist in formulating your reports:

- General knowledge of the Highway Code rules.
- General attitude to speed and the safety of other road users.

- General attitude to lessons and the driving test.
- General ability in vehicle control.
- General visual and perceptive ability.

As the driver training industry becomes more regulated, it is increasingly important to keep your own accurate records of pupils' achievements in line with the new logbook scheme and code of practice.

While most of the information can be handled manually, there are major advantages to be gained from having a computer database such as 'Driving School – The Business' (available from DeskTop Driving Ltd). An added advantage of this system is that it is linked to the DSA Web site, thereby ensuring that you receive the latest press releases and are kept up to date with all regulations.

'L' Driver Errors

Driving errors range from those with sometimes very simple causes to those caused by the pressures and stress built up by driving in complex traffic conditions.

Simple causes can range from unsuitable shoes being worn, to an incorrect seating position. Both of these could make control of the pedals extremely difficult and result in loss of concentration. Make sure your pupils seat themselves correctly when they get into the car.

The tensions caused by driving in difficult conditions can sometimes result in unusual and possibly dangerous decisions or actions being taken. This problem can easily be solved by ensuring your pupils are not taken into situations with which they are not yet able to cope.

Poorly developed perceptive skills frequently result in inexperienced drivers approaching hazards at excessive speeds. The outcome of this is rushed movements when carrying out the manipulative skills, resulting in errors in vehicle control. You can avoid this problem by giving your instructions early enough for pupils to respond and encouraging them to slow down sufficiently to get the car under proper control.

The types of errors committed by the 'L' driver vary considerably according to the particular stage of learning reached. The aptitude and attitudes of pupils also influence the mistakes made.

Most errors in the early stages of learning cannot seriously be considered as driving faults – they are usually caused through lack of knowledge or practice. However, unless these are nipped in the bud they may well develop into driving faults.

A lack of understanding of new information may also cause errors. Many such problems are intensified by insufficient practice in basic car control skills. This initial 'familiarisation' should be carried out in relatively safe surroundings on suitably quiet routes.

Particularly during the initial stages of learning, you must remain acutely alert for any unusual, sudden or excessive movements or reactions with the steering or other controls.

No matter how good your instructions may be, you should not assume that the pupil will carry them out. Initially, most learner drivers have difficulty in coordinating their hands, feet, steering and observations. You must allow for this and give full talk-through until the problems are overcome.

Some of the main causes of error are listed below:

- lack of correct knowledge;
- conflicting knowledge;
- underdeveloped perceptive skills;
- lack of or inadequate observations and/or misinterpretation of visual information;
- deficiencies in the basic manipulative (car control) skills;
- deficiencies in behaviour caused by timidity or irresponsible attitudes;
- poor health, fatigue, drink, drugs, emotional stress.

Note: The learner driver may often be subject to considerable pressure when having to interpret oral directions at the same time as attempting to assimilate other information and instructions on the move. Do not overload the pupil with too much to think about: it can result in lack of attention to the task in general.

General Errors

Poor car control Inadequate car control can usually be traced to insufficient practice at a basic skill; incorrect training and interference of previous knowledge/practice; lack of knowledge; poor co-ordination of body movements; hurried movements; and excessive speeds.

Persistent excessive use of speed Excessive speed is often attributable to incorrect attitudes; poor use of the footbrake; lack of awareness of potential or actual danger; poor perception of speed owing to the pupil being a regular passenger in a fast-driven vehicle.

Lack of awareness – of potential or actual dangers. These faults are very common and are generally caused by lack of experience; knowledge; imagination; or visual scanning. Passively observing a traffic scene does not imply active participation and attention to a developing traffic hazard.

Indecision – can be associated with lack of confidence; poor control skills; lack of knowledge; timidity; or conditions too busy for the pupil's ability. Indecision and/or unwillingness to give way, slow down or stop for a hazard is often caused because pupils lack confidence in their basic ability to move off again. They often fail to recognise that slowing down early will alleviate the situation by giving more time, and that this may also reduce the need to stop.

As a driving instructor, it is your responsibility to ensure that your pupils attain as high a standard as is possible, taking into consideration their own individual abilities. You also need to aim for high standards of driving at all times and at all levels. Try to offer as wide a scope of driver education as possible. Remember, this will mean that your work is more interesting, varied and satisfying.

8

Teaching People with Disabilities

This chapter gives an outline of the considerations to be made when teaching driving to people who have disabilities. It covers topics such as making preliminary assessments, vehicle modifications and adaptations, methods of teaching, notes on some common handicaps, how to apply for the driving test, how the test differs, and driver licensing.

Also listed in this chapter are factors which might affect the driver's performance, including teaching those with learning difficulties, physical stature, ill health, alcohol, drugs, stress, illness, and ageing.

ASSESSING THE NEEDS OF DRIVERS WITH DISABILITIES

Many thousands of people with disabilities have passed the driving test and are regular, safe and competent drivers. Teaching driving to people who have disabilities is essentially the same as teaching anyone else. The subject matter is exactly the same – you merely have to adapt how you teach it, and take into consideration each individual pupil's needs.

This type of driving instruction can be extremely rewarding. Very often pupils with some form of disability are much more highly motivated to do well and gain their independence.

You will need to assess your pupil's personal requirements with regard to any necessary vehicle adaptations. For many, all that may be required to control the car effectively could be:

- a car with automatic transmission;
- a steering ball on the wheel;
- power-assisted steering;
- left-foot accelerator.

261

For those with more severe disabilities, a range of more complex adaptations may need to be considered. Recent developments in technology, such as joystick steering and remote control devices, have given the freedom of driving to those with little movement or strength.

Preliminary Assessments

There are many centres in the UK offering advice, information and assessments. A list of these is given in the 'Useful Addresses' section of this book. They offer advice on the different vehicle adaptations available to compensate for physical limitations.

Minor adaptations may be all that is required for those with disabilities such as congenital limb deformity or those caused through spinal injuries. However, if there is a possible difficulty with a person's learning capability or ability to cope with the demands of driving, then a more comprehensive assessment will be required. This type of assessment may be particularly appropriate for those with:

- spina bifida;
- hydrocephalus;
- cerebral palsy;
- head injuries;
- marked general learning difficulties (even in the absence of physical disability).

The Driving Ability Assessment at Banstead Mobility Centre includes medical, visual and cognitive testing facilities as well as the physical and in-car tests for considering which vehicle adaptations may be required.

Most centres offer a free advice service; however, there is normally a charge for the assessments. This will depend on the scope of service and facilities required. It is sometimes possible to obtain a subsidy for these fees from an appropriate disability group, for example ASBAH (Association for Spina Bifida and Hydrocephalus). The Department of Social Services, or a local fundraising organisation such as the Rotary Club, may also be able to help.

It is certainly sensible to invest in a professional assessment as to the probabilities of driving, prior to investing large sums of money in a vehicle and adaptations.

An assessment centre should provide information on:

- eligibility to apply/reapply for a provisional or full driving licence;
- possible learning or other difficulties during the learning/retraining period;
- suitable cars and adaptations;
- conversion specialists and local driving instructors registered to teach those with disabilities.

Notes on common handicapping conditions

Cerebral Palsy This condition, present from birth, can be caused by birth injury or by the baby and mother having incompatible blood groups. It leads to stiffness, clumsy movement and difficulty with walking and speech. Speech problems sometimes mask an alert and lively intelligence.

Spina Bifida This is a failure of the spine to form normally and involves the spinal cord. At its most severe it can mean deformity of the spine, loss of feeling from the waist downwards and inability to control urine or faeces. Careful attention must be given to car seating. Students often have to be helped to transfer from wheelchair to driving seat and the presence of a urine drainage bag can be disconcerting if not anticipated.

Hydrocephalus This means 'water on the brain' and may be associated with Spina Bifida. It will have been treated medically by the time people are mature enough to drive. It sometimes leads to damage to parts of the brain dealing with concentration, memory and perception, which may make learning slower and more difficult.

Stroke Stroke is caused by a sudden blocking of the blood supply to the brain. A *cerebral vascular accident* is the event that blocks the blood supply. *Hemiplegia* refers to the resulting weakness and paralysis and indicates total paralysis. Partial paralysis is *Hemiparesis*. The 'hemi' (half) refers to the arm and leg of the same side.

Paraplegia Paraplegia involves the lower half of the body. This is nearly always caused by damage to the spinal cord from road or other accidents. The level of the lesion determines the amount of weakness and whether the result will be a spastic (stiff) or flaccid (floppy) weakness, ie whether it has affected the upper or lower motor-neurone.

Parkinson's Disease There are parts of the brain that control movement (motor areas), sensation (sensory areas) and co-ordination (cerebellum) which are all needed for accurate movement. Another group of cells, the basal ganglia, control initiation and co-ordination of movement. Patients with Parkinson's Disease have difficulty in starting movement, including walking. They may show a tremor, usually in the hands, which will decrease when a task such as picking up a cup is undertaken. This 'resting tremor' is characteristic of involvement of the basal ganglia.

Cerebellar Disease This leads to problems with co-ordination when patients may stagger and lurch when walking, have difficulty in speaking and are clumsy in movement. It is caused by a problem in the cerebellum such as a tumour, or can result from conditions such as Multiple Sclerosis.

Multiple Sclerosis This is a condition in which the insulating cover of the nerves of the central nervous system and brain is damaged. Once the cover (myelin sheath) is destroyed, conduction down the nerve is impaired. It can cause alteration of feeling, loss of balance, difficulty in vision and, in the later stages, deterioration of the mental processes. It is a disease that 'comes and goes', so thorough and frequent assessment is needed for driving.

Arthritis Arthritis means inflammation of the joints and there are two common forms. *Osteoarthritis* implies premature ageing and degeneration of the joints which may be precipitated by an injury in earlier life. In *Rheumatoid Arthritis* the lining of the joints and other tissues deteriorates with specific injury. There are many conditions allied to, though not identical with, rheumatoid arthritis. The question for drivers is whether the disability is fixed or unstable, so frequent checking may be necessary.

Myopathies This means disease of muscle and covers conditions in which there is progressive weakness. Most of these conditions are inherited. Often there is weakness round the shoulder and hips, so aids such as power-assisted steering may be needed. Frequent checks are needed to make sure a person has not become unfit to drive. There are not usually learning problems with this handicap.

Car Controls for the Disabled

There is a wide range and variety of modifications available for the disabled driver for either a manual or automatic car. The controls available have therefore been categorised under headings to explain the use of these controls. The majority of adaptations, however, will need to be fitted to automatic cars.

Steering

This can be lightened to either standard power-assisted steering or tailormade, power-assisted steering, depending upon the strength of the driver using the car. Most pupils using one hand to steer need standard power-assisted steering to assist them in various exercises, eg turn round in the road or reversing.

If only one hand is used for steering, the following modifications are available:

Steering ball for either right or left hand. This is usually placed at 10 o'clock for the left hand or 2 o'clock for the right hand, but it can vary, depending on the pupil's sitting position.

Steering aids come in various shapes and sizes to suit the pupil's disability, eg:

- Mushroom grip – this has a broader flat top.
- Steering peg.

- Quad grip – this is used by pupils who do not have any finger grip, but have sufficient strength in their wrists to turn a steering wheel.

A joystick system may be fitted to an automatic vehicle if a pupil is unable to turn the steering wheel. This can be fitted either to the right or left side of the steering column and will turn the steering wheel without actually touching it.

Foot steering may be used by pupils who have no useful function in their arms, but have two good lower limbs. In an automatic car, a steering disc can be placed to the left or right of the foot brake and, with a *stirrup* placed on a steering disc, either foot can steer the vehicle. The angle at which the steering wheel is placed can also be altered to suit; also a smaller steering wheel can be attached.

Brake and accelerator modifications

Foot pedals For those who cannot use the right foot on the accelerator/brake pedals, the accelerator may be moved over to the left of the footbrake. The use of flip-up pedals or wing nut fitting allows the accelerator to be switched back to the right for normal use. Both the accelerator and brake pedal can also be levelled to make operation easier; or the pedals can have raised edges to keep the feet in place, if using one foot over the brake and one over the accelerator. Foot pedals can be extended for a driver of short stature.

Knee controls If the feet are not reliable, but the knee joint is functional, adaptations can be fitted to allow a driver to operate the accelerator/brake controls with the knee.

Hand controls If the lower limbs cannot be used to accelerate/brake, then either hand can be used. The most popular modification is the *single combined lever* for accelerator/brake. This is placed near the steering wheel and the hand normally pushes away to brake, using the driver's body weight. The accelerator is controlled by pulling towards the steering wheel. There are, however, various types of hand control which include a *split control*, where the driver pulls the separate levers towards the steering wheel for both the accelerator and brake.

Another system is the *radial servo vacuum unit* in which the driver pushes down towards the floor to brake and pulls up to accelerate. The last two systems mentioned have power-assisted braking.

Joystick A joystick can also be placed either side of the steering wheel, if the driver is unable to use other methods mentioned for accelerating/braking. There is also a 4-way joystick system for use in an automatic vehicle which enables a disabled pupil with only one usable limb to drive. The joystick can be placed either side of the steering wheel and the driver pushes the stick to the right or left for steering and pushes forward and backwards for the accelerator/brake.

Tiller Another system which combines steering, accelerating and braking is called a tiller control. The steering wheel is replaced by two handles either side of the steering column and is steered like a motor cycle. Acceleration is achieved by twisting one of the handles, and braking is achieved by pushing the whole steering unit downwards.

Gear selector

This can be modified to suit a driver's restricted movement, either by extending the lever, removing the depressant button or lightening the tension required to move the lever. If this is not possible, an electric system can normally be fitted anywhere in the vehicle.

Handbrake

This can be moved to the right-hand side of the vehicle if the left hand cannot be used. If the left hand can reach the handbrake, but the button cannot be depressed, various aids can be fitted to assist with this.

There is a handbrake which is like a stick without a button. This is called a CAM handbrake. It is pushed forward to release or pulled back to secure. Electric handbrakes are available and can be placed anywhere within the car. An extension to the handbrake can be made for convenient use. A foot-operated parking brake can also be fitted to suit the driver.

Secondary controls

The most important and most used secondary control is the *indicator*.

The most popular modification for the indicator is the *trafficator thumb switch* attached to the top of the single combined lever. An *infra-red panel* is also popular and this, as well as indicating, operates windscreen wipers and washers, rear windscreen wipers, flash unit and horn. The infra-red panel is normally attached to a steering ball when the driver can only use one hand.

Both the above systems are very important from the driving instructor's point of view, as they enable the driver to indicate correctly and in good time, especially at roundabouts. All secondary controls, however, can be placed anywhere in the car to suit the driver's disability, including using the head.

Mirrors

Additional mirrors can be placed in or on the vehicle to suit a pupil who has a neck restriction. A *panoramic mirror* is most frequently used. This is fitted over the normal rear view mirror and gives more visibility, especially when reversing. This mirror, used properly in conjunction with the two side mirrors, will satisfy the safety standards required when taking a driving test. Other mirrors can be mounted internally or externally to enable safe observation at various types of junction and blind spot areas.

Impaired Vision

Distance vision

A person must be able to read a standard number plate in good daylight at 67 feet ($3^1/_8$ inches high) or 75 feet ($3^1/_2$ inches high). If a person has a defective or lazy (amblyopic) eye, at no time should he attempt to drive with his good eye covered (occluded).

When assessing whether the driver can read a standard number plate, it is advisable to note the following:

1. Whether the driver is screwing up his eyes noticeably. If so, this may indicate the need for glasses or a change of lenses. The driver should be referred to an optician. If glasses cannot bring the vision up to the required standard, sometimes contact lenses can.
2. Whether the driver is adopting a noticeable head posture which may be:
    (a) chin elevation or depression $\left.\right\}$ these may or may not
    (b) face turned to one side $\quad$ be combined together
    (c) head tilted to one side

    A head posture may be adopted for the following reasons:
    (a) to help overcome double vision (diplopia)
    (b) to bring a reduced field of vision to the central position
    (c) to steady a fine wobble in the eye (nystagmus) if this reduces the vision
    (d) to try to improve vision when incorrect glasses are worn.

    If the head posture is significant, it is advisable to suggest that the driver seeks the advice of an ophthalmologist regarding the cause and possible treatment.

3. Whether there is a tendency to close one eye. This may indicate diplopia (double vision). If so, and treatment cannot be given to eliminate it, the driver is permitted to cover one eye, provided the visual field in the uncovered eye is sufficient. If driving in this country, we advise covering the left eye when the vision in the right eye is satisfactory, as the field of vision to the right is the most useful.

    Sometimes only partial occlusion of one lens is all that is needed but the advice of an ophthalmologist should be sought. The presence of a squint does not necessarily mean that diplopia is likely to be a problem.

Squints These present no problem to driving, provided that a person sees adequately and that there is no double vision (diplopia).

Double vision There are varying degrees of diplopia depending on the level of vision in each eye and the separation of the images. Diplopia is usually at its worst when a person is tired and therefore, if control of the diplopia is possible, he should be instructed when feeling least tired. Prisms are often used to correct this and, if recently given, the driver may need a little time to get used to them. In all cases with constant diplopia, one eye must be covered (occluded) for driving.

Colour vision Defective colour vision is no bar to driving in most countries. However, it is always advisable to check that a person can assess traffic lights correctly by the position of the colours. Particular attention should be paid to Highway Code studies so that all types of signs can be recognised.

Visual fields Drivers may have constricted fields, provided that there is at least 120° in the horizontal field and that it spans the central area. No one may drive with *homonymous hemianopia* (half the field missing with a vertical or horizontal cut off through the centre of the field), or with a total quadrant loss (quarter missing).

Monocular vision These drivers have no depth perception (stereopsis). Forty degrees of their visual fields will be missing on one side and night-time driving may prove more difficult. They may also find it difficult to judge the speed of approaching vehicles.

Near vision Drivers who cannot see clearly at close range may be assisted by hand magnifiers for map reading. Learner drivers with reading difficulties may need help to learn the Highway Code.

Impaired Hearing

Deafness is not classed as a driver disability. No restrictions are placed on a full licence when a deaf driver passes the driving test.

It will be of benefit for those with any hearing problems, especially the profoundly deaf, to disclose this on the Driving Test Application form (DL26). This will ensure that the driving examiner is properly prepared.

Other Driving Impairments and Distractions
Illiteracy, dyslexia and non-English-speaking pupils

Some pupils have difficulty in reading – some may not be able to read at all. This is not a disability and does not necessarily mean that they will have difficulty in learning to drive.

There are various ways in which you can help these pupils and these are discussed in the 'Teaching Methods' section of this chapter.

Physical stature and ill health

Physical discomfort such as toothache, cramp and natural functions can distract drivers. The performance of even the most skilful of drivers can deteriorate when they are feeling unwell. Alcohol and drugs affect every aspect of the driver's physical and perceptive processes and some simple cold cures contain drugs which affect driving performance. Some common drugs to be avoided while driving are:

Sleeping pills	Tranquillisers	Antihistamines
Anti-depressants	Pain killers	Opiates
Amphetamines	Belladonna	

Drivers suffering from the following may be taking the above drugs:

Anxiety	Depression	Insomnia
Toothache	Indigestion	Headaches
Colds/flu	Hay fever	Asthma
Period pains and pre-menstrual tension		

One of the difficulties in helping clients with some of the less obvious handicaps is that they can often go unnoticed for a long time, throughout which period the learners simply struggle on as best they can. Another problem is that some people suffering from a minor handicap may be embarrassed by it and so do not mention it. Others may even deny a handicap through ill-founded fears that the instructor might be reluctant to teach them if they knew about it. Tact and understanding must be the order of the day in dealing with these problems. In some cases *a properly secured* cushion may be all that is required. Pedal extensions can be used for people with short legs or small feet. The floor of the car can easily be raised by placing a board (or similar object) under the carpet or mat.

Mirrors can often compensate for trunk and neck restrictions of movement.

None of us feel well all the time and your pupils will be no exception. Women in particular may feel less well one week in every four due to the menstrual cycle.

Mothers-to-be are not invalids and most of them will not appreciate being treated as such. However, they must be given some consideration, particularly with regard to ensuring the happy event does not occur during the driving test (or, for that matter during a lesson!). Plan the lessons and test sensibly – opinions in this respect vary considerably and the final discretion must be exercised jointly by the instructor and pupil in relation to both lessons and test. Where there is any doubt, the client should seek her doctor's advice.

Alcohol

Alcohol is a drug and is a contributory factor in over 30 per cent of road accidents. After just one drink a driver is less able to make decisions quickly or react promptly in an emergency.

After the second drink a driver will become more relaxed with less concern for normal restraint and attention to detail. There is a further deterioration in mental responses and physical reactions, combined with a slight degeneration in co-ordination and the execution of manipulative skills.

After the third drink a driver's emotions become more extreme and behaviour exaggerated. The driver becomes more confident, talkative, noisy or morose and there is a further deterioration in reactions, co-ordination and manipulative skill. Perceptive responses become slower and impossible feats are far more likely to be attempted.

After the fourth drink there is still further deterioration in co-ordination to the point of clumsiness. Confidence continues to increase while perceptive skills are unknowingly deteriorating. The driver's levels of attention and powers of discrimination and normal restraint are rapidly disappearing. Impossible feats are even more likely to be attempted.

After the fifth drink normal perception of moving and static objects becomes blurred. It takes longer for the eyes to focus and speeds and distances are severely misjudged. The driver's ability to make sensible decisions, and react promptly, is totally unreliable, resulting in high-accident-risk manoeuvres being unknowingly attempted.

Non-alcoholic drugs

Drugs impair driving ability by reducing attention levels, the perception of risk, and the ability to make sound decisions quickly and respond promptly to the road and traffic scene. Studies in the USA show that about 10 per cent of drivers involved in accidents take non-alcoholic drugs of some kind.

Instructors should be particularly cautious when new drivers are suffering from some temporary illness for which they may be taking drugs. New drivers should be advised to ask their doctors whether any prescribed drug will affect driving ability and also read instructions on the labels of non-prescribed drugs. It may also be appropriate to offer advice on the use of illegal drugs and their effect on driving.

Amphetamines speed up the nervous system and help users to 'keep going'. While taking this type of drug, users may feel more alert and confident, but when the effect wears off they are likely to feel very tired and depressed.

Barbiturates are used to calm the nerves. They have an effect similar to that of alcohol, but when the effect wears off depression may follow. A combination of barbiturates and alcohol can cause severe depression. Tranquillisers are used by people with nervous and emotional conditions. They cause drowsiness and the people who take them often combine their use with alcohol with the likelihood of severe or even fatal consequences.

Marijuana is an hallucinogen which can act as either a stimulant or depressant. It slows mental responses and physical reactions, affects the judgement of time and space and limits the ability to concentrate on more than one thing at a time.

Fatigue

Fatigue is a temporary condition that impairs the ability of all drivers. It reduces the ability to concentrate, impairs vision and the other senses, makes decisions more difficult and makes drivers more irritable and so less tolerant with other road users.

It can be caused by hard work, lack of rest, emotional stress, boredom or carbon monoxide poisoning. Contributory factors may include illness, overeating, an overheated car, driving for long distances without rest, bright sunlight or glare from oncoming headlights.

Carbon monoxide is discharged by the car's exhaust system. If this is leaking, or if boot seals are not effective, or if the tailgate of an estate or hatchback car is not fully closed, carbon monoxide may find its way into the passenger compartment. It is colourless, odourless, tasteless and poisonous. Keep plenty of fresh air circulating through the car.

The effects of fatigue on driving performance are not always obvious to the driver. They are:

- concentration becoming more difficult;
- the eyes becoming inactive;
- increased thinking time;
- a slowing of physical reactions;
- it becomes harder to make decisions.

Emotions and stress

Extremes of emotions, such as fear or anger, affect attention levels, perception and response to everyday traffic situations. They limit the driver's ability to reason quickly and logically.

Driving is in itself a stressful activity. High levels of frustration or stress are created by the vehicle and traffic environment. Stress can cause excessive overreaction which adds even more fuel to the fire. On the other hand these overreactions may (particularly in the case of new drivers in situations they are not yet competent to deal with) be associated with poorly developed hazard recognition skills, resulting in additional stresses due to late reactions and lack of confidence due to deficient car control skills.

Aggression is characterised by the hostile feelings or behaviour which some drivers display towards others. Normal mentally healthy people are able to tolerate a degree of aggression towards themselves without retaliation. Some experts claim aggression is linked to an individual's desire to dominate another and to compensate for feelings of inferiority or inadequacy. Others describe it as a surge of destructive feeling provoked by frustration. It is unlikely that aggression can be completely suppressed and when it manifests itself in new drivers, instructors should direct it towards the driver error rather than the person committing it.

Young people are generally more at risk because they are less able to control hostile feelings. However, aggressive behaviour is not restricted to any particular age group or gender if drivers are pushed beyond their limits.

Anxiety

Most normal people get upset and anxious from time to time, particularly when faced with a threat of some kind. Anxiety describes the psychological disturbance characterised by feelings of apprehension. Some people are more susceptible to anxiety than others. This may be due to feeling helpless and alone or experiencing a deep sense of inadequacy. These feelings are all normal in themselves but they have become over-obtrusive. Anxiety ranges in intensity from a vague restlessness to extreme uneasiness and is usually accompanied by some kind of physical distress such as a tightness of the chest, dryness of the throat, sweating, trembling or tears. It can be caused by financial or business difficulties, uncertainty about how to behave in some circumstances, fear of failure or fear of the consequences of an action. Intense anxiety can also be caused by seemingly insignificant matters such as meeting a stranger or having dirt on one's shirt or blouse. Such exaggerated cases may indicate some subconscious cause relating to forgotten experiences.

Anxiety makes it difficult for learners to think, reason or make judgements. It reduces their level of awareness and makes it difficult for them to concentrate on driving or any point under instruction. It results in a low level of retention of new information and skills, panic, reduced physical co-ordination, forced errors and a high degree of risk taking (to flee the situation).

Instructors can assist over-anxious students by creating a confident but relaxed and caring atmosphere, giving more reassurance and encouragement. Common sense over the task demands will help to build confidence. For example, let them drive more slowly on routes with reduced task demands until confidence grows. Shorter training periods and frequent breaks may help. Make sure students understand. Following the structure outlined on page 223, demonstrate and present information as graphically as possible.

Illness

Everyone suffers from temporary minor illness from time to time, such as colds, toothache, headache, tummy upsets. These can reduce attention, impair vision and upset judgements, timing and co-ordination.

Ageing

Ageing can reduce perception and impair manipulative co-ordination. Older people are more set in their ways and will generally find learning to drive more difficult. They tend to be more anxious and their reactions are generally slower. Instructors should not place them under too much pressure or compare their progress with younger learners.

Methods of Teaching

The rules, regulations and subject matter of driving remain the same. However, you will need to adapt your lessons and methods to suit the needs of each of your pupils.

Teaching those with physical disabilities

For those with severe handicaps, you may need to allow extra time for getting into and out of the car, and for finding the most comfortable driving position.

Some conditions cause people to tire during the day. It is important for you to discuss this with your pupil and arrange lessons at times of the day when they are likely to achieve the best results. This should also be taken into consideration when you apply for the driving test so that their concentration and confidence will be at a peak.

Teaching those with hearing problems

The following is an extract from *Teaching the Deaf to Drive* and is reproduced with the kind permission of The Institute of Master Tutors of Driving.

As the age of 17 must have been reached before a provisional licence can be issued, deaf youngsters, having received their education mainly in special schools or units, have some speech, although this may be difficult to follow. Usually sign language is used, and in addition they will be able to lip-read to a certain extent.

Lip-reading, however, depends as much on the clarity of the speaker's lip movements as on the ability of the deaf person. Young people may have a reading age much lower than the natural age. Consequently, the ability to read and write may be limited. They can, however, be just as bright and intelligent as their hearing peers, and with understanding and patience from the instructor will assimilate all that has to be learned to drive a motor vehicle.

The problem for the instructor is to learn the best way to impart the knowledge and the skill to the pupil. The essential is *what is the best way of communication*?

The instructor does not need to learn the sign language, but it is necessary for him or her to use simple straightforward words, which only have one meaning. For example, 'Do not hug the middle of the road'. The word 'hug' to the deaf has only the literal meaning of someone putting arms round another. Again, 'traffic jam' would not be understood; 'jam' is something one spreads on bread and butter.

It is essential to speak slowly and distinctly, and move the lips to form each word. Do not talk through your teeth. It will be appreciated that this approach means it has to be a face-to-face conversation and can therefore only be utilised in a stationary situation. Never shout – the pupil is deaf.

Due to the lack of hearing, it is vital that all 'conversations' be reinforced by demonstrations. Always be patient. Unsatisfactory response is likely to be the fault of the teacher rather than the pupil.

The deaf can normally speak but it is not always easy for the hearing to understand what they are saying. It is difficult for them to make the sounds which we are used to, as they are unable to hear their own voices. Always have a writing pad ready to hand, and ask the student to write down questions.

Learning the Highway Code can be helped by the instructor simplifying the language which is used. Formulate questions in written form and have the answers following in the same easy wording.

Instructors may benefit from getting in touch with local associations for the deaf or the Royal National Institute for Deaf People (RNID), 19–23 Featherstone Street, London EC1Y 8SL (tel: 0171 296 8000). They are always very ready to help with any problems which may arise.

Teaching those with reading and understanding problems

If you have any pupils with problems such as dyslexia or they are non-English speaking, there are various ways in which you can help.

Making more use of visual aids during in-car training sessions will help pupils to understand when introducing new topics. Showing them pictures of road signs and markings and explaining their meaning should also help. They will understand the Highway Code rules better if they can apply them to on-road situations as soon after learning them as possible.

It can be helpful to discuss with family or close friends the subjects currently under instruction and encouraging them to help the pupil by giving some in-between lesson revision and learning exercises.

If a student's command of English is inadequate for both training and testing purposes, try to develop some comprehension of the 'key words' described in Chapter 7. Keep your terminology as simple as possible and, to avoid confusion, make sure you are consistent with the words and phrases you use. It may be advisable to obtain the services of someone known to the pupil to act as interpreter. This can be particularly useful during the training stages because, when the pupil attends the driving test, you will not be able to act in this capacity and the person who has already been present on lessons would be familiar with what is required.

You should try to give as much encouragement as possible to all of your pupils, perhaps by emphasising their successes at the practical skills. In no way should you embarrass them or make them feel inadequate – this will do little to gain their confidence in you.

The book *Learn to Drive in 10 Easy Stages*, published by Kogan Page, is ideal for organising the learning into short, simple steps and for reinforcing the Highway Code rules in relation to the practical topics currently under instruction.

Applying for Tests for People with Disabilities

The procedure outlined in Chapter 9 should be followed when applying for tests for people with disabilities, taking into consideration the following notes. When completing the application form DL26, try to give as much information as possible about the disabilities. If there is not enough room on the form to explain the disability and how the candidate is affected by it, write the extra information out and attach it to the application form. Supplying this information in advance will avoid any possible embarrassment to both pupil and examiner by questions having to be asked on the day of the test.

If the candidate is dyslexic, supplying this information beforehand will allow a suitable means of communication to be devised. The senior examiner at the test centre should be informed at least two days before a test appointment where any of the following exist:

- impaired hearing;
- minor restrictions are experienced;
- abnormal stature;
- any disabilities not noted on the application form.

Providing such information may explain to an examiner why certain actions are taken by the candidate and allowances can therefore be made for them. For example, if an examiner knows in advance that a candidate has restricted neck movement, not classed as a disability, and uses the mirrors for making rear observations when manoeuvring, this will be expected and allowed for. If the information is not volunteered, then the examiner can only assume that correct observations are not made and there is no reason for it.

Before Attending the Test

By this time you should have ensured that the adaptations used by each individual pupil overcome, as far as possible, their disability. If they do not, then you should advise on any further adaptations which you think are necessary, allowing plenty of time to get used to them.

The time allotted for testing people with disabilities spans two normal test periods. You should bear this in mind when entering the appointment in your diary.

Attending the Test

Make sure you allow plenty of time for getting to the test centre if the candidate has difficulty getting out of and into the car. Where severe disabilities exist, you may go into the waiting room to inform the examiner that the pupil has arrived.

The content and length of the driving test are the same as for normal driving tests. (See Chapter 9 for the syllabus.) The extra time allotted is to allow:

- for the examiner to establish any extra details about the disability;
- to make a note of vehicle adaptations;

- sufficient time to repeat any manoeuvres if the examiner feels this is necessary;
- to complete the extra paperwork.

At the beginning of the test, the candidate will be asked if there are any additional disabilities which are not noted on the application form. Encourage your pupils to be frank about this as it will help the examiner to make an effective and objective assessment. The examiner will also ask about the vehicle's adaptations.

Where there are hand adaptations, more emphasis will normally be placed on downhill junctions to check that control is adequate. If a candidate has neck or vertebrae problems, emphasis is normally placed on the ability to make frequent observations at those junctions where sightlines are restricted.

At the End of the Test

The examiner has two decisions to make. These are:

1. Does the candidate have the ability to drive?
2. Do the adaptations overcome the disabilities?

If the examiner is satisfied that the candidate is competent to drive and the vehicle is unadapted, an unrestricted pass certificate for the category of vehicle tested on, and any additional categories covered, will be issued. If the examiner considers the candidate competent to drive unadapted vehicles of the category tested only, then the pass certificate will be issued for that particular category. The restriction will be noted on the form D255.

If the examiner considers that automatic transmission entirely overcomes the effects of the disability, the appropriate category letter will be noted. However, if it is considered that this is not the case, the appropriate category letter would be noted and the words 'with controls adapted to suit disability' and, if appropriate, the words 'and with suitably positioned mirrors'.

All candidates, whether they pass or fail, are given a copy of the Driving Test Report Form DL25A. If a candidate fails and the examiner feels that some other adaptation might enable them to pass, an indication of this may be given.

A pass certificate is not normally restricted solely because of abnormal stature, as this is not considered to be a disability in itself. However, there may be cases where extraordinary size may have an effect on the candidate's driving ability. Where adaptations have been made to overcome this, then the words 'with controls adapted to suit disability', would be included in the pass certificate.

Reporting of Driving Test Results

The results of all tests are reported to the DVLA at Swansea. Any restrictions noted by examiners are then itemised on candidates' driving licences.

Courses for Teaching People with Disabilities

If you are interested in teaching people with disabilities, special training courses are available at the Banstead Mobility Centre, Damson Way, Orchard Hill, Queen Mary's Avenue, Carshalton, Surrey SM5 4NR (tel: 0181 770 1151).

9

The Driving Test

This chapter contains information on the 'L' Test and includes:

- the test format;
- the Theory Test:
  - administration;
  - syllabus;
  - training;
  - application for a test;
  - attending for a test;
  - after passing;
- The Practical Test:
  - administration;
  - changes to the test;
  - syllabus;
  - application;
  - cancelling tests;
  - attending for a test;
  - driver errors;
  - at the end of the test.

THE FORMAT OF THE DRIVING TEST

The test for new drivers is conducted in two parts:

- the Theory Test;
- the Practical Test.

Candidates must pass the Theory Test before they can apply to take the Practical Test.

The Theory Test

Administration

The Theory Test is administered on behalf of the DSA by Sylvan Prometric and candidates may take it at the centre of their choice. There are currently over 150 test centres throughout the UK using touch screen terminals which are specially designed for ease of use by candidates.

Candidates can work through a practice session to get used to the system before starting the actual test and there are staff on hand if anyone has difficulties. Only one question appears on the screen at a time and candidates can move backwards and forward through them. This means they are able to go back to any they want to look at again or to change their answers. The system also alerts candidates if they have not completely answered a question. Those who have special needs may apply to have longer than the standard 40 minutes to take their test. Facilities include:

- being able to listen to questions being read in English through a headset. This will help those with dyslexia and other reading difficulties;
- being able to listen to the test in 15 other languages;
- a video of the test in British Sign Language for those with hearing difficulties.

The current fee (at October 2001) is £15.50 and the result is available immediately after the test.

The Theory Test Syllabus

A knowledge of the following subjects is tested:

Alertness:

- observation;
- anticipation;
- concentration;
- awareness;
- distraction.

Attitude:

- consideration;
- positioning;
- courtesy;
- priority.

Safety & the vehicle:

- fault detection;
- defects;
- safety equipment;
- emissions;
- noise.

Safety margins:

- stopping distances;
- road surfaces;
- skidding;
- weather conditions.

Hazard awareness:

- anticipation;
- hazard awareness;
- attention;
- speed and distance;
- reaction time;
- alcohol and drugs;
- tiredness.

Vulnerable road users:

- pedestrians;
- children;
- people with disabilities;
- motorcyclists;
- cyclists;
- horse riders.

Other types of vehicle:

- motorcycles;
- lorries;
- buses.

Vehicle handling:

- weather conditions;
- road conditions;
- time of day;
- speed;
- traffic calming.

Motorway rules:

- speed limits;
- lane discipline;
- stopping;
- lighting;
- parking.

Rules of the road:

- speed limits;
- parking;
- lighting.

Road and traffic signs:

- road signs;
- speed limits;
- road markings;
- regulations.

Documents:

- licence;
- insurance;
- MOT certificate.

Accidents:

- first aid;
- warning devices;
- reporting procedures;
- safety regulations.

Vehicle loading:

- stability;
- towing.

Theory Test Training

To prepare for the Theory Test your pupils will need to study:

- *The Highway Code;*
- *The Driving Manual;*
- *The Driving Test;*
- *The Official Theory Test for Car Drivers.*

As a driving instructor you should have a thorough knowledge of all the foregoing topics so that you can help your pupils prepare properly for their theory test. This applies even more if you have pupils with learning difficulties. You will sometimes need to encourage and help your learners' family or friends to assist.

There are many CD ROMS on the market to help with theory training. Some of these contain the entire DSA question bank and can be used to aid the learning process, particularly for pupils with difficulties such as dyslexia. Other CDs are aimed at the practical side of the ADI's job and relate to hazard recognition and awareness.

Programmes are available for both car and LGV/PCV drivers. Even if you have no computer skills or access to a PC, being able to offer CDs to your pupils is advantageous. Most learners now have access to a computer either at home or at college. Statistics show that more homes have a computer than have a dog!

Good instructors, who teach driving as a life skill, automatically incorporate most of the subjects covered in the theory test into their practical training courses. This helps learners to understand how to apply the rules and procedures. After all – *how can you teach driving without teaching the rules and regulations and encouraging safe attitudes?*

Application for a Theory Test

Application forms are available from test centres. Bookings can be made in one of three ways:

- by telephone;
- by post; or
- by fax.

If you apply for a test for a pupil by phone, you will need the pupil's:

- personal details;
- driver number; and
- credit card number – the cardholder will normally need to be present when the booking is made.

With a postal application a reply will normally be received within about 10 days.

Attending for a Theory Test

Candidates must present to the invigilator the following documents:

- a valid and current GB or Northern Ireland driving licence;
- signed, photographic proof of identity.

The test consists of 35 questions, some of which have more than one correct answer. Candidates are advised how many answers to select for each question and must get 30 questions correct to achieve a pass. The following are examples of questions:

Q You are the driver of a car carrying two adults and two children, both of whom are under 14 years of age. Who is responsible for ensuring that the children wear seatbelts?

(a) the children
(b) their parents
(c) the driver
(d) the front seat passenger

A The correct answer is:
(c) the driver (Highway Code rule number 76).

Q You are driving towards a zebra crossing. Pedestrians are waiting to cross. You should:

(a) slow down and prepare to stop
(b) give way to the elderly and infirm only
(c) use your headlamps to indicate they can cross
(d) wave at them to cross the road

A The correct answer is:
(a) slow down and prepare to stop (Highway Code rule number 171; *The Driving Manual*, page 109).

After Passing the Theory Test

Candidates receive their test results before they leave the centre. They are given feedback about any topic areas they answered incorrectly.

Candidates who pass are issued with a pass certificate which remains valid for two years. The certificate number must be quoted when applying for a practical test. If a practical test is not taken and passed within two years, a further Theory Test must be taken.

The Practical Test

Administration

This test is administered by the Driving Standards Agency, which is an executive agency of the DETR. The DSA conducts about 1.6 million 'L' tests on cars and motorcycles every year, as well as administering the vocational tests for LGV and PCV drivers. (Vocational tests are dealt with in Chapter 10 of this book, where more information is also given on motorcycle tests.) In Northern Ireland the DVTA conduct 50,000 driving tests at 17 test centres annually.

To ensure uniformity in the conduct of practical Driving Tests, all the DSA's Driving Examiners are trained at the Driving Establishment at Cardington, Bedford. They are monitored regularly and are sometimes accompanied on test by a senior member of staff.

The 'L' test syllabus

You will find this syllabus in full in *Driving Skills – The Driving Test*, which is available from most good bookshops. Alternatively, you can purchase in bulk from The Stationery Office for on-sale to your pupils.

The Driving Test describes in detail:

- the requirements of the test;
- the types of vehicle suitable;
- different categories of driver, eg those with disabilities, hearing and speech problems;
- general road procedures;
- the manoeuvre exercises;
- what the examiner will be looking for;
- the full syllabus for learning to drive;
- information on the motorcycle test.

Changes to the Driving Test

Spring 1999 saw the biggest changes being made to the practical driving test since it was introduced in 1935. The major changes are:

- *Length* – the test is now longer to enable a wider variety of roads to be included in the drive;
- *Routes* – to incorporate driving on higher speed roads and a broader range of hazards;
- *Recording of driving faults* – all driving faults are recorded and if a candidate accumulates more than 15 it will result in a failure. One serious or danger-ous fault will still result in failure;
- *Emergency stop* – is now conducted at random on one in three tests;
- *Reverse park* – pupils may be asked to reverse behind one car, between two cars, or the manoeuvre may be carried out in the test centre car park into a bay. This exercise may be done at the start, during or at the end of the test;
- *Manoeuvres* – two out of the three manoeuvres will be conducted;
- *Printed explanation of the driving test report* – will be given to all candidates;
- *Reverse parking* – into a parking bay at the test centre.

These changes have produced a test that is much more relevant in today's dri-ving conditions.

The 'L' Test syllabus includes:

- *Eyesight test* – make sure your pupils can read a number plate at the pre-scribed distance. It is advisable to check this a few weeks prior to the test.
- *Precautions* – driver checks including: doors; seat; mirrors; seatbelt; hand-brake; car in neutral; if a stall occurs the vehicle must be kept under control.
- *Control* – teach your pupils to handle all the controls smoothly. This includes use of the accelerator; clutch; gears; footbrake; handbrake and steering.

- *Moving away* – pupils will be tested on moving away safely; under control; on the level; from behind a parked car; and, where practicable, on a hill; with correct observations.
- *Emergency stop* – even and progressive braking is required, avoiding locking the wheels. In wet weather pupils should be aware that it could take twice as long to stop.
- *Reverse to the left or right* – full control and reasonable accuracy are expected; good all-round observations and correct response to others are looked for.
- *Turn in the road* – smooth control with full all-round observations. The correct response to others is expected.
- *Reverse parking* – pupils may be asked to reverse behind one car, between two cars or the manoeuvre may be carried out in the test centre car park into a bay. This exercise may be done at the start, during or at the end of the test.
- *Use of mirrors* – mirrors should be used regularly and pupils should be aware of the presence of others in their blind spots. Pupils' response to the all-round situation is tested. Early use of mirrors should be made before signalling; changing direction and/or speed; and as part of the mirror-signal-manoeuvre routine.
- *Signalling* – pupils should give signals clearly and in good time to warn other road users of intentions in accordance with the Highway Code.
- *Response to signs and signals* – pupils should understand and be able to react to all traffic signs and road markings; to check when proceeding through green lights; and to respond to signals given by police officers, traffic wardens, school crossing patrols and all other road users.
- *Use of speed* – safe and reasonable progress should be made according to the road, weather and traffic conditions, the road signs and speed limits. Candidates should always be able to stop within the distance they can see is clear.
- *Following distance* – a safe distance from the vehicle ahead should always be maintained in all conditions, including when stopping in traffic queues.
- *Maintaining progress* – pupils must be taught to drive at appropriate speeds for the type of road and the speed limit; the type and density of traffic; the weather and visibility. A safe approach to all hazards should be demonstrated without being over-cautious. All safe opportunities to proceed at junctions should be taken.
- *Junctions* – the correct procedure should be applied to all types of junctions. This includes applying the mirror-signal-manoeuvre routine and using the correct lanes. Good all-round observations should be made and safe response to other road users demonstrated.
- *Judgement* – the correct response should be applied when dealing with other road users including: overtaking; meeting oncoming traffic and turning across traffic. Other road users should not be made to slow down, swerve or stop.
- *Positioning* – correct position should be maintained at all times according to the type of road, the direction being taken and the presence of parked vehicles.

- *Clearance to obstructions* – plenty of room should be allowed when passing stationary vehicles and other obstructions that may be obscuring pedestrians.
- *Pedestrian crossings* – pupils should be able to recognise and respond correctly to the different types of crossing.
- *Position for normal stops* – pupils should choose safe and legal places to stop and not cause inconvenience or obstruction to others.
- *Awareness and planning* – you must teach your pupils to think and plan ahead and anticipate the actions of other road users. You should instil safe attitudes when dealing with vulnerable road users such as pedestrians, cyclists, motorcyclists and horse riders.
- *Ancillary controls* – pupils should understand the function of all the controls and switches, especially those that have a bearing on road safety. These include: indicators; lights; windscreen wipers; demisters; heaters.

Applying for Driving Tests

After making your assessments, and when you feel your pupils have reached a fairly consistent standard, you will need to advise them on applying for their driving test.

It is important that you make the decision jointly and that you fill in the application form together. This avoids problems arising such as pupils applying independently before they are ready, pupils not informing you of the date until it is too late to be postponed, being reluctant to delay the test once they have an appointment or their obtaining an appointment at a time when you may already have another test booked.

Whether or not to apply for the test is one of the most difficult and subjective decisions you may have to make. There are a number of reasons for this:

- From a business point of view, ie to make sure pupils stay with your school, you may often feel obliged to apply for tests early on during their training.
- Because of pupils' wishes, you may often be put under pressure to apply at the earliest possible date.
- If there is a particularly long waiting list for test appointments in your area, a combination of this with the above two reasons may also affect your decision.
- Where none of the above pressures exist to any significant degree, your decision may still not be easy. You must be fair to pupils and not impose standards so high as to absolutely guarantee a pass. It could well mean that pupils feel you are delaying the decision for purely monetary reasons.
- Pupils will make varying rates of progress at different stages of their training. For example, some make very rapid progress in the early stages, and later, when a higher degree of understanding is required, progress may slow down considerably. Others make very slow progress at first, then make very rapid headway after better understanding is achieved.

- The test waiting list is sometimes unpredictable in its length. If a new examiner is engaged at a test centre you use, you may get an appointment almost immediately. To ensure you do not get one before the pupil is likely to be ready, fill in the earliest date required.

It is as well to remember that if you apply for tests too early:

- the test may subsequently have to be postponed. This means extra administration, expense, time and possible ill-feeling, since pupils generally do not like having tests deferred;
- the pupil may not be ready and will probably fail. This may reflect back on you since you were saying, in effect, that when you applied you considered that the pupil was ready for the test.

When applying for a test where there is a long waiting list, you should emphasise that the booking is made on the assumption that a reasonable rate of progress will be maintained. Also, that the pupil's driving will have reached a suitable standard.

Having taken all of the foregoing into consideration, complete the application form (DL26 or DL3 in Northern Ireland). Make sure you fill in your driving school number as this will avoid problems with double-booked appointments.

The current fees for 'L' tests (at October 2001) are:

Weekday – £38.00   Saturday/Weekday evenings – £ 47.00

It is important to keep a record of test applications. If an appointment is not received within three weeks, get pupils to contact the DSA booking clerk to check. Make sure pupils inform you immediately they receive appointments so that they can be entered into your diary and the school car reserved accordingly.

If you are sending in the application, it is advisable to accept only cheques and postal orders payable to the 'Driving Standards Agency'. This will ensure that no misunderstanding occurs over the fees paid.

When the appointment card is received you should reserve the time in your diary. It is usual to give pupils a lesson immediately prior to the test. Ensure that pupils know that payment for this normally has to cover both the lesson and use of the school car for the test. Some pupils may think that payment of the test application fee also includes your fees.

Application forms (DL26) are available from driving test centres or in bulk from the DSA. Test centres and DSA offices are listed. Make sure all of the requested information is included to avoid any delays in the allocation of appointments.

The same application form is used when applying for tests for people with disabilities and for an extended test. It should be noted that the time for extended tests is double the length of the 'L' Test and the fees charged are higher.

For more information on how to apply for tests for people with disabilities see Chapter 8.

Driving test times

For cars, tests are conducted at: 8.40; 9.37; 10.44; 11.41; 13.33; 14.30; and 15.27.

Credit card booking facilities

Driving tests can be booked by credit card. This service offers the convenience of arranging your candidate's test over the telephone. The phone number for this service is 0870 01 01 372.

It is normal practice for the instructor to use the candidate's credit card when using this booking service. In this case, the booking clerk will normally need to speak directly to the card holder. Before dialling the special number, remember to have ready the credit card details together with the candidate's details, including the driver number. You will be given details of the appointment over the 'phone. It is advisable to immediately enter all the details in your diary. When making a telephone credit card booking, you do not need to send an application form. An appointment card will be sent to confirm the booking.

Cancelling and Postponing Tests

If you feel that a pupil is not yet ready to take the test, then it is in their interest as well as your own and other road users' that you postpone it. You should remember, however, that the contract is between the pupil and the DSA – you should never cancel a test without the pupil's consent.

You should advise the pupil of the need to cancel at least four weeks prior to the test and certainly not less than two weeks. The pupil may offer resistance to your advice. Be sympathetic and tactful, but firm. Be objective and give the pupil a realistic 'mock test'. This will usually convince even the most adamant that you are acting in their best interests. If the pupil still insists on going against your advice, then all you are entitled to do is withhold the use of your car.

It should be noted that driving examiners may not use the dual controls to avoid an accident unless there is a risk of danger – and then it may only be a last-second decision. Your car may be at risk! The school car is the 'tool of your trade'. It is imperative, therefore, that it is not off the road for unnecessary repairs because you let someone attend for a test too soon. There are also other considerations. Your reputation could be at risk if you regularly present candidates for test when they are not up to standard; you are also depriving other candidates of an appointment.

If you wish to postpone a test, 10 working days' notice is required to avoid forfeiting the fee. You may simply defer the test to a later date or you may cancel it. If a cancellation is made by telephone and a further appointment is not required, it must be followed up with a request in writing for a refund of the fee.

The fee will be withheld pending receipt of this request, which should be made within one week of the cancellation.

The DSA's Compensation Code

The DSA will refund a test fee or give a further appointment free under the following circumstances:

- if the DSA cancels the test;
- if the test is cancelled by the candidate with at least 10 working days' notice;
- if the appointment is kept but the test does not take place or is not finished, through no fault of the candidate or the vehicle being used.

It will also repay expenses incurred by the candidate on the day of a test cancelled by the DSA at short notice, unless the reason was bad weather. It will consider reasonable claims for:

- the cost of hiring a vehicle for the test including travelling to and from the test centre (generally up to a maximum of 1½ hours vehicle hire);
- any pay/earnings lost after tax (usually for half a day).

It will not pay, however, for any driving lessons arranged in relation to a particular test appointment or extra lessons taken while awaiting a re-scheduled appointment.

ATTENDING FOR THE TEST

The following is a checklist for you to follow to ensure that everything goes smoothly on your pupil's test day:

- ensure that the pupil has a valid, signed driving licence, their Theory Test pass certificate and some form of photographic identity;
- take the test appointment card in case any errors have been made;
- at least two weeks beforehand check that the pupil can read a number plate at the required distance;
- make sure your car is clean and tidy and has sufficient fuel;
- clean the windows, leaving one slightly open if there is a risk of condensation;
- make sure that the pupil knows where the ancillary controls are and how they work.

Make sure that your car is:

- roadworthy and has a current MOT certificate if applicable;
- fitted with front and rear seatbelts in working order, and adjustable head restraints;

- fully insured for the pupil to drive while on the test;
- properly taxed with the disc displayed in the correct position;
- displaying 'L' plates clearly visible to the front and rear;
- fitted with a rear view mirror for the driving examiner.

You should leave your ADI Registration Certificate or Trainee Licence in the windscreen when your car is being used for a test.

If you overlook any of the foregoing points, the test may be cancelled and the pupil will lose the fee. As they are your responsibility, you will then be obliged to pay for another appointment.

At the Test Centre

Take your pupil into the waiting room a few minutes prior to the time of the appointment. Keep them relaxed by chatting.

The examiner will come in and ask for your pupil by name, request some form of identification and get the candidate to sign the appropriate form. Examiners are trained to use their discretion about introducing themselves either on the way to, or in, the car. They will also decide whether or not it is appropriate to use first names.

The directions and instructions described in Chapter 7 are general guidelines and examiners may use slightly different terminology where appropriate to suit a particular candidate.

The candidate will be asked to sign the Driving Test Report form before the start of the test. This signature will serve as a declaration that the vehicle presented for test carries valid motor insurance in accordance with the Road Traffic Act 1988.

A reminder is given to candidates about motor insurance responsibilities on their test appointment card. However, it is sensible to remind your pupils, before they go into the waiting room, that this formality will take place. Confirm with them that your car is properly insured. If, for any reason, the candidate does not sign the declaration, the examiner will refuse to conduct the test and the fee will be forfeited.

Examiners are sympathetic towards candidates. They understand 'test nerves'. You should realise, however, that while nerves are frequently used as an excuse for failing, they are rarely the real cause. Provided your pupils are properly prepared, and know what to expect, nerves should not be too much of a problem. Conducting a realistic 'mock' test, to give pupils an insight into what will happen, can do much to prevent it.

The eyesight test will be conducted at the test centre. If the candidate fails this, the test will not be conducted. The drive will be of about 40 minutes' duration, when the topics listed previously will be assessed.

THE DRIVING TEST

Driving examiners are trained to look for the 'perfect driver'. At the moment of getting into the car every test candidate is considered to be perfect. Any deviations from this perfection are graded into three categories of fault: driving, serious and dangerous.

Faults are graded and recorded on the Driving Test Report form (DL25C), as they occur. Before any minor deviation from perfect is marked on the form, the examiner must consider its significance to the overall performance. In theory, a candidate could have numerous faults recorded and still pass the test. However, anyone committing a significant number of minor errors is almost certainly likely to commit a more serious one during the test.

Fault Categories

Faults committed during driving tests are assessed under the following categories:

1. *Dangerous fault*: recorded when a fault is assessed as having caused actual danger during the test. A single fault in this category will result in failure.
2. *Serious fault*: recorded when a fault is assessed as potentially dangerous. A habitual driving fault can also be assessed as serious when it indicates a serious weakness in a candidate's driving. A single serious fault is an automatic failure.
3. *Driving fault*: a less serious fault, which is assessed as such because of the circumstances at that particular time. Driving faults only amount to a failure when there is an accumulation of more than 15.

There is an obvious need for a degree of standardisation between the consistency of assessments made in training and those used for the driving test. It is essential therefore that you become familiar with this grading system.

In addition to the above grading system, and because there is a distinct difference between training 'L' drivers and examining them, you must also make allowances for another group of faults. These may not be of sufficient significance to warrant even a driving fault on the driving test. However, if they remain unchecked they could well develop into more serious problems later on in your pupil's driving career.

We will call this group of faults marginal errors.

Individually these errors may not affect road safety. Some may be of a fairly subjective, or even doubtful, nature even to justify the term error in its true sense. However, they may cause concern to the conscientious instructor who wishes to produce consistently good drivers. Where marginal errors are developing into patterns in relation to other serious errors, give them due attention and find a cure before things get too serious.

DECLARATION

I declare that my use of the test vehicle for the purposes of the test is covered by a valid policy of insurance which satisfies the requirements of the relevant legislation. Signed...

Driving Test Report

Candidate's Name

Vehicle Type

Registration No.

Driver Number

	S	D			S	D
1(a). Eyesight			12. Use of speed			
1(b). Highway Code (Categories F/G/H)			13. Following distance			
2. Precautions			14. Maintain progress by :-			
3. Control :- accelerator			driving at an appropriate speed			
clutch			avoiding undue hesitation			
gears			15. Junctions :- approach speed			
footbrake			observation			
handbrake			turning right			
steering			turning left			
balance m/c			cutting corners			
4. Move away :- safely			16. Judgement when :- overtaking			
under control			meeting traffic			
5. Emergency stop :- promptness			crossing traffic			
control			17. Positioning :- normal driving			
making proper use of front brake (m/c)			lane discipline			
6. Reverse to left or right :- control			18. Clearance to obstructions			
observation			19. Pedestrian crossings			
7. Turn in the road / control			20. Position for normal stops			
'U' turn (m/c) :- observation			21. Awareness and planning			
8. Reverse parking :- control			22. Ancillary controls			
R C observation						

9. Use of mirrors / rear observation (m/c) well before :-

- signalling
- changing direction
- changing speed

10. Give appropriate signals :-
- where necessary
- correctly
- properly timed

11. Response to signs and signals :-
- traffic signs
- road markings
- traffic lights
- traffic controllers
- other road users

Visitor

Total driving faults :-

23. Result of test   Pass   Fail   None

Route number

Examiner's signature

Extended test

Examiner's name

| 1 | 3 |
| 2 | 4 |

Supervision SDE   SE   AOM   ACDE

Test Terminated in the Interest of Public Safety		Pass certificate No.		ADI Number		Category
Test Terminated at Request of Candidate				Test Centre		
Examiner Took Action	Verbal Physical	Staff number		Date		M
Oral Explanation Given	Yes No			Time of Test		F

DL25A   DSA - An executive agency of the Department of the Environment, Transport and the Regions   5/00

© Crown Copyright 2000

JCN17147106

Guidance Notes

More detailed advice about the test requirements and the items marked for your attention overleaf are given in 'The Driving Test Report Explained', and also in the DSA products listed below :-

　　The Driving Test

　　The Motorcycling Manual

　　The Driving Manual

　　The Guide to Tractor and Specialist Vehicle Driving Tests.

These can be purchased from all good book shops.

Explanatory Markings

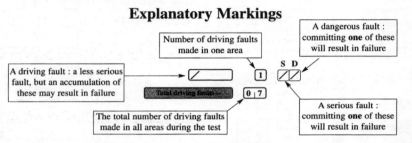

A dangerous fault : committing **one** of these will result in failure

Number of driving faults made in one area

A driving fault : a less serious fault, but an accumulation of these may result in failure

The total number of driving faults made in all areas during the test

A serious fault : committing **one** of these will result in failure

The result of your test is marked at Item 23 overleaf. the following statement only applies if your result is marked as a fail.

Statement of Failure to Pass Practical Test - Test of Competence to Drive
Road Traffic Act 1988.
This candidate named herein has been examined and has failed to pass the practical test/test of competence to drive prescribed under the Road Traffic Act 1988 (and for the purposes of Section 36 of the Road Traffic Offenders Act 1988 if an extended test).

Candidates are assessed against the items listed overleaf in deciding whether they are competent to drive. Items needing special attention are marked. You should study these along with the Guidance Notes above, and the 'Driving Test Report Explained' leaflet given to you by the examiner.
Unsuccessful candidates are required to wait a minimum period of ten clear working days before taking a further test in the same category.

Appeals

If you consider that your test was not properly conducted in accordance with the relevant Regulations, you may apply to a Magistrate's Court acting for the Petty Sessions Area in which you reside (in Scotland to the Sheriff within whose jurisdiction you reside) which (who) has the power to determine this point. If you reside in England or Wales you have six months from the issue of this Statement of Failure in which to appeal, and if you reside in Scotland, 21 days. If the Court finds that the test was not properly conducted it may order a refund of the fee and authorise you to undergo a further test forthwith (see Road Traffic Act 1988 Section 90).

You should note that your right to appeal to the Court under Section 90 is strictly limited to the question of whether the test was properly conducted in accordance with the relevant Regulations. **The examiner's decision and test result cannot be altered.**

Before you consider making any appeal you may wish to seek legal advice.

Details of DSA's service standards and complaints procedures are contained in our 'Customer Charter' and 'If Things Go Wrong' leaflets available in test centre waiting rooms.

The Driving Test Report Explained

1(a). Eyesight test

At the start of the test the examiner asked you to read a vehicle registration number. If you required glasses or contact lenses, you must wear them whenever you drive. If you had problems with the eyesight test, perhaps you should consider consulting an optician.

1(b). Highway Code / Categories F/G/H

If you didn't need to take a separate Theory Test, for example, to obtain a licence for a tractor or other specialist vehicle, you will have been asked questions on the Highway Code and other related motoring matters. You will have also been asked to identify some traffic signs. If you had difficulty with these questions make sure that you study properly by reading as wide a range of publications as you can find to increase your understanding. If you have already passed a theory test you will not have been asked Highway Code questions at the practical test stage - but you should still have a thorough knowledge of it.

2. Precautions

Make sure you always adjust the
- seat
- mirrors
- seat belt

so that you are comfortable and can reach all the controls. Before you start the engine make certain the doors are shut properly, the handbrake is on and the gear lever or selector is in neutral or park. If you need to restart your engine quickly, for example after a stall, you must make sure that you keep the vehicle under control.

3. Control

This section covers where appropriate, the use of the accelerator, clutch, gears, footbrake, handbrake and steering, and for motorcyclists - balance. Always try and use the vehicle controls as smoothly as possible. This means less wear and tear on your vehicle and a smoother ride for your passengers. Make proper use of the accelerator and clutch to make a smooth start. Always depress the clutch just before you stop. Select the correct gear to match the road and traffic conditions. Change gear in good time but not too soon before a hazard. Do not allow the vehicle to coast by running on in neutral or with the clutch down. There should be no need to look down at the gear lever when changing gear. Use the footbrake smoothly and progressively. Brake in plenty of time for any hazard. Make full use of the handbrake whenever it would help you to prevent the car rolling backwards or forwards, and if you are parking. Steer the vehicle as smoothly as possible. Avoid harsh steering, or steering too early or too late as it may cause you to hit the kerb or swing out towards another road user. If you are riding a motorcycle slowly, maintain a straight line and do not allow the machine to wobble towards other vehicles.

4. Move away

The Examiner will have asked you to move off safely and under control on level ground, from behind a parked vehicle and if practicable on a hill. Remember always to use your mirrors, and signal if necessary. Just before moving away check that it is safe by looking round for traffic and pedestrians in your blind spot. Move off in a controlled way making balanced use of accelerator, clutch and brakes, and steer safely. Make sure you are in the correct gear. Do not allow the vehicle to roll back.

5. Emergency stop

If you have to brake in an emergency remember to brake evenly and progressively and try to avoid locking the wheels. Remember that in wet weather it can take twice as long to stop safely. If you are riding a motorcycle you must make correct use of the front and rear brakes to make sure that you stop the machine as quickly as possible.

6. Reverse to the left or right

Whenever you are reversing a vehicle, you will need to control your speed. Steer a course reasonably close to the kerb. Remember that your vehicle will swing out as you turn the corner. Avoid hitting or mounting the kerb, or steering too wide. You must take good, effective, all-round observation throughout the manoeuvre and show consideration to other road users.

7. Turn in the road / Motorcycle U Turn

Keep a look out for traffic and pedestrians whenever you are turning your vehicle and be prepared to give way to them. Control your vehicle smoothly. Do not let the vehicle mount the pavement. Try not to touch the kerbs as this could damage your vehicle and endanger other road users and pedestrians.

8. Reverse parking

You must take good, effective, all-round observation and show consideration to other road users whilst parking your vehicle. Control your vehicle smoothly making proper use of the clutch, accelerator, brakes and steering. Remember, as you steer your vehicle into the parking space, the front of the car will swing out. Keep a special look out for cyclists and pedestrians who may pass close to the front of your vehicle.

9. Use of mirrors / rear observation

You should use your mirrors often, including exterior mirrors where necessary, and always be aware of what may be in your blind spots. Just looking is not enough. You must know what is happening all around you and act sensibly and safely on what you see. You must always check carefully before
- signalling
- changing direction
- changing speed.

Use the Mirrors Signal Manoeuvre (MSM) routine. Do not signal or act without first using the mirrors. Rear observation for motorcyclists is a combination of mirror checks and looking to the rear (Lifesaver).

10. Give appropriate signals

You must signal clearly to let others know what you intend to do. Signal
- only using signals shown in the Highway Code
- if it would help other road users, including pedestrians
- in plenty of time.

Other road users need to see and understand what you intend to do so that they can react safely. Your signals, or lack of signals, must not mislead others. Always ensure that the signal has been cancelled after the manoeuvre has been completed. Do not beckon to pedestrians to cross the road, you could put them in danger from other vehicles.

11. Response to signs and signals

You should understand and be able to react to all traffic signs and road markings. You must act correctly at traffic lights, and check that the road is clear before proceeding when the green light shows. Obey signals given by police officers, traffic wardens and school crossing patrols. Look out for signals given by other road users, including people in charge of animals, and be ready to act accordingly.

12. Use of speed

You should make safe, reasonable progress along the road bearing in mind the road, traffic and weather conditions and the road signs and speed limits. Make sure you can stop safely, well within the distance you can see to be clear. Do not speed. Remember that as a new driver, your licence will be revoked if you accrue six or more penalty points during the first two years, and you will have to retake and pass both your theory and practical tests.

13. Following distance

Always keep a safe distance between yourself and other vehicles. Remember, on wet or slippery roads it takes much longer to stop. When you stop in traffic queues leave sufficient space to pull out if the vehicle in front has problems.

14. Maintain progress

In order to pass your test you must show that you can drive at a realistic speed appropriate to the road and traffic conditions. You should be able to choose the correct speed for the
- type of road
- type and density of traffic
- weather and visibility.

You should approach all hazards at a safe, controlled speed, without being over cautious or interfering with the progress of other traffic. Always be ready to move away from junctions as soon as it is safe and correct to do so. Driving excessively slowly can create dangers for yourself and other drivers.

15. Junctions (including roundabouts)

You should be able to judge the correct speed of approach so that you can enter a junction safely and stop if necessary. Position your vehicle correctly. Use the correct lane. If you are turning right, keep as near to the centre of the road as is safe. Avoid cutting the corner when turning right. If turning left, keep over to the left and do not swing out. Watch out for cyclists and motorcyclists coming up on your left and pedestrians who are crossing. You must take effective observation before moving into a junction and make sure it is safe before proceeding.

16. Judgement when overtaking, meeting oncoming traffic, turning across traffic

Only overtake when it is safe to do so. Allow enough room when you are overtaking another vehicle. Cyclists and motorcyclists need at least as much space as other vehicles. They can wobble or swerve suddenly. Do not cut in too quickly after overtaking. Take care when the width of the road is restricted or when the road narrows. If there is an obstruction on your side or not enough room for two vehicles to pass safely, be prepared to wait and let the approaching vehicles through. When you turn right across the path of an approaching vehicle, make sure you can do so safely. Other vehicles should not have to stop, slowdown or swerve to allow you to complete your turn.

17. Positioning

You should position the vehicle sensibly, normally well to the left. Keep clear of parked vehicles and position correctly for the direction that you intend to take. Where lanes are marked, keep to the middle of the lane and avoid straddling the lane markings. Do not change lanes unnecessarily.

18. Clearance to obstructions

Allow plenty of room to pass stationary vehicles and be prepared to slow down or stop. A door may open, a child may run out or a vehicle may pull out without warning. Keep a safe distance from builders' skips or other large obstructions, as you may not be able to see pedestrians or workers close to the obstruction.

19. Pedestrian crossings

You should be able to recognise the different types of pedestrian crossing and show courtesy and consideration towards pedestrians. At all crossings you should slow down and stop if there is anyone on the crossing. At zebra crossings you should slow down and be prepared to stop if there is anyone waiting to cross. Give way to any pedestrian on a pelican crossing when the amber lights are flashing. You should give way to cyclists as well as pedestrians on a toucan crossing.

20. Position for normal stops

Choose a safe, legal and convenient place to stop, close to the edge of the road, where you will not obstruct the road and create a hazard. You should know how and where to stop without causing danger to other road users.

21. Awareness and planning

You must be aware of other road users at all times. You should always think and plan ahead so that you can
- judge what other road users are going to do
- predict how their actions will affect you
- react in good time.

Take particular care to consider the actions of the more vulnerable groups of road users such as pedestrians, cyclists, motorcyclists and horse riders. Anticipate road and traffic conditions, and act in good time, rather than reacting to them at the last moment.

22. Ancillary controls

You should understand the function of all the controls and switches, especially those that have a bearing on road safety. These include
- indicators
- lights
- windscreen wipers
- demisters
- heaters.

You should be able to find these controls and operate them correctly when necessary, without looking down.

© Crown Copyright 2000

You can include in this group of faults slight errors in co-ordination; inefficient or uneconomic driving style; and other errors which do not fall into the Driving Standards Agency grading system.

In order to help you differentiate more clearly between the various groups of faults we have defined, study the following carefully:

Example 1 – Marginal error The pupil is approaching a junction to turn right into a fairly wide side road. Visibility into the road is good and, after making all the necessary safety checks, the pupil makes the turn. While the corner is not actually cut, the car was very close to the give way lines. Although no fault would be recorded on a driving test, your responsibilities go further than the examiner's.

If this had been a 'one-off' type of error which had not been previously committed by this pupil, you may decide not to mention it unless it occurs again. If it has occurred previously, then it should be mentioned rather than recorded.

Example 2 – Driving fault The pupil is approaching the same right turn as in example 1. Visibility into the road is good and, after ensuring it is safe to turn and the side road is free of traffic movement, the learner turns into the side road cutting the corner very slightly. No potential danger was caused to other road users because the pupil had checked the situation before turning. On a driving test this would be recorded as a driving fault. It would not result in failure.

Example 3 – Serious fault The pupil is approaching the same right turn. This time visibility into the side road is severely restricted by parked vehicles. These make it impossible for the pupil to see whether the junction to the right is clear of approaching traffic. The pupil blatantly cuts the corner into this unknown situation. No actual danger occurred because no other road user appeared from the side road. This, however, was purely good luck and not an assessed judgement. The incident involved potential danger and the learner would fail the test.

Example 4 – Dangerous fault In exactly the same circumstances as example 3 above, the learner cuts the corner. This time, another vehicle appears approaching the end of the side road. The other driver has to brake to avoid a collision. This incident involved actual danger and, of course, the learner would fail the test.

Driving, Serious or Dangerous? It is not necessary for you to be able to grade errors exactly to DSA Driving Test criteria. While some degree of standardisation is desirable, it is not absolutely essential to get it right all the time and you need not worry unduly over this matter.

In any event, the difference between serious and dangerous is purely academic, because in both instances the result is the same – failure.

The difference between a driving fault and a serious fault in this situation, however, could mean the difference between pass and fail. Using again examples 2 and 3 above, for comparison, we will define the errors in a different way.

The essential difference between the two incidents is that the driver committing the driving fault in example 2 was able to see that the new road was clear. In example 3, the fault was a serious fault because the driver was unable to see if the new road was clear, but was prepared to take a risk.

The fault really is not a difference between two people cutting a corner with one of them getting away with it. One of them was able to see and might well have acted differently had the visibility been restricted – the other proved himself to be totally unaware of the danger caused by the parked vehicles.

It is only possible to assess the actions of a driver in the light of the prevailing situation.

Summary of 'L' driver errors

The DSA driving skills book, *Your Driving Test*, states under each subject heading some of the most common causes for driving test failure. The following is a summary of some of these:

- *Eyesight test:* unable to read a vehicle number plate at 67 feet (20.5 metres).
- *Highway Code:* knowledge of the Highway Code (and application of it during the drive) weak or wrong.
- *Precautions before starting engine:* handbrake not applied, neutral not selected, when starting or re-starting the engine.
- *Make proper use of acceleration:* erratic, fierce or jerky use; poor coordination with clutch.
- *Clutch:* not depressed far enough, causing noisy changing or stalling, poor co-ordination with accelerator.
- *Foot-brake:* not used when needed, used late, harshly or erratically.
- *Gears:* incorrect selection, coasting, not in neutral when needed. Harsh control of the gear lever, looking at lever, reluctant to change, incorrect use of selector on automatic.
- *Hand-brake:* not applied when required, not released when moving, used before stopping.
- *Steering:* (position of hands on wheel) one hand off, both hands off; hands on spokes, rim or centre; hands crossed unnecessarily, elbow on window ledge.
- *Steering:* (oversteer) erratic control of steering, wandering on wheel, late correction, over or under steering, jerky or fiddling movements.
- *Moving off – angle, hill, level, straight:* not done smoothly, not safe, not controlled. Causing inconvenience or danger to others, not using mirrors, not looking round or not acting sensibly on what is seen. Not signalling when needed, incorrect gear, lack of co-ordination of controls.
- *Emergency stop:* slow reactions, like a normal stop, footbrake/clutch used in a manner likely to cause a skid, handbrake used before stopping, both hands off the wheel.

- *Reverse: left/right:* rushed, stalling, poor co-ordination of accelerator and clutch, incorrect course, mounting kerb, steering wrong way: too wide or close (not realised), not looking around before/during reverse, not acting on what is seen.
- *Turning in road:* rushed, stalling, poor co-ordination of accelerator and clutch, not using handbrake, incorrect steering, mounting or bouncing off kerb, uncontrolled footbrake or accelerator, more moves than needed, lack of observation before or during manoeuvre, danger or inconvenience to others, looking but not acting sensibly on what is seen.
- *Reverse park:* rushed; poor co-ordination of controls, incorrect course, too wide or too close to parked car, lack of effective observations before/during exercise, poor response to other road users, not using handbrake, not finishing exercise correctly.
- *Effective use of mirrors:* not looking in good time, not acting on what is seen. Omitted or used too late, used as or after movement is commenced. Not used effectively before signalling, changing direction, slowing or stopping. Omitting final look when necessary.
- *Give signals correctly:* signals omitted, given wrongly, or given late. Too short to be of value, not cancelled after use, not repeated when needed. Arm signal not given when needed.
- *Prompt action on signals:* failing to comply with signals or signs: Stop, Keep Left, No Entry, Traffic lights, Police signals, School Crossing wardens, signals given by other road users.
- *Use of speed:* not exercising proper care in use of speed; too fast for conditions or speed limits. Too close to vehicle in front, in view of speed, weather, road conditions.
- *Making progress:* not making normal progress, too low speed for conditions, crawling in low gear, no speed build up between gears, speed not maintained, undue hesitation at junctions, over cautious to point of being nuisance.
- *Crossroads and junctions:*
  - Incorrect regulation of speed on approach, late appreciation of, or reaction to, junctions or crossroads.
  - Not taking effective observation before emerging at a crossroad or junction. Not being sure it is safe to emerge, before doing so. Incorrect assessment of speed and distance of other vehicles, including cyclists.
  - Incorrect positioning for right turns, at or on approach, position taken late, too far from centre, wrong position out of narrow road, or from one way street, wandering, wrong position at end of right turn. Incorrect positioning for left turns, at or on approach, too far from near kerb, swinging out before turning, striking or running over kerb, swinging out after turn.
  - Cutting right turns when entering or leaving.

- *Overtaking/meeting/crossing other traffic:* overtaking unsafely, wrong time or place, causing danger or inconvenience to others, too close or cutting in afterwards. Inadequate clearance for oncoming traffic, causing vehicles to swerve or brake. Turning right across oncoming traffic unsafely.
- *Normal position:* unnecessarily far out from kerb.
- *Adequate clearance:* passing too close to cyclists, pedestrians or stationary vehicles.
- *Pedestrian crossings:* approaching pedestrian crossings too fast, not stopping when necessary, or preparing to stop if pedestrian waiting, overtaking on approach, not signalling (by arm if necessary) when needed. Giving dangerous signals to pedestrians.
- *Normal stops:* stopping unsafely or in inconvenient place. Not parallel to kerb, too close to other vehicles or hazards, compounding hazards.
- *Awareness and anticipation:* lack of awareness or anticipation of others' actions. (This is marked when the result of bad planning or lack of foresight involves the test candidate in a situation resulting in late, hurried or muddled decisions.)
- *Use of ancillary controls:* not using equipment that is necessary for the conditions.

AT THE END OF THE TEST

DL25C (DL9A in Northern Ireland) – Driving Test Report

During the test this form is used by the examiner to record any driving errors. Other information regarding the conduct of the test is also itemised. At the end of the test a copy of the marking sheet is given to the candidate. The examiner may also discuss the reasons for failure with the candidate and the instructor. The form lists the main subjects outlined in *The Driving Test*. It should be used as a guide for both you and your pupil.

When Your Pupil Passes

The examiner will record all driving faults on form DL25A, and a duplicate (DL25C) is handed to the candidate. The examiner will discuss any relevant points and the instructor will be invited to listen to this explanation.

The reverse of the form gives an explanation of the markings, and an outline of the appeals procedure.

A Certificate of Competence to Drive (D10) will also be issued which allows the candidate to drive unaccompanied on any type of road, without 'L' plates.

You should advise your pupils to apply for a full licence as soon as possible, and in any case within two years, otherwise the D10 will become invalid.

The examiner will hand the pupil a leaflet describing the 'Pass Plus' scheme. This is your opportunity to encourage them to take further training in those areas of driving not already covered within your syllabus. For example, motorway driving.

If Your Pupil Fails

A copy of the Driving Test Report form will be issued by the examiner, who will also normally give a verbal report on the reasons for failure. You may sit in and listen to this explanation if you wish. This may help you advise the pupil in any further training requirements.

Application for a re-test can be made immediately, but the test must not be taken within 10 working days.

Book the pupil a lesson as soon as possible so that your analysis and correction of weaknesses is more valid. This also allows the current standard of driving to be maintained.

DSA Complaints Procedure

The Driving Standards Agency's aims are to give their customers the best possible service. They would like to know when they have done well or if a candidate has not been satisfied. Comments, both positive and negative, are welcomed.

If a candidate feels dissatisfied with the conduct of a driving test, the local supervising examiner should be contacted with the details. If they are then not satisfied with the reply, or they would like to comment on other matters, they should write to the regional manager.

None of the above removes the candidate's right to take the complaint to their Member of Parliament or to a Magistrate's Court (in Scotland to the Sheriff in whose jurisdiction they live).

After the Test

Whether the pupil has passed or failed, it is sensible and advisable for you to do the driving. The reasons for this are:

- you can vacate the parking spaces for other test candidates;
- if the pupil has passed, they will be feeling very elated and may be unable to concentrate properly;
- if the pupil has failed, they will be feeling disappointed, angry or frustrated – none of which are conditions conducive to good driving;
- the test centre area is not ideal for carrying out 'post-mortems'.

Remember that whenever you are driving, use the opportunity to demonstrate how it should be done!

Conclusion: The 'L' Test is a test of basic competence. It is your responsibility to prepare your pupils for 'safe driving for life'. Do your best to convince them that further training under the 'Pass Plus' scheme, or in preparation for an advanced driving test, is in their interest. (Please note there is no 'Pass Plus' scheme in Northern Ireland.)

Driving Lorries, Buses and Motorbikes

The contents of this chapter include:

- Lorries:
  — driving licences;
  — test syllabus;
  — staged licencing and testing;
  — theory test;
  — minimum test vehicles;
  — new young driver scheme;
  — Advanced Commercial Vehicle Test;
  — instructors' qualifications;
  — voluntary register of instructors.
- Buses:
  — driving licences;
  — tests – practical and theory;
  — instructor qualifications.
- Motorbikes and mopeds:
  — licences;
  — Compulsory Basic Training;
  — tests – practical and theory;
  — direct access;
  — instructor qualifications.

LORRIES

Driving Licences

A new driver who passes the car test receives a full licence entitlement to drive cars and goods vehicles up to 3.5 tonnes gross weight (Category B), and passenger-carrying vehicles with up to eight seats.

Drivers whose full licence was issued before 1997 have entitlement for goods vehicles up to 7.5 tonnes (subject to the minimum age limit). There are restrictions on the weight of any trailer to be used.

A full car licence is needed before you can apply for provisional LGV entitlement and a full rigid vehicle licence (Category C) must be obtained before driving artics or drawbar outfits. The first application for LGV entitlement must be accompanied by a medical report.

Car drivers who wish to drive large vehicles have to pass a separate test for each category and must meet higher medical standards. Full details of the licence requirements are shown in the D100 leaflet, 'What you need to know about driving licences'.

Driving licence categories

Definitions of vehicles	New category	Old group or class	Minimum age
Goods vehicles Maximum authorised mass of between 3.5 and 7.5 tonnes	Cl	Group A	18
Large goods vehicles Maximum authorised mass more than 3.5 tonnes	C	HGV class 2 or 3	21
As above with drawbar trailer For rigid vehicles towing trailers of more than 750 kg and with more than one axle	C + E (limited to drawbar trailers)	HGV class 2 or 3	21
Articulated goods vehicles	C + E	HGV class 1	21

Health Standards

The health standards are much higher for drivers of large vehicles. This is mainly because accidents involving LGVs are often much more serious than those involving cars. A medical report is required for each application for a licence and with each renewal. By law, a vocational licence (for lorries or buses) cannot be issued to anyone who:

- has had an epileptic attack since reaching the age of five;
- is being treated by insulin for diabetes;
- has visual acuity less than 6/9 in the better eye and less than 6/12 in the worse eye. If corrective lenses are worn, the uncorrected acuity must be no less than 3/60 in each eye.

Some of the other conditions which may make it unsafe to drive these types of vehicles and which may cause the licensing authority to refuse a licence, include disorders of the heart, circulation, brain and nervous system, mental illness and addiction to alcohol or drugs.

Application for a Licence

Before applying for provisional entitlement for LGVs you must already hold a full car licence. The application must be accompanied by:

- the full car licence (or a provisional licence together with a test pass certificate);
- a completed medical report form (D4);
- the appropriate fee.

A first provisional LGV licence is now valid for category C (rigid) vehicles only. A full category C licence is needed before a provisional for artics or trailers can be issued. The theory test must be passed before taking a practical rigid vehicle test, but is not necessary for upgrading from rigid to articulated vehicles.

The licence application is normally processed by DVLA within about 10 days and you have to wait for the licence to arrive before you can drive the larger vehicle. Licence entitlement for LGVs is normally valid to the driver's 45th birthday. For drivers over 45, the licence lasts for five years. From the age of 65 a licence is renewed annually. A medical report is required with each application or renewal.

When learning to drive an LGV, the learner must:

- hold provisional licence entitlement for that category of vehicle;
- be supervised by a driver who holds a full licence for that category;
- display 'L' plates on the front and back of the vehicle.

Minimum Test Vehicles

Vehicles used for LGV tests must be capable of 80 kph and must conform to the following requirements:

Category C1	4 tonnes maximum authorised mass (mam).
Category C1 + E	As above, with a trailer of 2 tonnes mam – combined length must be at least 8 metres.
Category C	10 tonnes mam and at least 7 metres in length.
Category C + E	18 tonnes mam and at least 12 metres in length.
Category C + E (drawbar)	As for Category C with a trailer at least 4 metres in length. Minimum total weight of 18 tonnes.

The LGV Test

Application for a test can be made by post, fax or telephone. Forms are available from the DSA or commercial driving schools. The current fee (October 2001) is £76.

If you apply by post you will need to send a cheque or postal order. Applications by phone or fax can be made using a credit card. In either case, the driving licence details are required unless the application is made under the 'trainer booking' system. In this case the test is allocated to the training organisation and the candidate is nominated at a later stage.

LGV driving tests are conducted by a team of experienced examiners who are specially trained for the requirements of goods vehicles. A list of test centres is provided on the test application form.

The candidate has to provide a suitable vehicle for the test and it must comply with the following requirements:

- The vehicle must be unladen and of the correct category for which the licence is required.
- It must display 'L' plates on the front and rear.
- It must have sufficient fuel for the test lasting up to 1½ hours.
- It must be in a thoroughly roadworthy condition with all stop lamps and direction indicators working properly.
- Seating accommodation must be provided for the examiner.
- It must not be working on trade licence plates.
- The vehicle must not exceed 60 ft in length.

Test syllabus

The DSA book *The Goods Vehicle Driving Manual* is available from most bookshops and training organisations. It explains the contents of the LGV test and how to prepare for it. You should read it in conjunction with *The Driving Test*, which gives advice on correct vehicle control and road procedures for candidates on both car and lorry tests.

In order to pass the test you must:

- demonstrate to the examiner that you can handle the vehicle safely and competently in both town and country conditions;
- show courtesy and consideration for other road users, no matter what the situation;
- show that you have complete control of the vehicle throughout the test, whatever the weather and road conditions.

The test is in three parts:

1. A test of the driver's ability to control the vehicle in a confined space. This part of the test is conducted at the test centre on a special area of about 300 ft × 60 ft.
2. A drive over a route covering various road and traffic conditions. During this part of the test (which lasts about one hour), the examiner will ask the candidate to carry out several special exercises.

3. For drivers of articulated vehicles and drawbars, a practical exercise in coupling and uncoupling the trailer is now included in the test.

Manoeuvring tests – reversing The candidate is expected to drive in reverse along a course marked out by cones, involving the use of right and left steering lock, and finishing in a bay 1½ times the width of the vehicle. The object of the exercise is to complete the manoeuvre smoothly, without touching any of the cones and to stop with the extreme rear of the vehicle within a 3 ft marked area. Throughout the exercise the driver should maintain all-round observation.

Braking The candidate drives forward over a distance of about 200 ft to a speed of about 20 mph. After passing the marker cones, the brakes are applied, stopping the vehicle as quickly as possible, with safety, under full control.

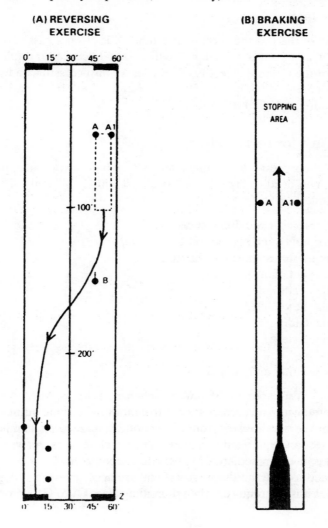

(A) REVERSING EXERCISE

(B) BRAKING EXERCISE

On the road During the 'on-road' section of the test, the candidate will be asked to carry out various exercises together with normal driving over a route of approximately 25 miles. These include an uphill and downhill start and a gear change exercise. In order to show that *all* gears can be used when necessary, the driver is required to demonstrate progressive downward gear changes until the lowest has been selected. During this exercise it is not necessary to use any auxiliary transmission systems.

Depending on the size of the vehicle used for the test, some degree of tolerance in positioning before and after turning is permitted. However, care must be exercised so as not to endanger or inconvenience other road users.

The test route may include a section of motorway driving.

After the test

At the end of the test the successful candidate is given a pass certificate which enables the applicant to exchange the provisional licence for a full licence entitlement for the relevant category of vehicle. An unsuccessful candidate is issued with a statement of failure on which the examiner will have marked the points which require particular attention.

Theory Test for Lorry Drivers

The LGV theory test must be taken and passed before you can apply for a practical test. You need to take the practical test within two years. The theory syllabus includes:

- vehicle weights and dimensions;
- drivers' hours and rest periods;
- braking systems and speed limiters;
- in the event of an accident;
- vehicle condition;
- leaving the vehicle;
- vehicle loading;
- restricted view;
- overtaking;
- windy weather and heavy rain.

The Theory Test paper has 35 multiple choice questions. Most of the questions are answered with one correct answer from four, with some questions requiring two or more correct answers from a selection. You are given 40 minutes to complete the test and you need to achieve 30 correct answers. As with the car test, the result is given immediately after the test is completed.

You need to take the theory test if you are applying for a Category C or C1 licence, but it is not required when upgrading from C1 to C, or from C to CE.

LGV Theory Test Sample Questions

1/ Under EC rules, when may you interrupt daily rest periods?

Mark one answer.
a) When part of it is taken on board a ferry or train.
b) When loading and unloading the vehicle.
c) When there is not more than a 1 hour gap between rest periods.
d) When your journey includes night driving.

2/ An LGV is found to be overloaded. Who is liable to be prosecuted for this offence?

Mark one answer.
a) The person who loaded the vehicle.
b) Both the driver and the operator.
c) The operator only.
d) The driver only.

3/ What could prevent air pressure building up in the air brake system in cold, frosty weather?

Mark one answer.
a) Moisture in the air may form bubbles in the brake fluid.
b) The air will contract, reducing the pressure.
c) Moisture drawn in with the air may freeze and cause a blockage.
d) The dampness may cause valves to rust.

4/ How far can a load overhang at the rear before you must use triangular projection markers?

Mark one answer.
a) 1 metre (3 ft 4 ins)
b) 1.5 metres (5 ft)
c) 2 metres (6 ft 8 ins)
d) 2.9 metres (9 ft 6 ins)

LGV Instructor Qualifications

In order to accompany a learner LGV driver, the supervising driver must:
- be at least 21 and have held a full driving licence for at least three years;
- hold a full licence for the category of vehicle being driven.

This is the *minimum* legal requirement. However, most LGV instructors hold other voluntary qualifications, including the ADI certificate, RTITB approval and other training qualifications from the Armed Forces.

Voluntary register of LGV instructors

The scheme, which was introduced in 1997, is very similar to the ADI register in its administration and testing systems. For example, the candidate takes three separate tests: a theory test, a practical test of own driving and a practical test of instructional ability. At present there is no theory test, although this is planned for a later date.

The syllabus for the practical instructional ability test includes:

- fault assessment, fault analysis, remedial action;
- level of instruction;
- planning a lesson;
- control of the lesson;
- communication;
- question/answer techniques;
- feedback and encouragement;
- use of controls;
- attitude and approach to pupil.

As on the ADI examination, the test involves the examiner playing the part of a learner driver and covering a range of topics:

- safety precautions on entering the vehicle;
- location, function and use of the controls;
- moving away/stopping;
- braking exercise;
- traffic signs, signals, road markings;
- reversing, gear changing exercises;
- use of all mirrors;
- uncoupling and re-coupling;
- judgement of speed;
- positioning the vehicle correctly during normal driving;
- approaching and turning into and out of T junctions;
- approaching and turning at crossroads and roundabouts;
- meeting and overtaking other traffic;
- anticipating the actions of other road users;
- remedial lesson, having failed an LGV test.

The candidate's knowledge and ability will be assessed on the following:

- the method, clarity, adequacy and correctness of the instruction given;
- the observation and correction of the pupil's driving errors;
- general manner and attitude when dealing with the pupil.

The current cost at October 2001 is £58.75 for the theory test and £70 for each of the practical tests, together with a further registration fee of £117.50.

Registration is for 3 years, after which another set of exams has to be taken. Each part of the exam has to be passed within a 6 month period.

The New Young Driver Scheme

The normal minimum age for driving vehicles with a gross weight of more than 7.5 tonnes is 21 years. However, the Young Drivers' Scheme is now available as a result of co-operation within the industry, involving the Department of Transport, the Road Haulage and Distribution Training Council, the Road Haulage Association, the Freight Transport Association and the various trades unions.

Under the scheme, trainees between the ages of 18 and 21 receive quality driver training and an opportunity to obtain an NVQ. This enables the driver to gain experience and licences for the various categories of vehicles from B through C1 and C to C+E.

Further details of the courses are available from the RHDTC on 01923 858484.

The IAM Advanced Driving Test for Commercial Vehicle Drivers

The advanced commercial vehicle test is run by the Institute of Advanced Motorists (IAM) and can be taken on any type of commercial vehicle. On passing the test, the driver qualifies for membership of the IAM. Some specially qualified drivers are exempt and may apply for membership without taking the test. These include LGV driving examiners, members of the Armed Forces and the Fire Service who hold an instructor's qualification, and holders of the RTITB Instructor's Certificate.

The test lasts about two hours and covers a route of approximately 40 miles. The route includes a variety of road and traffic conditions, as well as incorporating some reversing manoeuvres.

After passing the test, drivers may display the IAM badge on the vehicle, and qualify for the usual membership benefits.

Further details of the test are available from the IAM at 359 Chiswick High Road, London W4 4HS (tel: 0181 994 9249).

BUSES AND COACHES

Licences

A full car licence (Category B) is needed before you can apply for a provisional licence for buses, coaches and minibuses.

PCV licence entitlement is needed for any vehicle with more than 16 passenger seats and for a vehicle with more than 8 passenger seats which is used for hire or reward.

Large buses which are used for hire or reward require Category C entitlement. Buses with large trailers and articulated buses need the additional category E entitlement.

Driving licence categories

Definitions of vehicles	New category	Old group or class	Minimum age
Small passenger-carrying vehicles (between 9 and 16 passenger seats) not used for hire or reward	D1	Group A	21
Small passenger-carrying vehicles (between 9 and 16 passenger seats)	D (limited to 16 passenger seats)	New category	21
Passenger-carrying vehicles (more than 8 passenger seats but not longer than 5.5 metres)	D (not more than 5.5 metres long)	PSV class 4	21
All large passenger-carrying vehicles (more than 8 passenger seats and longer than 5.5 metres)	D	PSV class 3	21
Articulated buses and buses towing trailers of more than 750 kg	D + E	PSV class 1 or 2	21

Minimum Ages

Passenger vehicles: The minimum age for driving a vehicle with more than 8 seats is normally 21. However, it is 18 years for some smaller buses and on limited service routes.

Health Standards

The health standards for drivers of LGVs and PCVs are much higher than those required for car drivers. This is because accidents involving larger vehicles are usually more serious than those involving smaller vehicles. A medical report is required for each application for a licence and with each renewal.

Application for a PCV Licence

To apply for a PCV provisional licence you need to hold a full licence for Category B (cars). The application has to be accompanied by a completed medical report (Form D4) and the appropriate fee, as well as the full licence.

The licence application is processed by DVLA at Swansea usually within about 10 days and is valid until the driver's 45th birthday. For drivers over 45 the licence usually lasts for five years. From the age of 65 the licence is renewed annually. A medical report is needed with each application.

Minimum Test Vehicles

Category D1	More than 8 passenger seats, up to 9 metres in length.
Category D	More than 8 passenger seats, at least 9 metres in length.
Category D + E	As Category D above, with a trailer of at least 1.25 tonnes.

Application for the test is made on form DLG 26 which can be obtained from offices of the Driving Standards Agency (DSA) or from a commercial driving school. The current fee is £76.00.

The PCV Driving Test

The driving test for bus and coach drivers is conducted by the same examiners and at the same centres as for goods vehicles. The content of the test is similar to the goods vehicle test, but with several variations which are specific to the driving of PCVs. The purpose of the test is to assess the driver's competence to drive in a manner which shows consideration for the safety and comfort of passengers and without danger to other road users. The safety and comfort of passengers should be reflected in the candidate's smooth use of the controls and steering. The vehicle should be driven so as not to strike a kerb or to mount the pavement unless this is necessary due to the large size of the vehicle combined with a restricted space in which to manoeuvre. Under such circumstances, the vehicle must be controlled and the manoeuvre completed safely.

Before granting a licence, the licensing authority have to be satisfied not only that the applicant can drive to a high standard, but also that he or she is medically fit and of good character. The applicant's previous driving history and non-motoring offences may be taken into account when considering the issue of a PCV driving licence.

The applicant for a test must hold a full ordinary licence and provisional entitlement for the category of PCV on which the test is to be taken.

The candidate for test has to provide a suitable vehicle which must comply with the following requirements:

- It must be at least 9 metres overall length and capable of reaching at least 80 kph (50 mph).
- It must be thoroughly roadworthy with all stop lamps and direction indicators working correctly.
- It must be properly insured and display a valid vehicle excise licence.
- Seating accommodation must be provided for the examiner.
- The examiner must have a clear view of the road behind without having to rely on mirrors.

- The examiner must be able to speak to the driver while he or she is driving.
- It must have enough fuel for the test of approximately 1½ hours.

Before taking the test, candidates should make sure that they know the dimensions of the vehicle (height, width and weight) and the position of the fuel emergency cut-off and of the fire extinguishers. They should ensure that all doors are properly closed and that any equipment carried is properly stowed and secured.

The 'on-road' section is similar to that of the goods vehicle test, but with several variations. For example, a 'snatch' gear change may be needed after an uphill start. At bus stops, the vehicle should be stopped with the platform or entrance positioned correctly in relation to the stopping place.

After the test

At the end of the test the successful candidate is given a pass certificate which enables the applicant to exchange the provisional licence for a full licence entitlement for the relevant category of vehicle. An unsuccessful candidate is issued with a statement of failure on which the examiner will have marked the points which require particular attention.

Theory Test for Bus and Coach Drivers

The theory test for buses is similar to that for LGVs (see page 306) with an additional section covering 'Carrying Passengers'. This includes:

- passenger comfort;
- vehicle stability;
- driver attitude;
- special passengers;
- safety equipment.

You need to take the Theory Test if you are applying for a Category D or D1 licence.

MOTORCYCLE TRAINING AND TESTING

Although motorcyclists make up only a very small percentage of road traffic, they account for a quarter of serious road injuries and one-seventh of all road deaths. In an effort to deal with the problem, the DSA has implemented a series of changes in the training and testing of motorcycle riders.

Compulsory basic training is now required for all riders of mopeds, motorcycles (including those with sidecars) and scooters. The learner is required to undergo a course of off-road and on-road basic training before riding on the roads. On successful completion of the basic training, the pupil is issued with a certificate which validates the provisional licence.

This compulsory basic training (CBT) now applies to anyone riding a motorcycle or moped on 'L' plates, irrespective of when their licence was issued, and includes full Category B (car licence) holders who have not passed the motorcycle test.

After basic training, learners may ride on the road, but are limited to machines of up to 125 cc and up to 11 kw power output. 'L' plates must be displayed and pillion passengers are not permitted on solo machines. CBT certificates issued after 1 February 2001 are valid for 2 years. Both the theory and practical tests have to be passed within the two-year period.

Motorcycle Categories

Category A1: light motorcycle – not exceeding 125 cc and a power output of 11 kw. This type of licence can be obtained by taking the CBT, followed by a test on a bike between 75 cc and 120 cc.

Category A: standard motorcycle – any motorcycle. The test must be taken on a bike over 120 cc and which is capable of at least 100 kph. For the first two years of the licence the rider is restricted to a bike of 25 kw unless they take the Direct Access route to obtaining a licence.

Direct access

Direct Access is a means of achieving an unrestricted licence within the two-year period. It is available only to anyone over the age of 21 and must be taken on a motorcycle which exceeds 35 kw. Training can only be taken under the direct supervision of a certified Direct Access instructor on another bike who is able to communicate by radio. Both instructor and pupil must wear reflective or luminous jackets.

Theory test

Even if you hold a full car licence, you now need to take and pass a separate theory test before applying for the practical test.

Licence application

Provisional licence entitlement for motorcycles is normally granted for a maximum period of two years. Learners are not permitted to ride on the road until the successful completion of a training course, except when under the supervision of an authorised instructor during CBT.

Mopeds may be ridden at 16 years and are included in the CBT regulations.

A full car licence includes provisional entitlement for motorcycles but a CBT certificate is needed to validate the licence. A full car licence issued before the end of January 2001 includes full entitlement for mopeds and CBT is not required in those circumstances. If you passed the car test after 1st February 2001 you need to take CBT before riding a moped.

Compulsory basic training (not applicable in Northern Ireland)

The training is carried out by approved training bodies at sites which have been approved by the Driving Standards Agency. Motorcycle instructors are specially trained, qualified and tested. Their work is checked regularly by the DSA and their results are monitored carefully. The maximum permitted ratio is one instructor to four pupils for off-road training and one instructor to two pupils for on-road training.

The emphasis in compulsory basic training is on the continuous assessment of the pupil's ability, rather than testing. As a result, the duration of a course is not specified; the syllabus must be covered adequately, taking into account the aptitude of the trainee.

CBT syllabus

Trainees must attain a satisfactory standard in each objective before moving on the next.

Introduction Aims of the course: eyesight requirements, equipment and clothing, conspicuity, motorcycles on the public roads, vulnerability, speed can kill, eyesight test.

Practical on-site training Familiarisation with the machine, basic machine checks (on and off the stand), wheeling machine – left–right balance – braking.

Practical on-site riding OSM–PSL routine, left and right turns, figure of eight, slow riding, emergency braking.

Practical on-road riding Explanation of basic defensive riding techniques, road procedure, value of rear observation, anticipation of other road users, road surface, intelligent use of speed, weather, practical road riding.

Instructor Qualifications

Instructors who conduct the on-road part of the compulsory training, and who issue the certificate of completion of training, must have held a full motorcycle licence for a minimum of two years. At least one instructor from the organisation must have attended a motorcycle instructor course at the DSA Training Establishment at Cardington. The Cardington-trained instructor is then responsible for the training and supervision of other instructors. An instructor with less than two years' riding experience may be trained as an Assistant Instructor, and can be authorised to conduct only the off-road, on-site elements of the course. Standards of training are closely monitored by the DSA, and instructors who fail to train and assess to those standards are liable to have their appointment withdrawn.

The Motorcycle Test

The on-road accompanied rider test is undertaken by specially qualified Driving Standards Agency examiners at most of the driving test centres. The validation certificate, which is issued at the end of the compulsory basic training, must either be sent with the application or produced to the examiner on the day of the test. Application for the test is made to the DSA using the form DL26 – the same form which is used for the car test. Alternatively, the test may be booked by telephone using the credit card booking facility.

The Driving Standards Agency is normally able to offer a test appointment within four weeks of applying so that the training organisation can link the training more closely to the on-road test. Block-booking arrangements are also available to appointed training bodies.

The test is normally conducted with the examiner accompanying the candidate on another motorcycle, although in some areas the accompanying vehicle may be a car.

A separate theory test must be passed before you can apply for a practical motorcycle test.

Practical test syllabus

The test is carried out over a route covering a wide variety of traffic conditions and includes some special requirements:

Braking Correct combination of front and rear brakes. Correct braking techniques and their use.

Emergency stop Apply the front brake just before the rear. Apply both brakes effectively. Stop as quickly as possible without locking either wheel.

U-turn Ride in a U–turn and stop on the other side of the road.

Slow ride Ride as you would in slow-moving traffic for a short distance.

Rear observation Look over the appropriate shoulder to check the position of the traffic before signalling, changing direction, slowing down or stopping.

Test procedure

The examiner maintains contact with the candidate and gives directions by way of mobile radio communication equipment. Radios are worn by candidates in an adjustable waist belt and earpieces are fitted into the rider's helmet. All equipment is fitted by the examiner and is checked before the start of each test. The radio allows one-way communication only: the candidate is not able to talk back to the examiner. If a candidate does not understand an instruction or direction he should pull over to the side of the road and wait for the examiner.

Applicants who have disabilities and those who are profoundly deaf should give full details on the application form. Riders who are unable to hear directions through an earpiece are asked by the examiner to stop from time to time and are then given written route directions. Candidates who do not speak or understand English should make this clear on the application form. They should bring along an interpreter to relay instructions. The examiner will then conduct the test from a car.

Useful Addresses

Driving Standards Agency

Headquarters
Stanley House
56 Talbot Street
Nottingham NG1 5GU
Tel: (0115) 901 2500
Fax: (0115) 901 2600

**National Number Driving Tests and
Other Enquiries**

Driving Standards Agency
PO Box 280
Newcastle-upon-Tyne NE99 1FP
Tel: (0870) 01 01 372
Fax: (0870) 01 02 372
Welsh speakers: (0870) 01 00 372
Minicom users: (0870) 01 07 372

ADI Consultative Organisations

AA – The Driving School
Customer Service Centre
26–32 Park Row
Fanum House
Bristol BS1 5LJ
Tel: (0800) 607080

ADI Business Club
3 Greenacre Close
Wyke
Bradford
West Yorkshire BD12 9DQ
Tel: (01274) 672 850

Approved Driving Instructors
National Joint Council (ADINJC)
41 Edinburgh Road
Cambridge CB4 1QR
Tel: (01223) 359079

The British School of Motoring Limited
RAC House
Feltham
Middlesex
TW13 7RR
Tel: (020) 8540 8262

Driving Instructors' Association (DIA)
Safety House
Beddington Farm Road
Croydon
Surrey CR1 4XZ
Tel: (020) 8665 5151

Driving Instructors' Scottish Council
(DISC)
74 Ardross Place
Glenrothes
Fife KY6 2SQ
Tel: (01592) 772863

Motor Schools' Association (MSA)
182A Heaton Moor Road
Stockport
Cheshire SK4 4DU
Tel: (0161) 443 1611
Freephone: (0500) 53 37 57

Training Aids & Services

Margaret Stacey – Autodriva
(Books & Training Aids)
35 Bourne Square
Breaston
Derbyshire DE72 3DZ
Tel/Fax: (01332) 874111
e-mail:
mstacey@autodriva.freeserve.co.uk

Millers Motor School
57 North Street
Chichester
West Sussex PO19 1NB
Tel/Fax: (01243) 784715

DeskTop Driving Ltd
81 North Lane
East Preston
Littlehampton
West Sussex BN16 1HD
Tel: (01903) 859137
Fax: (01903) 783967

Driving School Aids
East View
Broadgate Lane
Horsforth
Leeds LS18 4DD
Tel: (0113) 258 0688

Driving School News
PO Box 469
Maidstone
Kent ME16 9PU
Tel: (01622) 728898

Driving School Supplies
2–4 Tame Road
Witton
Birmingham B6 7DS
Tel: (0121) 328 6226

F I N D
(NVQ Assessment Centre)
121 Marshalswick Lane
St Albans
Herts AL1 4UX
Tel/Fax: (01727) 858068

He-Man Dual Controls
23–27 Princes Street
Northam
Southampton SO14 5RP
Tel: (01703) 226952

Her Majesty's Stationery Office
Publications Centre
PO Box 276
London SW8 5DT
Tel: (020) 7873 0011

Porter Dual Controls
Boar's Head Business Park
Brent Way
Brentford
Middlesex TW8 8ES
Tel: (020) 8568 2345

RCM Marketing Ltd
20 Newtown Business Park
Albion Close
Poole
Dorset BH12 3LL
Tel: (01202) 737999

Royal Society for the Prevention
of Accidents (RoSPA)
Edgbaston Park
353 Bristol Road
Birmingham B5 7ST
Tel: (0121) 248 2000

Wholesale Book Supplies
Britannia House Shop
King Edward Street
Barmouth
Gwynedd LL40 1AD
Tel: (01341) 281292

Disabled Driver Services

Disability Action
2 Annadale Avenue
Belfast
Northern Ireland BT7 3TH
Tel: (01232) 491011

Disability Scotland
Princes House
5 Shandwick Place
Edinburgh EH2 4RG
Tel: (0131) 229 8632

Disability Wales
Llyfifor Crescent Road
Caerfili
Mid Glamorgan CF3 1XL
Tel: (01222) 887325

Disabled Living Foundation
380–384 Harrow Road
London W9 2HU
Tel: (020) 7289 6111

Disabled Drivers' Assessment Centres

Banstead Mobility Centre
Damson Way
Fountain Drive
Carshalton
Surrey SM5 4NR
Tel: (020) 8770 1151

Cornwall Friends Mobility Centre
Tehidy House
R C H (Treliske)
Truro
Cornwall TR1 3LJ
Tel: (01872) 254920

Derby Regional Mobility Centre
Kingsway Hospital
Kingsway
Derby DE3 3LZ
Tel: (01332) 371929

Edinburgh Driving Assessment Service
Astley Ainslie Hospital
133 Grange Loan
Edinburgh EH9 2HL
Tel: (0131) 537 9192

Mobility Advice & Vehicle
Information Service (MAVIS)
Department of Transport
TRL
Crowthorne
Berks RG11 6AU
Tel: (01344) 770456

The Mobility Centre
Regional Neurological Rehabilitation
Centre
Hunters Moor Hospital
Hunters Road
Newcastle-upon-Tyne NE2 4NR
Tel: (0191) 219 5694

Mobility Information Service
National Mobility Centre
Unit 2
Atcham Estate
Shrewsbury SY4 4UG
Tel: (01743) 761889

Stoke Mandeville Drivers'
Assessment Centre
Occupational Therapy Department
Stoke Mandeville Hospital
Mandeville Road
Aylesbury
Bucks HP21 8AL
Tel: (01296) 315000

Wales Disabled Drivers' Assessment
Centre
Rookwood Hospital
Fairwater Road
Llandaff
Cardiff CF5 2YN
Tel: (01222) 615276

Motoring Organisations
The Automobile Association
Fanum House
Basingstoke
Hampshire RG21 2EA
Tel: (0990) 448866

320 Useful Addresses

The Royal Automobile Club
RAC House
1 Forest Road
Feltham
Middlesex TW13 7RR
Tel: (020) 8917 2500

Index